T0214170

# Lecture Notes of the Institute for Computer Sciences, Social Informatics and Telecommunications Engineering 309

More information about this series at http://www.springer.com/series/8197

Honghao Gao · Kuang Li ·
Xiaoxian Yang · Yuyu Yin (Eds.)

# Testbeds and Research Infrastructures for the Development of Networks and Communications

14th EAI International Conference, TridentCom 2019
Changsha, China, December 7–8, 2019
Proceedings

 Springer

*Editors*
Honghao Gao
Shanghai University
Shanghai, China

Xiaoxian Yang
Shanghai Polytechnic University
Shanghai, China

Kuang Li
School of Software
Central South University
Changsha, China

Yuyu Yin
Hangzhou Dianzi University
Hangzhou Shi, Zhejiang, China

ISSN 1867-8211        ISSN 1867-822X  (electronic)
Lecture Notes of the Institute for Computer Sciences, Social Informatics
and Telecommunications Engineering
ISBN 978-3-030-43214-0        ISBN 978-3-030-43215-7  (eBook)
https://doi.org/10.1007/978-3-030-43215-7

This Springer imprint is published by the registered company Springer Nature Switzerland AG
The registered company address is: Gewerbestrasse 11, 6330 Cham, Switzerland

# Preface

We are delighted to introduce the proceedings of the 14th EAI International Conference on Testbeds and Research Infrastructures for the Development of Networks & Communities (TridentCom 2019). This conference has brought together researchers, developers, and practitioners from around the world who are interested in the field of Testbeds and Research Infrastructures.

The technical program of TridentCom 2019 consisted of 16 papers in oral presentation sessions at the main conference tracks. The conference sessions were: Session 1 - AI and Internet Computing; Session 2 - QoS, Reliability, Modeling and Testing; and Session 3 - Wireless, Networking and Multimedia Application. Apart from high-quality technical paper presentations, the technical program also featured one keynote speech which was delivered by Prof. Shaohua Wan from Zhongnan University of Economics and Law, China.

Coordination with the steering chair, Prof. Imrich Chlamtac, was essential for the success of the conference. We sincerely appreciate this constant support and guidance. It was also a great pleasure to work with such an excellent Organizing Committee and we thank them for their hard work in organizing and supporting the conference. In particular, we thank the Technical Program Committee (TPC), led by our TPC co-chairs: Kuang Li and Xiaoxian Yang, who completed the peer-review process of technical papers and made a high-quality technical program. We are also grateful to the conference manager, Lukas Skolek, for his support, and to all the authors who submitted their papers to TridentCom 2019.

We strongly believe that the TridentCom conference series provides a good forum for all researcher, developers, and practitioners to discuss all science and technology aspects that are relevant to communications and networking. We also expect that the future TridentCom conferences will be as successful and stimulating, as indicated by the contributions presented in this volume.

February 2020

Honghao Gao
Kuang Li
Xiaoxian Yang
Yuyu Yin

# Organization

## Steering Committee

### Chairs

Imrich Chlamtac      University of Trento, Italy
Victor C. M. Leung      The University of British Columbia, Canada
Honghao Gao      Shanghai University, China

## Organizing Committee

### General Chairs

Honghao Gao      Shanghai University, China
Yuyu Yin      Hangzhou Dianzi University, China

### Program Chairs

Kuang Li      Central South University, China
Xiaoxian Yang      Shanghai Polytechnic University, China

### Workshop Chairs

Yusheng Xu      Xidian University, China
Yucong Duan      Hainan University, China

### Publications Chair

Youhuizi Li      Hangzhou Dianzi University, China

### Local Arrangement Chair

Li Kuang      Central South University, China

### Web Chair

Xiaoxian Yang      Shanghai Polytechnic University, China

### Conference Manager

Lukas Skolek      European Alliance for Innovation, Belgium

## Technical Program Committee

| | |
|---|---|
| Li Kuang | Central South University, China |
| Xiaoxian Yang | Shanghai Polytechnic University, China |
| Fekade Getahun | Addis Ababa University, Ethiopia |
| Jue Wang | Computer Network Information Center of CAS, China |
| Kai Lin | Dalian University of Technology, China |
| Lianyong Qi | Qufu Normal University, China |
| Limei Peng | Ajou University, South Korea |
| Nianjun Zhou | IBM T. J. Watson Research Center, USA |
| Qing Wu | Hangzhou Dianzi University, China |
| Stephan Reiff-Marganiec | University of Leicester, UK |
| Wan Tang | South-Central University for Nationalities, China |
| Xiaobing Sun | Yangzhou University, China |
| Bin Cao | Zhejiang University of Technology, China |
| Congfeng Jiang | Hangzhou Dianzi University, China |
| Guobing Zou | Shanghai University, China |
| Jiwei Huang | China University of Petroleum, China |
| Youhuizi Li | Hangzhou Dianzi University, China |
| Yuyu Yin | Hangzhou Dianzi University, China |
| Yiping Wen | Hunan University of Science and Technology, China |
| Yueshen Xu | Xidian University, China |
| Han Ding | Xi'an Jiaotong University, China |

# Contents

## Wireless, Networking and Multimedia Application

# AI and Internet Computing

# Evaluating the Effectiveness of Wrapper Feature Selection Methods with Artificial Neural Network Classifier for Diabetes Prediction

M. A. Fahmiin[(⊠)] and T. H. Lim

Universiti Teknologi Brunei, Bandar Seri Begawan, Brunei Darussalam
fahmiinabdullah96@gmail.com, lim.tiong.hoo@utb.edu.bn

**Abstract.** Feature selection is an important preprocessing technique used to determine the most important features that contributes to the classification of a dataset, typically performed on high dimension datasets. Various feature selection algorithms have been proposed for diabetes prediction. However, the effectiveness of these proposed algorithms have not been thoroughly evaluated statistically. In this paper, three types of feature selection methods (Sequential Forward Selection, Sequential Backward Selection and Recursive Feature Elimination) classified under the wrapper method are used in identifying the optimal subset of features needed for classification of the Pima Indians Diabetes dataset with an Artificial Neural Network (ANN) as the classifying algorithm. All three methods manage to identify the important features of the dataset (Plasma Glucose Concentration and BMI reading), indicating their effectiveness for feature selection, with Sequential Forward Selection obtaining the feature subset that most improves the ANN. However, there are little to no improvements in terms of classifier evaluation metrics (accuracy and precision) when trained using the optimal subsets from each method as compared to using the original dataset, showing the ineffectiveness of feature selection on the low-dimensional Pima Indians Diabetes dataset.

**Keywords:** Feature selection · Wrapper methods · Diabetes classification

## 1 Introduction

The application of Artificial Intelligence (AI), Machine Learning (ML) and Internet of Things (IoT) encompasses a wide range of industrial fields that have benefitted from the results of data mining, data acquisition and accurate predictions brought up by said technological advances. The healthcare sector is no different worldwide. The use of AI and ML into early detection and prediction of harmful diseases, notably non-communicable diseases such as diabetes, have greatly improved the diagnostics accuracy for healthcare professionals which conversely improves the standard of living for their patients through the means of prevention over treatment [1, 2].

An important stage of performing machine learning for classification and detection is to determine the specific feature that would help to speed up and improve the

© ICST Institute for Computer Sciences, Social Informatics and Telecommunications Engineering 2020
Published by Springer Nature Switzerland AG 2020. All Rights Reserved
H. Gao et al. (Eds.): TridentCom 2019, LNICST 309, pp. 3–17, 2020.
https://doi.org/10.1007/978-3-030-43215-7_1

detection rate. Additional machine learning algorithms are usually applied to determine the most important or relevant features that contributes the most towards performing correct classifications. By selecting the correct features, overall training time is reduced as well removing the problem of overfitting to the diabetes dataset, enabling better generalizability for new inputs of patient data. However, another issue arises from the case of low dimensional datasets, defined as datasets with low number of features relative to the number of instances. In this case, feature selection arguably does not contribute much towards improving the classification algorithm [2].

In this paper, we evaluated a multi-layer wrapper feature selection methods using Sequential Forward Selection (SFWS), Sequential Backward Selection (SBS) and Recursive Feature Elimination (RFE)) and proposed the use of Artificial Neural Network (ANN) to classify diabetic patients trained on the Pima Indians Diabetes dataset. The main contribution of the paper is to evaluate the reliability of the different feature selection methods statistically and compare the performance of the algorithms in selecting the relevant features for classification of diabetes. The relevant subset of features selected by these methods is compared against the results of previous literatures on the same diabetic dataset. The results have shown that all methods are able to identify the two most important features with varying other additional features. The second contribution is showing the effectiveness of feature selection on low-dimensional diabetic dataset, where the results concluded with little to no improvement on the classification model evaluation metrics. We believe this is the time that the wrapper feature selections methods have been evaluated statistically.

The organization of the paper is as follows. Section 2 of the paper explains previous works related to the current study. Section 3 introduces the feature selection methods used in this paper, followed by an introduction to ANN in Sect. 4. In Sect. 5, the proposed methodology is explained and with its results discussions found in Sect. 6. Statistical analysis of the results obtained is done in Sect. 7, while Sect. 8 concludes the paper with a discussion of the contributions and prospects for future work.

## 2   Literature Review

In current literatures, there are numerous studies done towards the application of AI and ML in the case for diabetes mellitus, Vijayan et al. [3] used a combination of multiple algorithms to produce a model that can classify patients likely to contract diabetes mellitus for up to 80.7% accuracy rate, while Wei et al. [4] obtained the highest accuracy of 77.9% amongst five different individual algorithms (Neural Net-work, Support Vector Machine, Decision tree, Logistic regression and Naïve Bayes). Sowjanya et al. [5] and Duke et al. [6] created their own unique web and mobile inter-faces for diabetes diagnostics in addition to constructing the machine learning models. From the above studies, data preprocessing beforehand is proven to be an important factor that the authors have acknowledged when it comes to achieving better results.

In order to extract the correct feature, Gacav et al. [7] propose the Sequential Feature Selection (SFS) to extract the most important subset of distance vectors on facial expressions for classification purposes. Their method yields an 89.9% mean class recognition accuracy. Zheng et al. [8] also applied the backward variation of SFS with the addition of Information Gain for a hybrid approach to determine an optimal subset of diabetic patient risk factors from the Korean National Health survey. 10 out of their 33 initial features were determined to be optimal for classification, yielding 95.6% in accuracy. SFS and its variances showed positive effects in selecting the most optimal features necessary for accurate prediction results.

The recursive feature elimination (RFE) method involves fitting a model and evaluating the contribution of each feature towards the accuracy of prediction. The least important feature is then removed, and the process is repeated until the desired number of features is reached. Lv et al. [9] made use of a Support Vector Machine (SVM) based RFE to construct a low dimensional face image feature for face recognition which obtained 93.5% recognition accuracy with feature reduction from 720 to only 60. Zhang et al. [10] proposed a Random Forest (RF) based RFE to extract the key feature subset of transient stability assessment of New England 39-bus power system. They have obtained a 99.1% accuracy score with reduction of features from 263 to 45 using said method. From the studies mentioned, the combination of RFE with different classifier models can improve on the feature selection methods.

Similar works have also been done on the publicly available Pima Indians Diabetes dataset [11]. Dutta et al. [12] performed an in-depth analysis of feature importance for the using Random Forest, the algorithm in which they obtained the best result from. They have determined that five of the eight given features having the most importance towards classifying diabetics and non-diabetics. In the work done by Balakrishnan et al. [13], they have used a classification algorithm known as the Support Vector Machine with feature reduction technique, where the accuracy of prediction is assessed after each subsequent elimination of the least important feature of the Pima Indians Diabetes dataset. They have obtained a 1.88% increase in accuracy when removing 37. 5% of the features in the dataset. These studies have shown the usage of feature selection in areas of diabetes prediction but with minimal contribution to improvement of the classifying model.

## 3   Feature Selection Wrapper Methods

Different Feature Selection Wrapper (FSW) methods have been evaluated for its capabilities in obtaining the important features of the dataset and determining the effectiveness of improving the evaluation scores for a classifying algorithm such as Artificial Neural Network (ANN) using the optimal subsets obtained from the tests. Under feature selection techniques, wrapper methods consider the different combinations of subset of features to determine the best combination which resulted in the overall improvement of the evaluation metrics for the specific classifying algorithm. This would result in a more accurate selection than other methods [14]. In this paper, three wrapper methods, proven to be effective based on previous literatures mentioned in Sect. 2, are used for the tests in selecting relevant features from the Pima Indians Diabetes dataset.

**Sequential Feature Selection (SFS)**

This method of feature selection makes use of a classifier's performance to determine the most optimum feature subset that gives the best result. SFS have two variances which are Sequential Forward Selection (SFWS) and Sequential Backward Selection (SBS). In SFWS, the feature subset started off empty and features from the collection, which results in the best classifier performance, is added until a terminating condition has been reached.

> *let* complete dataset: $D = \{d_1, d_2, d_3, \ldots, d_n\}$
> *let* new subset: $S = \{\ \}$
> *for* k iterations *do*
>     $s_{add} = \text{best } F(S+s)$, where $s \in D - S$
>     $S = S + s_{add}$
>     $k = k + 1$

Similarly, in SBS, the process works in reverse where a feature, which contributes to the best result for the classifier performance upon removal, is removed from the feature subset. The final optimal subset is then fed into the ANN where its scoring metrics can be determined.

> *let* complete dataset: $D = \{d_1, d_2, d_3, \ldots, d_n\}$
> *let* new subset: $S = D$
> *for* k iterations *do*
>     $s_{minus} = \text{best } F(S-s)$, where $s \in S$
>     $S = S - s_{minus}$
>     $k = k + 1$

**Recursive Feature Elimination (RFE)**

In this method, features of least importance is iteratively removed, and the model reconstructed until the desired number of inputs is reached. The dataset is put through RFE using four common estimators (Logistic Regression, Support Vector Machine, Gradient Boosting and RandomForest) and its subset of classified important features is then be fed into the ANN and its scoring metrics determined after. The number of optimal features to be selected is determined by introducing cross-validation into the RFE and scoring different feature subsets before selecting the best scoring collection.

> *let* complete dataset: $D = \{d_1, d_2, d_3, \ldots, d_n\}$
> *let* new subset: $S = D$
> *for* k iterations *do*
>     train F(S), rank S according to importance
>     $S = S - s_{minus}$, where $s_{minus} = \text{least important feature}$
>     $k = k + 1$

## 4    Artificial Neural Network

In order to evaluate the FWS, it is necessary to feed the features extracted into an machine learning algorithm. Artificial Neural Network (ANN) is an machine learning algorithm that attempts to emulating the inner workings of the human brain in which the model learns through its experience and taking corrective measures in reducing the errors in prediction over each cycle. Supervised learning will be used in this paper where outputs are known during training and the weights of each neuron in the hidden layer to be adjusted iteratively to bring about the lowest difference in measurement between network output and desired output. The output being a single Boolean neuron that represents either the patient is diabetic or not (Fig. 1).

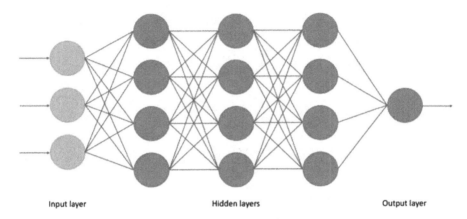

**Fig. 1.** Representation of an Artificial Neural Network (ANN)

In other literatures, Jayalakshmi et al. [15] made use of ANN as the predicting model for diabetes mellitus of the same dataset while Dey et al. [16] obtained a high accuracy score when predicting diabetics from their local dataset. In both cases, the dataset was preprocessed but does not implement any feature selection techniques. Accounting for this, ANN is chosen in this paper for the classifying algorithm.

## 5    Methodology

In this paper, three distinct steps are proposed to evaluate the performance of the FWS and predict the diabetes patients. Initially, the data is preprocess before the feature selection algorithm is applied. Finally, classification using the chosen predictor model is executed as shown in Fig. 2.

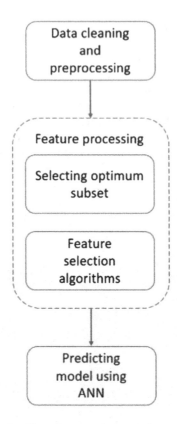

**Fig. 2.** Flow diagram of proposed approach

**Data Preprocessing**

As most real-world data comes with its own errors due to external influences, the datasets procured are generally considered as unclean which would result in a worse performance for the classifying model. From inspecting the Pima Indians diabetes dataset, there are missing data for some feature columns. A common method to clean this dataset would be to replace all zero or null values in each column with the median of that feature column. Another important consideration to note would be the different ranges of values contained in each feature column. Preferably, these values would need to be rescaled in order better the performance of the predicting model which entails transforming the ranges of values of each column to be in the span of 0 and 1.

**Feature Preprocessing**

The next step of would be the implementation of the wrapper methods for selecting the relevant features from the dataset. For the four common estimators used, each of them would have a different optimal number of features, k, that gives the best classification results. In SFWS and SBS, the terminating condition is only reached when a certain number of k features is reached where $k < N$ (number of features in the dataset). A similar number of k is also used for the RFE method for picking up the top k features from the N number of features in the dataset.

This can be determined by obtaining a cross-validation score against the number of features used to obtain said score. Logistic Regression classifier requires the greatest number of features (7) to perform optimum classification, followed by Random Forest (5), Support Vector Machine and Gradient Boosting (both 4) (see Figs. 3, 4, 5 and 6).

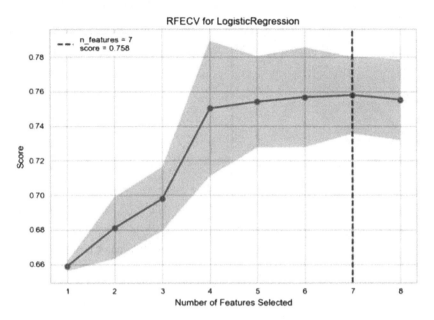

**Fig. 3.** Optimum number of features for Logistic Regression

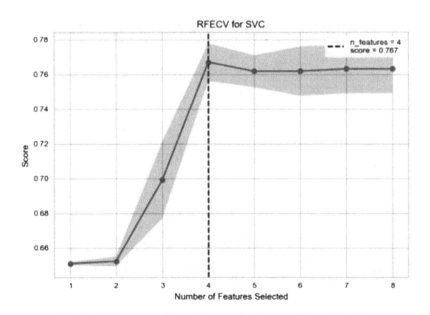

**Fig. 4.** Optimum number of features for Support Vector Machine

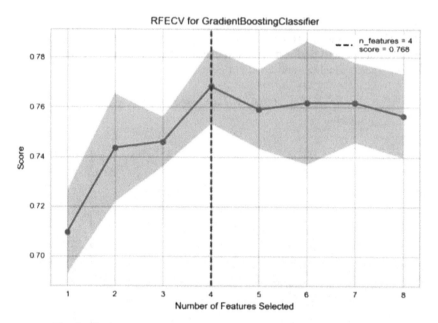

**Fig. 5.** Optimum number of features for Gradient Boosting Classifier

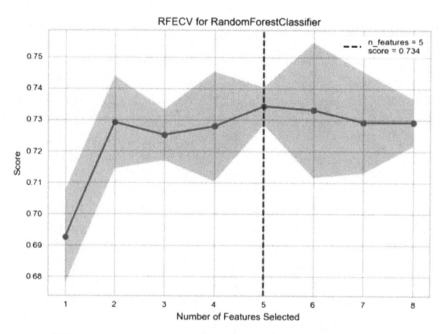

**Fig. 6.** Optimum number of features for Random Forest Classifier

**Scoring Evaluation Metrics**

The evaluation metrics of a classifying model are commonly dictated by the accuracy and prediction scores of the classifying model. This establishes the effect of each subset of features have on the model, which in turn determines the effectiveness of the wrapper methods.

The ANN model is built on the Keras Sequential model [17]. A suitable amount of dense neural network layers is added to the model with the Rectified Linear Unit (RELU) activation function and Adam optimizing algorithm before the end classification. This process of training will be repeated for at least 1000 times with an added condition of stop training if the error loss value difference does not change for 5 consecutive iterations.

The training test split is 7:3 respectively and evaluated based on the accuracy and precision values. A 10-fold cross validation is integrated to the predicting mode as well to remove the problems of overfitting and bias. For the purpose of the experiments, the hyperparameters are kept as a constant, removing its effect of prediction improvement unrelated to feature selection.

## 6    Results and Discussion

In SFWS and SBS, the scoring metric are based on accuracy scores of each classifier, while in RFE, the features are chosen based on its importance ranking. Features selected 75% of the time throughout all classifiers is accounted as one of the chosen features to be used in the ANN. The following Tables 1, 2 and 3 shows the results obtained from the tests.

**Table 1.**  Feature ranking through SFWS.

| Features | Importance ranking | | | | Chosen features |
|---|---|---|---|---|---|
| | LR | SVM | GB | RF | |
| Pregnancies | ✓ | | ✓ | | |
| Glucose | ✓ | ✓ | ✓ | ✓ | ✓ |
| Blood pressure | | ✓ | | ✓ | |
| Skin thickness | ✓ | | | ✓ | |
| Insulin | ✓ | | | | |
| BMI | ✓ | ✓ | ✓ | | ✓ |
| DiabetesPedigreeFunction | ✓ | | ✓ | ✓ | ✓ |
| Age | ✓ | ✓ | | ✓ | ✓ |

**Table 2.** Feature ranking through SBS.

| Features | Importance ranking | | | | Chosen features |
|---|---|---|---|---|---|
| | LR | SVM | GB | RF | |
| Pregnancies | ✓ | | | ✓ | |
| Glucose | ✓ | ✓ | ✓ | ✓ | ✓ |
| Blood pressure | ✓ | ✓ | | | |
| Skin thickness | ✓ | ✓ | | ✓ | ✓ |
| Insulin | ✓ | | ✓ | | |
| BMI | ✓ | ✓ | ✓ | ✓ | ✓ |
| DiabetesPedigreeFunction | ✓ | | | | |
| Age | | | ✓ | ✓ | |

**Table 3.** Feature ranking through RFE.

| Features | Importance ranking | | | | Chosen features |
|---|---|---|---|---|---|
| | LR | SVM | GB | RF | |
| Pregnancies | ✓ | ✓ | | | |
| Glucose | ✓ | ✓ | ✓ | ✓ | ✓ |
| Blood pressure | ✓ | | | ✓ | |
| Skin thickness | ✓ | | | | |
| Insulin | | | | ✓ | |
| BMI | ✓ | ✓ | ✓ | ✓ | ✓ |
| DiabetesPedigreeFunction | ✓ | ✓ | ✓ | ✓ | ✓ |
| Age | ✓ | | ✓ | | |

The model is run for 50 10-fold cross validation iterations and the scores averaged out. Table 4 tabulates the results obtained from the neural network evaluations with its own feature subsets. Figures 7 and 8 shows the boxplot distribution of the readings

**Table 4.** Evaluation of predicting model.

| Feature ranking method | Mean accuracy (%) | Mean precision (%) |
|---|---|---|
| Unfiltered (UNF) | 78.85 | 73.34 |
| SFWS | 78.41 | 72.07 |
| SBS | 76.18 | 70.42 |
| RFE | 77.13 | 71.19 |

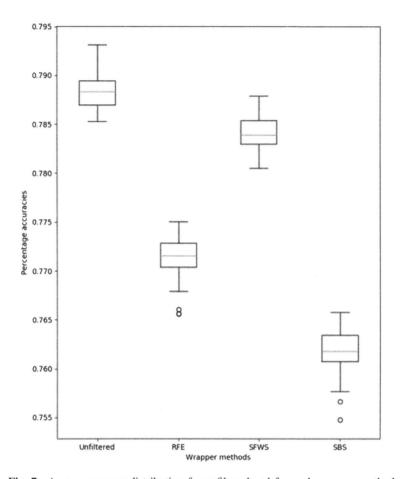

**Fig. 7.** Accuracy scores distribution for unfiltered and for each wrapper methods

From the above tables and figures, the best performing wrapper method would be the SFWS in both accuracy and precision scores of the ANN model. However, none of the feature selection methods yielded any significant improvement compared to using the existing dataset – in fact, the metrics have decreased, though only slightly.

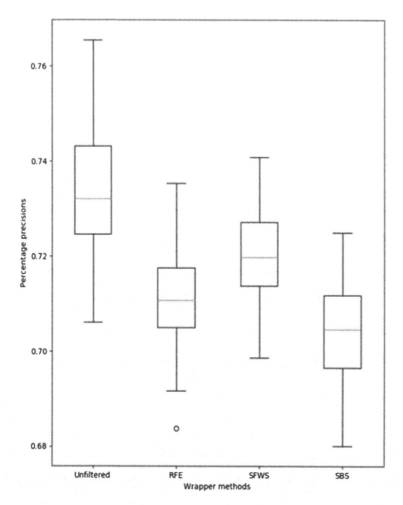

**Fig. 8.** Precision scores distribution for unfiltered and for each wrapper methods

## 7  Statistical Analysis

In order to evaluate the statistical significant of our result, a t-test statistical test is applied. According to Lim et al. it is necessary to apply significant testing in order to ensure that the test results are scientifically and statistically significant [18]. Using the t-test, we can determine the difference between the means of the results obtained to one another, and the significance of these differences [19]. A null hypothesis stating that

*There is no difference between the accuracy and precision scores of each wrapper method*

is formulated, while an alternate hypothesis states that the results obtained are unique form one another. The hypothesis can be rejected if the *p*-value $\leq \alpha$, where the common value of $\alpha$ is 0.05, indicating a 95% confidence of a valid conclusion for the test. The $t$-score is the scale of difference between the two groups, a larger value of $t$ indicates the repeatability probability of the results. The results obtained are tabulated in Table 5.

**Table 5.** t-score and $p$-values for the ANN readings

| Wrapper methods | Metrics used for the ANN model | | | |
|---|---|---|---|---|
| | Accuracy | | Precision | |
| | $t$-score | $p$-value | $t$-score | $p$-value |
| UNF-RFE | 43.144436 | 1.484971e−65 | 9.456317 | 1.832930e−15 |
| UNF-SFWS | 12.404437 | 8.354766e−22 | 5.701209 | 1.257081e−07 |
| UNF-SBS | 65.519795 | 9.891198e−83 | 12.012385 | 5.647437e−21 |
| SFWS-RFE | 34.657911 | 8.362349e−57 | 4.365991 | 3.140681e−05 |
| RFE-SBS | 22.706234 | 8.068926e−41 | 3.469553 | 0.000776444 |
| SFWS-SBS | 58.863079 | 2.773827e−78 | 7.542704 | 2.366585e−11 |

The resulting p-values from the tests fall way below the threshold of $\alpha = 0.05$, concluding the validity of readings from the ANN model for each wrapper method to be statistically significant and the test results to be valid.

# 8 Conclusion

The paper concluded that feature selection using wrapper methods is effective at determining the important features from the Pima Indians Diabetes dataset, that is being Plasma Glucose Concentration and BMI reading of the patients, as proven according to previous literatures seen in the works of Choubey et al. [20] and Rubaiat et al. [21]. As this paper only evaluates the wrapper methods separately, future improvements to produce a more robust feature selection method would be through an introduction of multi-stage process which incorporates all the above methods or in combination with filter and embedded methods. For the latter, SFWS is a prime candidate to be used as the wrapper component of the hybrid technique, considering that this method performs the best overall.

The paper also shows the ineffectiveness of the optimal subset of features derived from the feature selection methods in improving the evaluation scores of the ANN. Considerations for future research would include comparing different classification algorithms using the same methodology discussed on different low-dimensional data-sets to further determine the true benefits of feature selection.

# References

1. Norhafizah, D., Pg, B., Muhammad, H., Lim, T.H., Binti, N.S., Arifin, M.: Non-intrusive wearable health monitoring systems for emotion detection. In: 2017 12th IEEE Conference on Industrial Electronics and Applications (ICIEA), Siem Reap, pp. 985–989 (2017)

2. Adenin, H., Zahari, R., Lim, T.H.: Microcontroller based driver alertness detection systems to detect drowsiness. In: Proceedings of SPIE 10615, Ninth International Conference on Graphic and Image Processing (2018)
3. Veena Vijayan, V., Anjali, C.: Prediction and diagnosis of diabetes mellitus—a machine learning approach. In: IEEE Recent Advances in Intelligent Computational Systems (RAICS), Trivandrum, India, 10–12 December 2015 (2015)
4. Wei, S., Zhao, X., Miao, C.: A comprehensive exploration to the machine learning techniques for diabetes identification. In: IEEE 4th World Forum on Internet of Things (WF-IoT), Singapore, Singapore, 5–8 February 2018 (2018)
5. Sowjanya, K., Singhal, A., Choudhary, C.: MobDBTest: a machine learning based system for predicting diabetes risk using mobile devices. In: IEEE International Advance Computing Conference (IACC), Bangalore, India, 12–13 June 2015, pp. 297–402 (2015)
6. Duke, D.L., Thorpe, C., Mahmoud, M., Zirie, M.: Intelligent diabetes assistant: using machine learning to help manage diabetes. In: IEEE/ACS International Conference on Computer Systems and Applications, Doha, Qatar, 31 March–4 April 2008, pp. 913–914 (2008)
7. Gacav, C., Benligiray, B., Topal, C.: Sequential forward feature selection for facial expression recognition. In: 24th Signal Processing and Communication Application Conference, Zonguldak, Turkey, 16–19 May 2016 (2016)
8. Zheng, H., Park, H.W., Li, D., Park, K.H., Ryu, K.H.: A hybrid feature selection approach for applying to patients with diabetes mellitus: KNHANES 2013–2015. In: 5th NAFOSTED Conference on Information and Computer Science, Ho Chi Minh City, Vietnam, 23–24 November 2018 (2018)
9. Lv, X., Wu, J., Liu, W.: Face image feature selection based on gabor feature and recursive feature elimination. In: Sixth International Conference on Intelligent Human-Machine Systems and Cybernetics, Hangzhou, China, 26–27 August 2014 (2014)
10. Zhang, C., Li, Y., Yu, Z., Tian, F.: Feature selection of power system transient stability assessment based on random forest and recursive feature elimination. In: IEEE PES Asia-Pacific Power and Energy Engineering Conference, Xi'an, China, 25–28 October 2016 (2016)
11. Pima Indians Diabetes Dataset. https://www.kaggle.com/mehdidag/pimaindians/home
12. Dutta, D., Paul, D., Ghosh, P.: Analysing feature importances for diabetes prediction using machine learning. In: IEEE 9th Annual Information Technology, Electronics and Mobile Communication Conference, Vancouver, BC, Canada, 1–3 November 2018 (2018)
13. Balakrishnan, S., Narayanaswamy, R., Savarimuthu, N., Samikannu, R.: SVM ranking with backward search for feature selection in type II diabetes databases. In: IEEE International Conference on Systems, Man and Cybernetics, Singapore, Singapore, 12–15 October 2008 (2008)
14. Kohavi, R., John, G.H.: Wrappers for feature subset selection. Artif. Intell. **97**, 273–324 (1997)
15. Jayalakshmi, T., Santhakumaran, A.: A novel classification method for diagnosis of diabetes mellitus using artificial neural networks. In: International Conference on Data Storage and Data Engineering, Bangalore, India, 9–10 February 2010 (2010)
16. Dey, R., Bajpai, V., Gandhi, G., Dey, B.: Application of Artificial Neural Network (ANN) technique for diagnosing diabetes mellitus. In: IEEE Region 10 and the Third international Conference on Industrial and Information Systems, Kharagpur, India, 8–10 December 2008 (2008)
17. Keras Sequential Model. https://keras.io/models/sequential/
18. Hoo, T., Lim, I.B., Timmis, J.: A self-adaptive fault-tolerant systems for a dependable Wireless Sensor Networks. Des. Autom. Embedded Syst. **18**(3–4), 223 (2014)

19. Lim, T., Lau, H., Timmis, J., Bate, I.: Immune-inspired self healing in wireless sensor networks. In: Coello Coello, C.A., Greensmith, J., Krasnogor, N., Liò, P., Nicosia, G., Pavone, M. (eds.) ICARIS 2012. LNCS, vol. 7597, pp. 42–56. Springer, Heidelberg (2012). https://doi.org/10.1007/978-3-642-33757-4_4
20. Choubey, D., Paul, S., Kumar, S., Kumar, S.: Classification of Pima indian diabetes dataset using Naive Bayes with genetic algorithm as an attribute selection, pp. 451–455 (2016)
21. Rubaiat, S.Y., Rahman, Md.M., Hasan, Md.K.: Important feature selection & accuracy comparisons of different machine learning models for early diabetes detection. In: International Conference on Innovation in Engineering and Technology (2018)

# Food Recognition and Dietary Assessment for Healthcare System at Mobile Device End Using Mask R-CNN

Hui Ye[1] and Qiming Zou[2(✉)]

[1] School of Computer Engineering and Science,
Shanghai University, Shanghai 200444, China
[2] Computing Center, Shanghai University, Shanghai 200444, China
kim@shu.edu.cn

**Abstract.** Monitoring and estimation of food intake is of great significance to health-related research, such as obesity management. Traditional dietary records are performed in manual way. These methods are of low efficiency and a waste of labor, which are highly dependent on human interaction. In recent years, some researches have made progress in the estimation of food intake by using the computer vision technology. However, the recognition results of these researches are usually for the whole food object in the image, and the accuracy is not high. In terms of this problem, we provide a method to the food smart recognition and automatic dietary assessment on the mobile device. First, the food image is processed by MASK R-CNN which is more efficient than traditional methods. And more accurate recognition, classification and segmentation results of the multiple food items are output. Second, the OpenCV is used to display the food category and the corresponding food information of unit volume on the recognition page. Finally, in order to facilitate daily use, TensorFlow Lite is used to process the model to transplant to the mobile device, which can help to monitor people's dietary intake.

**Keywords:** Food image processing · Dietary monitoring · Mobile terminal recognition

## 1 Introduction

An unhealthy diet is one of the critical reasons for health problems. Obesity, diabetes, and other chronic diseases are all caused by unhealthy eating habits. According to the WHO [1], in 2016, more than 1.9 billion adults, 18 years and older, were overweight. Of these over 650 million were obese. One of the most important causes of this phenomenon is that many people have unhealthy lifestyle and poor eating habits, such as excessive intake of high-calorie and high-fat foods. Most people are reluctant to take the time to estimate their food intake due to the tedious methods which lack of real-time feedback. Traditional dietary methods require people to record intake manually, and subjective estimates limit the accuracy. So fewer people know their daily intake.

The development of technology provides iOS and Android systems with sufficient computing power to perform real-time image recognition. More and more applications

H. Gao et al. (Eds.): TridentCom 2019, LNICST 309, pp. 18–35, 2020.
https://doi.org/10.1007/978-3-030-43215-7_2

are developed and widely used under these systems. The spread of social platforms such as Facebook, Instagram, Weibo, and WeChat have enabled people to develop the habit of taking pictures and sharing before eating the food. This paper is also based on the increasing property of mobile device, and the growing reliance of people on them. After obtaining the food image through the mobile device, the information contained in the food image can be extracted to provide a useful reference for people's diet.

Image processing is a hot research direction because of the rapid development of AI. In recent years, it has made some progress in the field of automatic bounding-box object detection, recognition, and classification of food items from images by PC. Some researchers have used CNN to recognize and classify food and made the results more and more accurate. However, the results of these research methods show that only one food item for the whole image was recognized and there's no precise segmentation of multiple food items of the image. Some studies have already developed health recognition and management applications on mobile devices, but they still require users' involvement, such as framing the location of the food items manually, which degrades the user experience. Besides, the processing of food images is a fine-grained image processing problem. The existing methods for food image recognition generally use a single CNN, which is relatively troublesome in dealing with multiple kinds of classification problems. So,its accuracy is limited.

The paper is to achieve accurate segmentation, recognition, and classification of multiple food items of one image. The integrated network can provide more accurate results while considering the demand, such as Mask R-CNN [2] which is well known for its instance segmentation. However, it has not been applied to food images in existing researches to complete the recognition and classification of food items. Based on the above research status, this paper proposes a real-time food intake monitoring system using modern mobile devices with more powerful computing power and advanced target recognition technology, which offer a feasible method to help people manage their health. It can capture food image which will be classified in real-time by mobile devices, then display the type of food items and the intake information of per unit volume on the image.

The rest of the paper is organized as follows. Section 2 introduces the related work, and Sect. 3 gives an overview of the proposed system and details the implementation method. Section 4 introduces the experiment and results, and Sect. 5 summarizes the paper.

## 2 Related Work

### 2.1 Food Recognition

For food recognition, Parrish et al. [3] may be the first to use computer vision technology for food analysis tasks back to 1977. In 2010, Yang et al. [4] proposed a method using pair-wise local feature statistics for single-category food classification. They divided the image soft pixel level into eight components with labels such as bread and beef. To understand these spatial relationships, pair-wise local features based on distance and orientation between ingredients can be used. A multidimensional histogram can be used to represent how these features are distributed. SVM is further used as a classifier. Matsuda et al. [5] in 2012 proposed a method to recognize multiple food items in two steps by detecting candidate regions. The first step was to detect candidate regions by the circular detector and JSEG region segmentation. Then, image features such as food texture, gradient, color, etc. in the candidate area were extracted, and multi-core learning was used for recognition to train the model. Martinel et al. [6] proposed a wide-band residual network for food identification in 2018. They thought that the food has a vertical food layer regardless of the form of cooking, and they learn from residuals to achieve food recognition. For multi-food items recognition, He et al. [7] proposed a multi-core SVM method for multi-food images in 2016, which is a food recognition system based on a combination of part model and texture model. Part-based model is a common method for rigid target detection and classification. Considering the differences in food appearance and texture, the authors chose STF texture filters for integration into component-based detectors. Mask R-CNN is an integrated network that can recognize and classify multiple targets in an image. In this paper, Mask R-CNN is used to achieve accurate segmentation through the branch network which can generate mask of multiple food items.

## 2.2   Food Intake Monitoring

Dietary assessments or diet logs provide valuable reference for preventing many diseases. Most traditional methods rely on questionnaires or self-reports. These methods may cause inaccurate results due to subjective judgments, such as underreporting or miscalculating food consumption. With the development of computer technology, more and more methods are adopted based on these more efficient diet health management methods.

The first method to estimate food intake through digital photography was proposed by Williamson et al. [8] in 2003. They used a digital camera in a cafeteria to record food choices and post-meal residues to measure food intake. The registered dietitian analyzes the image based on the USDA data and enters the estimating size of the food into the computer application that has been designed to calculate the food's metrics. In 2011, Noronha et al. [9] launched a diet system platform for analyzing nutrients in food images, but it is still a semi-automatic method that requires the participation of registered dietitians.

To automate the monitoring, Zhu et al. [10] proposed a technology-assisted diet estimation system in 2008 to evaluate the type and consumption of food by obtaining food images before and after eating. There are also some similar approaches which estimate the amount of food for scene reconstruction and multi-view reconstruction. In recent years, more and more diet-related researches have provided nutrition-related information. Some foods are also labeled with relevant nutrients to help people get a healthier eating habits. The method proposed in this paper is to take the food image taken by the user before meal. The analysis output is carried out by the backend server, the food items in the image are automatically segmented, recognized and classified, and the nutritional information of per unit volume is displayed.

## 2.3    Food Recognition on Mobile Devices

Due to the increase in diet-related diseases such as obesity, many simple healthy diet applications have been developed, from manual monitoring of dietary activity analysis to the transmission of monitored information to web applications for immediate analysis.

To make it easier to monitor what people eat, Joutou et al. [11], in 2009, were the first to propose an algorithm for monitoring diet on mobile devices. They introduced multi-core learning into food recognition and then classified food images according to feature weights. In the same year, Puri et al. [10] proposed a system for food recognition and volume estimation, realizing food recognition by acquiring image data and voice data through mobile devices. However, this system only collects image and voice information by mobile devices, and the operation of image processing is still carried out by the server. Different from the above method, in 2012, Kong et al. [12] only implemented two functions according to the image. Users capture three pictures from different angles or surrounding videos of food through the mobile device, and then the obtained image information will be sent in XML format to the server for the remaining processing operations.

In 2013, Kawano and Yanai et al. [13] developed a lightweight food recognition mobile application for the first time. After the user pointed the camera at the food, manually framed the detection area, segmented the image using GrubCut, extracted the color histogram, and identified it based on the SURF feature pack. They continued to optimize this project in 2015 [14]. Pouladzadeh et al. [15] proposed a method similar to Kong's. Users need to record two photos of food from the top and side, extract each segment of food image by k-means clustering and texture segmentation, extract color features by edge detection and k-means, and extract texture features by Gabor filtering.

# 3    System Structure and Method

The ultimate goal of the system is to support users to capture types and nutrition information of food in real-time through general mobile devices before the meal which can help users to monitor their diet and manage their health.

The overall structure of the system can be seen in Fig. 1. The food image, which is taken by the mobile camera or existing already, is input into the mobile device. After the food image is pre-processed to a uniform size by the server of the system, the feature map of the whole image is extracted by five shared convolution layers. The network outputs five feature map for the entire image and FPN merges the feature maps to generate five fusion feature layers for subsequent model training and region generation. The RPN layer will operate on the bottom feature map to generate various anchors for each pixel after feature extraction of the input image. And also, the remaining feature layers are input into the sibling convolutional network for rough classification and rough bounding-box object detection to output a certain amount of optimized RoIs, namely the target item to be detected in the food image. The RoI Align operation is performed on the screened candidate boxes so as to match the feature maps of each food target with the original images and RoIs more accurately. The last three branches of the network implement multi-category classification of these RoIs, and perform border regression again for fine bounding-box object detection and mask generation. In terms of displaying food information, types of food items and corresponding nutritional information such as calorie, which is obtained from the BooheeNet [16], are stored in a food information database in advance. The food types obtained from the classification process are used to search in the food information database and get the corresponding food information. Finally, the classification results of food items and the obtained food information are sent to the client for display.

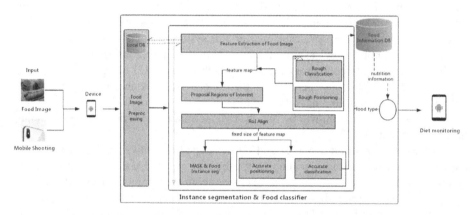

**Fig. 1.** System architecture diagram.

The network structure (see in Fig. 2) is used to train the model of food image processing. Corresponding food information is obtained from the food database through the classification results, which will be displayed to the users by OpenCV and PIL method at the same time. For the convenience of daily use, TensorFlow Lite is used to transplant the pc-trained model to the mobile terminal. Next section will detail the main approaches to implementing this process.

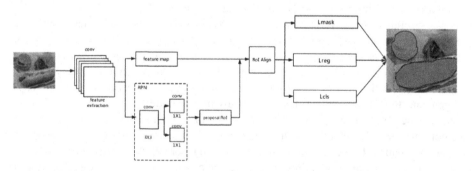

**Fig. 2.** Network model diagram.

### 3.1   Feature Extraction and Target Detection

In this paper, we adopt ResNet50+FPN as the backbone network to improve recognition accuracy. The food image is pre-processed into the size of 1024 * 1024 and extracted feature maps of the whole picture through five shared convolution layers. Here we divide ResNet50 into five stages to output five graphs that would be used next in the FPN network. FPN network is used to make better fusion feature map. Normal networks are directly using feature map output by the lowest layer because of its strong semantics. However, it is not easy to detect small items because of low location and resolution. So, five-layer fusion feature maps are carried out after that FPN deals with the five-layer feature maps output by the ResNet through reverse bounding-box object detection procession.

The lowest feature layer is used to generate nine different sized anchor boxes for each pixel in the image, and use a small network as a sliding window to detect item on the feature map generated before. For each point, the network generates nine anchors of different three areas and three aspect ratios, and get the coordinate values. The specific coordinates of each anchor box can be calculated as long as knowing the coordinates of the sliding window. In order to generate anchors for a pixel point, a base anchor is used to determine constant area at first and make the length-width ratios as 1:1, 1:2 and 2:1 to obtain three anchors. Figure 3 shows that nine anchors can be generated for each pixel with three areas and three ratios.

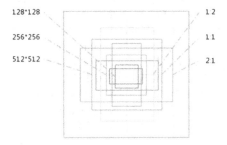

**Fig. 3.**  Nine anchor boxes with different three aspect ratios and three areas.

In the part of target detection, the remaining feature maps output from top to bottom is used to train RPN. The trained RPN realizes the simple bounding-box object detection and classification of target items. The extracted food image feature maps are input into the 512d convolution layer for processing firstly and then input to two 1 * 1 sibling convolution layers which one is for classification and another is for bounding-box object detection.

To achieve simple classification, the 256-dimensional features obtained before are input into the 1 * 1 cls layer. The softmax layer of cls layer is used for each anchor box to assign a binary degree to distinguish the foreground and background. There're two types of anchor boxes, they are assigned positive labels as the foreground. One is the anchor box whose IoU overlaps with any ground truth (GT) box more than 0.7. And the another is the anchor box with the highest IoU overlaps with a GT box (maybe less than 0.7). Therefore, a GT box can correspond to multiple anchors of positive labels as is shown in Fig. 4. Besides, negative labels are assigned to the anchors whose IoU with GT boxes are less than 0.3 as the background. In order to reduce redundancy, the anchor boxes with positive and negative labels are output and the remaining anchors are removed. At this time, the output is 18 (2 * 9) dimensions in total. After obtaining nine anchors for each pixel point, the cls layer outputs 2k scores for each region to estimate the probability if it's the target item. The scores will be used next.

**Fig. 4.** Comparison example of anchor box and GT.

As for achieving simple bounding-box object detection, the anchors of target items are input to the 1 * 1 reg layer for fine-tuning in the image. Each anchor box has $[x, y, w, h]$ 4 values corresponding to 4 offsets related to bounding-box object detection and size, where $(x, y)$ is the coordinate of the center point and $(w, h)$ is the width and height. As mentioned above, the $GT$ boxes are set to help detect the target items in the food image. However, the foreground anchors may have a great deviation from the $GT$. So, it is necessary to fine-tune the generated foreground anchor boxes so that they're more closely with the GT boxes. For each anchor, smooth loss is adopted for regression correction. The foreground anchor boxes are carried out before, and then translation parameter $(d_x, d_y)$ and scaling parameter $(d_w, d_h)$ are regression corrected to make the original anchor box $A$ adjust to be $GT'$ which is closer to $GT$. Namely for anchor box $A[A_x, A_y, A_w, A_h]$, there is a mapping $f$, make $f(A_x, A_y, A_w, A_h) = (GT'_x, GT'_y, GT'_w, GT'_h)$, where $(GT'_x, GT'_y, GT'_w, GT'_h) \approx (GT_x, GT_y, GT_w, GT_h)$. The output value is not the absolute coordinate of the anchor, but the offset correction relative to the $GT$.

Of course, for the output anchors to be detected, it is also necessary to determine whether exceeds the, and remove which is exceeded seriously. The scores obtained by the softmax loss before are sorted from large to small, and the top 2000 are extracted. Then, the NMS operation is performed on the top 2000 and redundancy is removed to obtain the anchors which are the local maximum values. At last, 300 anchors to be detected are output after being sorted again, and the area to be tested is preliminarily determined. Since workload for training all the anchors is relatively large, the program selects 128 positive label anchors and 128 negative label anchors randomly for training among the appropriate anchors during the training process.

## 3.2    Food Identification and Classification

Food recognition is a challenging task because that even if it is the same type of food, their shapes maybe vary depending on the way they are cooked, the eating habits of different countries or regions and the way they are dished up. The factors of different lighting conditions and shooting angles when taking food pictures can also lead to the challenge of food recognition. Besides, the integrated network such as the Mask R - CNN has not yet to be directly used in existing research of food processing. On the one hand, there're external factors above-mentioned may cause some recognition difficulties for food image. On the other hand, although the integrated network has advantages of good effect and high precision, their structures are more complicated than the simple classification and identification network. Under the calculation condition of mobile device support a few years ago, the performance of application on food recognition cannot keep up.

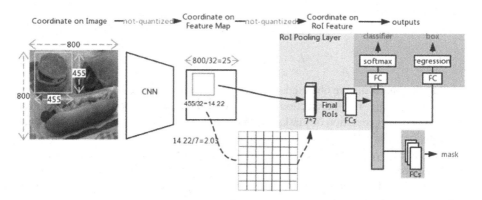

**Fig. 5.** Food identification, recognition and segmentation process.

In this paper, after filtering out some useless candidate RoIs, the process of image processing can be seen in Fig. 5. In order to consistently maintain a clear single-pixel spatial relationship, RoI Align operation is performed on the remaining candidate RoIs. In order to match the original image with the feature map obtained earlier and to match the feature map with the fixed size RoI, the RoI size in the feature space can be corrected by two quantization operations, and the floating-point pixel value appearing during the conversion process can be quantized (rounded). However, due to the high probability of rounding errors, the two quantized errors of images and features may have a large impact on the final matching. To avoid the errors caused by quantization, the "bilinear interpolation" method is used to solve the floating-point pixel values in the transform and make the RoI of the feature space corresponding to the original image more precisely.

The so-called "bilinear interpolation" method uses the four existing real pixel values around the virtual point to jointly determine a pixel value in the target image (see in Fig. 6). After adopting this method, the deviation caused by rounding can be well avoided. It is not necessary to quantize the RoI for the first time, but map to the feature map to divide the bin of 7 * 7 directly and accurately. The bilinear interpolation is performed on each bin to obtain four points, and then perform max pooling after inserting the value to get the final 7 * 7 RoI. That means the process of RoI Align has completed. The RoIs in the feature space are processed by RoI Align to output RoIs matching the original image, the full feature map, and the RoI feature.

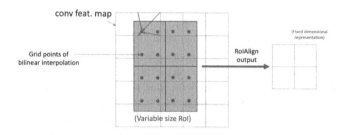

**Fig. 6.** RoI Align implementation.

Due to the addition of a mask branch, the loss function for each RoI is (1).

$$L = L_{cls} + L_{reg} + L_{mask} \tag{1}$$

After the final RoIs are obtained, the processing outputs of the full connection layer are input into the full connection layers for classification, bounding-box object detection and the generation of masks. Because that classification process is earlier than segmentation, it is only necessary to split it semantically if each RoI corresponds to only one category, which is equivalent to instance segmentation. Although for each RoI, the mask branch can complete the k-category classification, we hope that the segmentation and classification are implemented separately, so only take the foreground and the background as a two-category semantic segmentation. The other two branches are the final exact classification and bounding-box object detection.

### 3.3 Food Index Coefficient

The final purpose of this paper is to transplant the research contents above to mobile devices and add food-related information to monitor the users' diet. The local food database, on the one hand, can improve the recognition efficiency and reduce the pressure on the server. On the other hand, the food which is not stored locally will be saved in the same mode to the database, which can expand the variety of food and provide more data foundation for future identification.

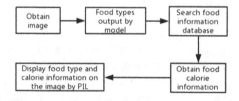

**Fig. 7.** Process of displaying the final output results.

After the PC-side model is trained, the recognition result and the corresponding food information need to be present at the same time to improve the users' use. After getting an image of an approximate video stream of food, then use the OpenCV library, which is provided in Python, to capture real-time food images and process on them. Figure 7 shows the process of displaying the final output results. The results of the model recognition are used to search in the database to obtain the corresponding food information, and call the PIL library to display the obtained food information and the recognition result together in the food image.

## 4  Food Recognition

### 4.1  Model Training of PC End

All ten categories of food in the COCO2017 [17] data set are prepared for the experiments in this paper, each category with a different quantity. Some categories do not have independent images but are labeled in other images. In the experiment, 8k images are selected for training and 1k are for verification. Through training, we hope to achieve bounding-box object detection, segmentation for one or more types of foods present in the image and classify them accurately.

In the experiments, ResNet50+FPN is selected as the basic network for the sake of accuracy. Of course, considering the image processing work on the mobile terminal, the lighter network YOLO will be used as the backbone network in the future work, which can improve the recognition efficiency and provide relatively more flexible model.

**Fig. 8.** The output of bounding-box object detection process. (a) Anchors for each pixel. (b) Anchors after filtering according to IoU. (c) (d) Refine some anchors out of bounds. (e) Anchors after NMS operation. (f) Final output result.

After extracting the feature map of entire image, the bounding-box object detection process is output at first. Candidate regions are generated for each pixel point by the RPN. Figure 8(a) shows the anchors of different proportions produced by the RPN. Each point generates nine candidate anchors of different areas and aspect ratios. Then the IoU of the generated candidate region with the GT is calculated to perform further screening to obtain more accurate anchors, which aim to achieve coarse bounding-box object detection of the food items in the image. Figure 8 shows the process and final results of bounding-box object detection by generating bounding boxes.

It is known from the introduction of experiment methods in Sect. 3 that the bounding-box object detection and classification are carried out through two parallel networks in the RPN. When classifying the food items in the image, the initial results are very confusing. Therefore, as shown in Fig. 9, the NMS method is also used to correct the outputs after removing all which are out-of-boundary or non-positive and negative labels to eliminate the redundancy. Finally, more accurate classification results are output.

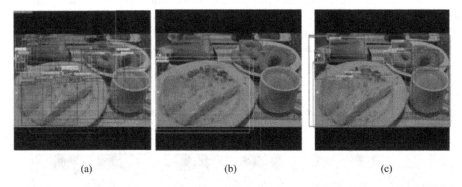

       (a)                                (b)                               (c)

**Fig. 9.** The output of the classification process. (a) The result of classification before refinement. (b) The result of classification after refinement. (c) The final result of classification after NMS.

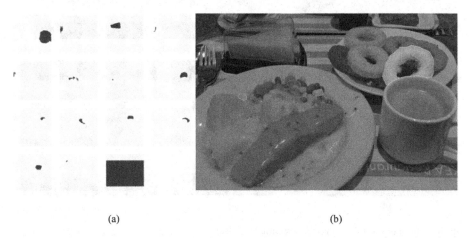

                  (a)                                     (b)

**Fig. 10.** The output of the segmentation process. (a) Mask target of different food items. (b) Mask result of each food item.

Except bounding-box object detection and classification, it's also necessary to output a binary mask corresponding to each final RoI, which can segment multiple food items of the image. The mask targets and results corresponding to RoI are shown in Fig. 10.

After bounding-box object detection, segmentation, and classification are completed, it's necessary to display categories and corresponding food nutrition information at the same time on the image. The nutrition information of 10 kinds of food had stored in advance in the food information database, and adopt the methods mentioned in Sect. 3.3 for the experiment. Figure 11 shows the final training output on the PC that food-related information was presented with the categories on the food image at the same time.

**Fig. 11.** The final result of processing food image on the PC-end.

## 4.2 Food Recognition on Mobile End

AI applications for mobile devices typically have features such as no network latency, more timely response, and higher data privacy. After training the model on the PC side, it's time to consider how to transplant it to the mobile terminal and implement the same functions on the mobile side as the PC. TensorFlow Lite is a cross-platform lightweight solution released by Google that runs machine learning on mobile devices. It can help transplant the PC models trained by TensorFlow to mobile and embedded devices, which support multiple platforms including Android, iOS, etc. Because there is no cellular network delay with minimal runtime library, the application can run more smoothly, and its high portability supports not only PC-side but also mobile devices operation. It's useful for implementing the same AI-related functions on the PC side and the mobile terminal.

The model trained by TensorFlow on the PC side cannot be directly used by the mobile terminal because of incompatible formats with each other. In this paper, after the process of training model on the PC side is completed, the generated .pb model file of saving constant and the .ckpt model file of saving variables are format converted. At first, the two model files are frozen into a .pb graph file, and then quantized the frozen file by the toco tool mentioned above to generate a callable lite model file. the model file, which is generated before, can be directly called when developing system through the Java interface provided in Android studio. The TensorFlow Lite provides both C++ and JAVA APIs, but the transplant process is the same regardless of the API's type for that the task to be done is to load the model and then run the model. In the experiments, the Interpreter class of JAVA API is used to complete the process of loading and running. The following (see in Fig. 12) is the recognition results carried out by using the virtual device in Android Studio. It's known that the system can process and output all food item of the image. Not only display the results on the image, but also show in the text output box below the image. If there are food items of the same type in one image, each processing result will be output on the image while the bottom text will only output once.

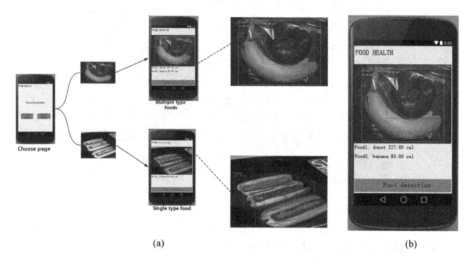

(a)                                                                                      (b)

**Fig. 12.** (a) Food detection results at the mobile terminal simulator. (b) Main process result screen of the proposed system.

## 5   Experiment

In this section, we describe experimental results regarding recognition accuracy and spending time. In the experiments, we have selected ten-category food dataset randomly from the training dataset and validation dataset of the COCO2017, which has more than 100 testing images per category that have been pre-processed into standard size already. The total number of food images in the dataset is 2000. Appropriate number of food image dataset have been used to calculate the classification error rate for each food item separately and the recognition accuracy of four plate situations.

## 5.1 Evaluation on Recognition Accuracy

The food classifier's accuracy is affected by many factors, such as fault segmentations, failing classification to a different shaped food type, misinterpretations between similar shaped food types, and food information missing in database. Therefore, the proposed method was tested with different types of test cases to cover as many situations as possible. Then, the overall accuracy was estimated.

Firstly, we evaluate recognition accuracy by ten types of food items as ten test cases. For a certain food, 100 image data are input and get the classification results at first, and then the classification error rate is calculated by function (2). TN is the number of positive classes classified as positive classes while FN is the number of positive classes classified as negative classes. As shown in Table 1, the rates of food items like sandwich, which is closer to a specific shape, is much higher than the rates while items with a variable shape like broccoli. The system has achieved a reasonable error of about 3.82% on average.

$$P_{error} = 1 - (TN/(TN + FN)) \tag{2}$$

**Table 1.** Classification error rates of ten types of food items.

| No. | Food items | Error rate (%) | No. | Food items | Error rate (%) |
|-----|-----------|----------------|-----|-----------|----------------|
| 1 | Apple | 2.37 | 6 | Carrot | 0.63 |
| 2 | Banana | 2.12 | 7 | Hot dog | 2.33 |
| 3 | Sandwich | 0.23 | 8 | Pizza | 7.91 |
| 4 | Orange | 4.45 | 9 | Donut | 1.57 |
| 5 | Broccoli | 9.86 | 10 | Cake | 6.78 |

After classification error rate of different types of food items was tested, the food image dataset is divided into four test situations of fast food, fruits, salad and dessert, which are include 400 for each plate situation removing mix-types images and redundance. Each situation is divided into 5 categories according to the amount of food in an image, and each category has 80 food images. Figure 13 shows that the average lowest classification accuracy rate of each plate situation which is with the same number of food items. It is clear that, when the number of food items increases of plate, the accuracy rate will drop. Besides, we just average the lowest classification rates without considering the number of food items, and obtain the average lowest classification rates of each plate situation. As shown in Fig. 13 and Table 2, another fact is that the method performs better on shaped food items like fast food, fruits and dessert when the number of food items is the same. The salad is hard to be classified for it usually does not have plated with a standard pattern. In general, the proposed method can achieve the lowest recognition accuracy of 90% for standard shape food items and 79% for irregular shape food items, which improves the accuracy of food recognition to 88%.

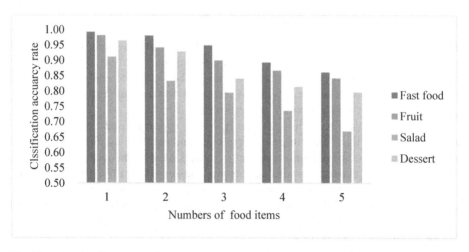

**Fig. 13.** The classification accuracy rate of different plate situations with the number of food items.

**Table 2.** The classification accuracy rate regard to different plate situations.

| Plate situation | Fast food | Fruit | Salad | Dessert | Average |
|---|---|---|---|---|---|
| Accuracy rate (<1.000) | 0.935 | 0.907 | 0.789 | 0.869 | 0.875 |

In this experiments, we compare the proposed system with server-side recognition system by Martinel et al. [6] and mobile-end recognition system by He et al. [7]. We randomly selected 250 food images from the test dataset to compare the three methods. Among these food images are the mixture of four kinds of plate situations mentioned above.

An comparison with existing methods based on the COCO2017 dataset is shown in Table 3. Top1 accuracy refers to the probability that the maximum probability of the prediction result is the correct result, while top5 accuracy means the probability that there is correct result in the top five prediction results. Results demonstrates that the proposed method performs better than the newest server-side recognition method by achieving a Top1 accuracy of more than 92%. Besides, our method on mobile-end is also showing a better recognition accuracy than Multi-SVM proposed in latest mobile-end food recognition system and the Top 1 accuracy can be more than 90%.

**Table 3.** Top1 and Top5 performance obtained by server-end and mobile-end approaches separately on test dataset.

| Method | Top1 | Top5 |
|---|---|---|
| WISeR [6] | 90.27 | 97.84 |
| ResNet+FPN (proposed on pc-end) | 92.35 | 99.87 |
| Multi-SVM [7] | 88.86 | 95.72 |
| ResNet+FPN (proposed on mobile-end) | 90.21 | 99.16 |

## 5.2   Evaluation of Processing Time

The system is implemented as an Android application required 36 MB memory (31 MB is mainly for except image processing and 5 MB is mainly for image processing) for the Android virtual mobile device which has a quad-core CPU and using Android 5.0 operation system. Click the button "Choose a food image" at the choose page and input a food image prepared in advance to the system, which will output the results among 2 s and 15 s depending on the size of image and the number of images. As shown as in Fig. 14, the number and size of the input image are the factors that affect the spending time. Firstly, we selected 25 food images of the same size for the affection of images' number. Figure 14(a) shows that the more images we input, the longer the time spend. Input image number which is close to the maximum, and the normal processing spend time is close to 5 s. In addition, although the number of images we output is small, it takes a long time because the food items which need to be recognized are difficult to process. Secondly, we selected 10 food images of different sizes to test the influence of image size. As shown as in Fig. 14(b), the larger the input image size is, the longer the time spend, and the longest time is close to 6 s. Except that spending time increases linearly with size, there are also exceptions due to the difficulty of processing food items. Overall, the system can help a user obtain food information faster than traditional methods.

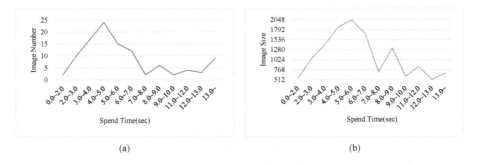

(a)                              (b)

**Fig. 14.** Spend time of different image numbers and different sizes.

From the aspect of memory feasibility, if the system proposed in this paper only needs about 40M memory as an independent application, the main memory consumption is used to call the camera interface, request the server, etc., and the memory consumption in image processing is small, only about 1/4 of which is consumed. Therefore, if the existing image is used for processing, the memory cost is very feasible. In terms of time feasibility, it can be seen from the above that when the image size is not more than 2M, the processing time will not exceed 5 s, and the fastest time can be less than 1 s. Therefore, when it is used in daily life to process food images, it is within the acceptable range in terms of time, because it is also feasible in terms of time cost.

## 6 Summary and Future Work

This paper has realized to output the types of food items and the corresponding nutrition information on the food image, which is taken real-timely by the mobile terminal, to help people monitor diet and eat healthier. Although the experiment results are not very mature, and there is still a long way to go. Same as many seniors who have brought many methods and ideas of this field, we hope that our efforts can not only provide a theoretical foundation for managing people's health and life, but also help people who interested in this direction continue related study base on it.

To improve the flexibility of the model and the lightness and efficiency of the mobile application, the new real-time target detection network YOLO will be considered as the backbone network in the next work to make the system more applicable. And the way of 3D modeling will be used to optimize the system and make a more detailed estimate of the volume of food to get more accurate food information.

## References

1. WHO Homepage. https://www.who.int/zh/news-room/fact-sheets/detail/obesity-and-overwe ight. Accessed 20 Oct 2019
2. He, K., Gkioxari, G., Dollar, P., et al.: Mask R-CNN. IEEE Trans. Pattern Anal. Mach. Intell. **PP**(99), **1** (2017)
3. Parrish, E., Goksel, A.K.: Pictorial pattern recognition applied to fruit harvesting. Trans. ASAE **20**, 822–827 (1977)
4. Yang, S., Chen, M., Pomerleau, D., et al.: Food recognition using statistics of pairwise local features. In: The Twenty-Third IEEE Conference on Computer Vision and Pattern Recognition, CVPR 2010, San Francisco, CA, USA, 13–18 June 2010. IEEE (2010)
5. Matsuda, Y., Hoashi, H., Yanai, K.: Recognition of multiple-food images by detecting candidate regions. In: 2012 IEEE International Conference on Multimedia and Expo (ICME). IEEE (2012)
6. Martinel, N., Foresti, G.L., Micheloni, C.: Wide-slice residual networks for food recognition. In: Proceedings of 2018 IEEE Winter Conference on Applications of Computer Vision, WACV 2018, vol. 2018-January, pp. 567–576, December 2016
7. He, H., Kong, F., Tan, J.: DietCam: multiview food recognition using a multikernel SVM. IEEE J. Biomed. Health Inf. **20**(3), 848–855 (2017)
8. Williamson, D.A., Allen, H.R.: Digital photography: a new method for estimating food intake in cafeteria settings. Eat. Weight Disord. – Stud. Anorexia Bulimia Obes. **9**(1), 24–28 (2004)
9. Noronha, J., Hysen, E., Zhang, H., Gajos, K.Z.: Platemate. In: Proceedings of the 24th Annual ACM Symposium on User Interface Software and Technology - UIST 2011, p. 1 (2011)
10. Puri, M., Zhu, Z., Yu, Q., et al.: Recognition and volume estimation of food intake using a mobile device. In: IEEE Workshop on Applications of Computer Vision (WACV 2009), Snowbird, UT, USA, 7–8 December 2009. IEEE (2009)
11. Joutou, T., Yanai, K.: A food image recognition system with multiple kernel learning. In: IEEE International Conference on Image Processing. IEEE Press (2009)
12. Kong, F., Tan, J.: DietCam: automatic dietary assessment with mobile camera phones. Pervasive Mob. Comput. **8**(1), 147–163 (2012)

13. Kawano, Y., Yanai, K.: Real-time mobile food recognition system. In: 2013 IEEE Conference on Computer Vision and Pattern Recognition Workshops. IEEE (2013)
14. Kawano, Y., Yanai, K.: FoodCam: a real-time food recognition system on a smartphone. Multimed. Tools Appl. **74**(14), 5263–5287 (2015)
15. Pouladzadeh, P., Shirmohammadi, S., Arici, T.: Intelligent SVM based food intake measurement system. In: IEEE International Conference on Computational Intelligence & Virtual Environments for Measurement Systems & Applications. IEEE (2013)
16. Boohee Homepage. http://www.boohee.com/food/. Accessed 20 Oct 2019
17. COCO dataset Homepage. http://cocodataset.org/. Accessed 20 Oct 2019

# Power Micro-Blog Text Classification Based on Domain Dictionary and LSTM-RNN

Meng-yao Shen, Jing-sheng Lei, Fei-ye Du, and Zhong-qin Bi[(✉)]

College of Computer Science and Technology,
Shanghai University of Electric Power, Shanghai, China
zqbi@shiep.edu.cn

**Abstract.** The micro-blog texts of the national grid provinces and cities will be analyzed as the main data, including the micro-blogs and corresponding comments, which will help us understand the events of power industry and people's attitudes towards these events. In this work, the data set is composed of 420,000 micro-blog texts. Firstly, the professional vocabulary of electric power is extracted, and these vocabulary are manually labeled, thus proposing a new field dictionary closely related to the power industry. Secondly, using the new power domain dictionary to classify the 2018 electric micro-blogs, and we can find that classification accuracy increased from 88.7% to 95.2%. Finally, a classification model based on LSTM (Long Short-Term Memory) and RNN (Recurrent Neural Network) is used to deal with the comments under the micro-blog. The experimental result shows that the classification of the LSTM-RNN is more accurate. The rate was 83.1%, which was significantly better than the traditional LSTM and RNN text classification models of 78.4% and 73.1%.

**Keywords:** Text classification · Power micro-blog · Domain dictionary · Word vector · Classification accuracy · LSTM-RNN

## 1 Introduction

The so-called micro-blog emotional analysis is to identify personal emotions [1, 2] from the micro-blog published by users, so as to judge the emotional tendencies of micro-blog texts [3–5], or to get the views expressed by users are "agree", "neutral" or "oppose". Aiming at the problem of feature selection in emotional analysis of micro-blog, Ning, Yang and Zhao [6] proposed the construction method of emotional dictionary based on Synonym Words Forest and micro-blog retrieval system. Cherishing [7] proposed a multi-strategy approach based on emoticons and emotional dictionaries to calculate the emotional tendency of micro-blog texts by counting the number of emoticons and emotional words. However, this approach has some limitations in dealing with micro-blogs that do not obviously contain emotional features.

The language model can be divided into word level and character level according to the prediction results of the output terminal. In the existing studies, most of the language models are at the lexical level [8–11], but a small number of studies focus on the character level. For example, Karpathy, Johnson and Fei-Fei [12] demonstrated the learning ability of LSTM by using character-level model, while Ballesteros, Dyer and

H. Gao et al. (Eds.): TridentCom 2019, LNICST 309, pp. 36–45, 2020.
https://doi.org/10.1007/978-3-030-43215-7_3

Smith [13] constructed LSTM by replacing pronouns with characters, which improved the accuracy of dependency analysis.

In building language model, Socher, Lin and Ng [14] uses RNN to parse syntax. Irsoy and Cardie [15] builds RNN into a deep structure and becomes a typical three-tier deep learning model. However, RNN has the problems of gradient explosion and disappearance [16, 17], and is not suitable for long text [18]. So later researchers put forward LSTM (Long Short-Term Memory) [19], which is a time recursive neural network, and is suitable for processing or predicting time series. Important events with relatively long intervals. Today, LSTM has been applied in many fields, such as emotional classification [20, 21], machine translation [22, 23], semantic recognition [24], intelligent question and answer [25]. In short, LSTM-based natural language processing has become the mainstream research direction.

## 2  Introduction of LSTM-RNN

In this section, the structure and modeling method of LSTM-RNN neural network model will be described.

### 2.1  LSTM Text Classification Model

LSTM is widely used in NLP, and has many mature applications in machine translation and text classification. LSTM neural network model is specially designed to deal with the problem of long-term dependence absence. It differs from traditional RNN network model in that LSTM has different cyclic unit module structure, which is different from traditional RNN network model. Some module structures are stored in four interacting layers of neural networks. Specifically, LSTM can effectively control the historical information by improving the structure of RNN, adding memory unit and three gated units, instead of removing the hidden layer state of the previous moment every time as RNN does. These improvements enhance the ability of LSTM to process long text sequences and solve the problem of gradient disappearance.

The cell model structure of LSTM is shown in Fig. 1.

- Forget Gate

In text categorization, sometimes it is necessary to label words as singular or plural. At this time, LSTM can achieve the desired effect.

$$\Gamma_f^{(t)} = \sigma\left(W_f\left[a^{(t-1)}, x^{(t)}\right] + b_f\right) \tag{1}$$

$W_f$ is the parameter that controls the forget gate. The value of $\Gamma_f^{(t)}$ is [0, 1]. The forget gate vector multiplies the previous cell $c^{(t-1)}$. Therefore, if the value of $\Gamma_f^{(t)}$ is 0 (or close to 0), this means that LSTM will remove the information previously stored in the cell; if the value of $\Gamma_f^{(t)}$ is 1, it Represents retaining information in a cell.

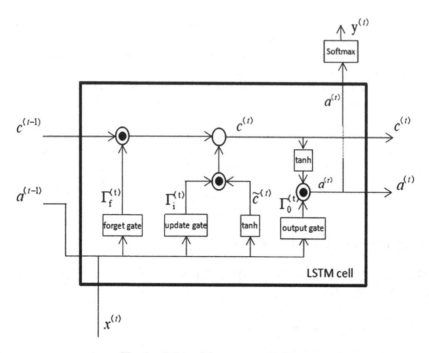

**Fig. 1.** Cell model structure of LSTM.

- Update Gate

If in forget gate the nature of the object is not required Singular (i.e. forgetting singular information) requires update gate to update the state of the object to be complex. The formula is as follows:

$$\Gamma_u^{(t)} = \sigma\left(W_u\left[a^{(t-1)}, x^{\{t\}}\right] + b_u\right) \tag{2}$$

The value of $\Gamma_u^{(t)}$ is [0, 1]. At the same time, the product of $\tilde{c}^{(t)}$ and the element is used to calculate $c^{\langle t \rangle}$.

- Update Cell Status

First, a vector is used to save the state of the previous cell:

$$\tilde{c}^{\langle t \rangle} = \tanh\left(W_c\left[a^{(t-1)}, x^{\langle t \rangle}\right] + b_c\right) \tag{3}$$

The state of the new cell is:

$$c^{(t)} = \Gamma_f^{(t)} * c^{(t-1)} + \Gamma_u^{(t)} * \tilde{c}^{(t)} \tag{4}$$

- Out Gate

The value used to determine the final output:

$$\Gamma_o^{(t)} = \sigma\left(W_o\left[a^{\langle t-1\rangle}, x^{(t)}\right] + b_o\right) \tag{5}$$

$$a^{(t)} = \Gamma_o^{(t)} * \tanh\left(c^{(t)}\right) \tag{6}$$

## 2.2   LSTM-RNN Model

The structure of LSTM-RNN model is shown in Fig. 2.

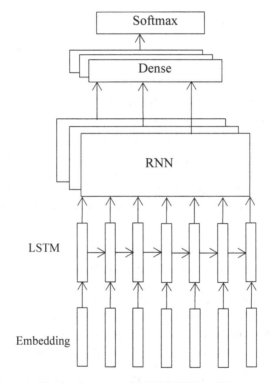

**Fig. 2.** Structure of LSTM-RNN model.

Firstly, the trained word vectors are input into Embedding layer, and then the output vectors of Embedding layer are input into an initial LSTM layer for semantic feature extraction. Because the original corpus is processed by Padding, the LSTM output needs to be multiplied by Mask matrix to reduce the impact of Padding. Since the RNN can process the data directly, the output of the LSTM will then be used directly as input to the RNN for further feature extraction. Finally, the output of RNN convolution layer will be aggregated to a smaller latitude, and the output will be positive tag 1, neutral tag 0 and negative tag −1, so as to obtain the required text classification results.

## 3 Experiment

### 3.1 Experimental Preparation

The experiment in this paper is carried out under Windows 10 system. The CPU used is Inter Core i5-2450M 2.5 GHz, and the memory size is 6 GB. The experimental programming language is Python 3.5, the development tool is Pycharm, and the depth learning framework used is Tensorflow 1.0.1.

### 3.2 Experimental Design

This section mainly based on the severity of the power accident, to analyze the micro-blog text corpus and get three types.

**Data Set for Micro-Blog Text.** Using selenium-based micro-blog crawlers, this paper collects all relevant texts and letters published by Sina micro-blog in 2018 from the State Grid and other provinces, include Jiangsu, Jiangxi, Henan, Zhejiang, Hunan, Shanghai, Beijing, Xiamen, Shaanxi, Chongqing. Interest, a total of 420,000 data.

**Establishment of Emotional Dictionary in Electric Power Field.** Domain dictionary is mainly used to store real words with clear distinction. Because of the particularity of power industry, it is difficult to process them directly by using existing dictionaries. Therefore, we construct a new emotional dictionary in power field. The main flow chart is shown in Fig. 3.

By focusing on the official micro-blog accounts of 11 different provinces and municipalities, the micro-blog published in 2018 is regarded as the corpus content, and the special vocabulary of the power industry is analyzed and annotated artificially. For example, the vocabulary of precision, order, efficiency, environmental protection, automation, power saving and operation is added into the active category, while the vocabulary of damage and operation is damaged. Words such as sudden drop, fall, blackout, electricity theft, lightning strike, emergency repair, arrears and so on were added to the negative category. At the same time, it combines NTUSD Emotional Dictionary of Taiwan University, CNKI Emotional Dictionary and Tsinghua University Chinese Commendatory and Degradation Dictionary to get an Emotional Dictionary for the field of electricity. Using the emotional dictionary in the field of power, this paper carries out emotional analysis on power-related micro-blogs. The idea is as follows: to segment each micro-blog text document, find out the emotional words, negative words and degree adverbs, and then judge whether there are negative words and degree adverbs in front of each emotional word. In each group, if there is a negative word, the emotional weight of the emotional word is multiplied by −1. If there is a degree adverb, the emotional weight of the emotional word is multiplied by the degree value of the degree adverb. Finally, the scores of all groups are added up, that is, the micro-blog. Emotional score of text. Experiments show that the accuracy rate of text categorization by using emotion dictionary in power field is 95.2%, which is significantly higher than 88.7% when using ordinary emotion dictionary for text categorization.

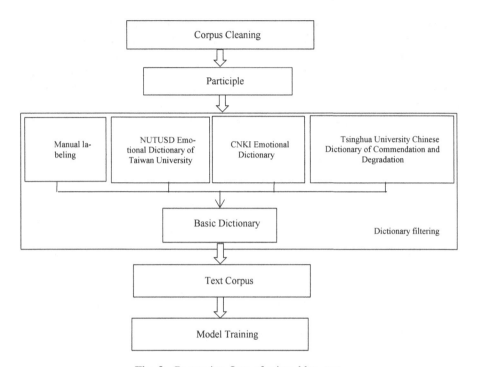

**Fig. 3.** Processing flow of micro-blog text.

**Processing Comments.** Firstly, the text of power micro-blog is divided into three categories: first, there are casualties; second, there are no casualties but financial losses; third, there are no casualties or financial losses. Correspondingly, all comments on micro-blog are classified into the same three categories, thus three sets of power micro-blog comment data sets are obtained. Next, we can use LSTM-RNN model to classify the comment text of power micro-blog.

Due to the limitation of comment length on micro-blog, most of the comments on power-related micro-blog are relatively short. At the same time, there are also many special emoticons. In view of these characteristics of power micro-blog text, this paper considers using word vector to process micro-blog text.

Firstly, the trained word vectors are input into Embedding layer, and then the output vectors of Embedding layer are input into an initial LSTM layer for semantic feature extraction. Because the original corpus is processed by Padding, the LSTM output needs to be multiplied by Mask matrix to reduce the impact of Padding. Since the RNN can process the data directly, the output of the LSTM will then be used directly as input to the RNN for further feature extraction. Finally, the output of RNN convolution layer will be aggregated to a smaller latitude, and the output will be positive tag 1, neutral tag 0 and negative tag −1, so as to obtain the required text classification results.

### 3.3    Experimental Result

In order to make a more intuitive comparison between LSTM-RNN and LSTM and RNN, this paper uses Matplotlib, a third-party library of Python, to draw graphics.

As can be seen from Fig. 4, when LSTM model and RNN model are trained by gradient descent method, the loss value of function decreases gradually, and finally tends to stable convergence state. Compared with the original LSTM-RNN model, the initial loss value of LSTM-RNN model increases with the increase of model complexity, but the convergence rate increases significantly.

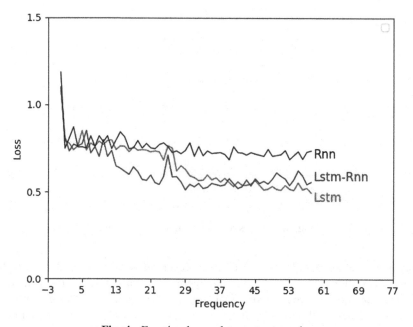

**Fig. 4.** Function loss value contrast graph.

As can be seen from Fig. 5, the convergence speed of the classification accuracy of LSTM-RNN micro-blog comment model based on word vector is faster than that of traditional LSTM model and RNN model, and the final classification accuracy is also higher. The classification accuracy of LSTM-RNN model is 83.1% after 460 iterations, while that of LSTM model and RNN model is 78.4% and 73.1% respectively.

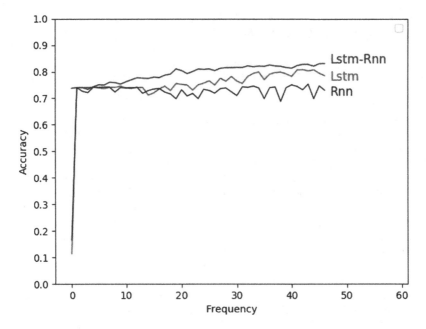

**Fig. 5.** Model accuracy contrast diagram.

## 4 Conclusion

The method based on emotional dictionary can make full use of existing emotional resources and has a good effect on emotional classification of normative texts, but this method depends largely on the quality and coverage of emotional dictionary. In this paper, we propose an emotional dictionary in the field of electric power, so as to get a higher accuracy of text categorization of electric power micro-blog. In view of the many characteristics of micro-blog comment text, this paper proposes a text classification model based on word vector LSTM-RNN. Compared with the traditional LSTM model and RNN model, the results show that this method can significantly improve the classification accuracy of micro-blog comment text, thus effectively improve the quality of micro-blog sentiment analysis.

## References

1. Ding, Y., Jia, Y., Zhou, B.: Survey of data mining for Microblogs. J. Comput. Res. Dev. **51** (4), 691–706 (2014)
2. Hou, M., Teng, Y., Li, X., et al.: Research on the language characteristics and emotional analysis strategies of topic-based weibo. Lang. Charact. Appl. **2**, 135–143 (2013)
3. Song, S., Li, Q., Lu, D.: A sentiment analysis method for hot events in microblogging. Comput. Sci. **6A**, 226–228 (2012)
4. Zhang, Y., Zheng, J., Huang, G., et al.: Microblog sentiment analysis method based on a double attention model. J. Tsinghua Univ. **58**(2), 122–130 (2018)

5. Qing, F., Wang, H.C.X., Wang, X.: Microblog sentiment analysis based on linguistic context. Comput. Eng. **43**(3), 241–252 (2017)
6. Ning, H., Yang, S., Zhao, Y., et al.: Study of microblog sentiment analysis based on semantic feature. Appl. Sci. Technol. **43**(3), 70–74 (2016)
7. Xie, L., Zhou, M., Sun, M.: Hierarchical structure based hybrid approach to sentiment analysis of Chinese micro blog and its feature extraction. J. Chin. Inf. Proc. **26**(1), 73–84 (2012)
8. Kombrink, S., Mikolov, T., Karafiát, M., et al.: Recurrent neural network based language modeling in meeting recognition. In: Proceedings of the 12th Annual Conference of the International Speech Communication Association, Florence, Italy, pp. 2877–2880 (2011)
9. Mikolov, T., Kombrink, S., Burget, L., et al.: Extensions of recurrent neural network language model. In: Proceedings of the IEEE International Conference on Acoustics, Speech and Signal Processing, Prague, Czech Republic, pp. 5528–5531 (2011)
10. Shi, Y.Z., Zhang, W.Q., Liu, J., et al.: RNN language model with word clustering and class-based output layer. EURASIP J. Audio Speech Music Process. **2013**, 22 (2013)
11. Zhao, M., Du, H., Dong, C., et al.: Dietary health text classification based on word2vec and LSTM. Agric. Mach. **48**(10), 202–208 (2017)
12. Karpathy, A., Johnson, J., Fei-Fei, L.: Visualizing and understanding recurrent networks. arXiv preprint arXiv:1506.02078 (2015)
13. Ballesteros, M., Dyer, C., Smith, N.A.: Improved transition-based parsing by modeling characters instead of words with lstms. Comput. Sci. **8**(9), e74515 (2015)
14. Socher, R., Lin, C.Y., Ng, A.Y., et al.: Parsing natural scenes and natural language with recursive neural networks. In: Jonny, P., Rob, B. (eds.) International Conference on International Conference on Machine Learning, pp. 129–136. Omni Press, Haifa (2011)
15. Irsoy, O., Cardie, C.: Deep recursive neural networks for compositionality in language. Adv. Neural. Inf. Process. Syst. **3**(5), 2096–2104 (2014)
16. Hochreiter, S., Bengio, Y., Frasconi, P., et al.: Gradient Flow in Recurrent Nets: The Difficulty of Learning Long-Term Dependencies, pp. 237–243. Wiley/IEEE Press (2001)
17. Pascanu, R., Mikolov, T., Bengio, Y.: On the difficulty of training recurrent neural networks. In: Sanjoy, D.D. (ed.) Proceedings of the 30th International Conference on Machine Learning, vol. 28, pp. 1310–1318. JMLR Org, Atlanta (2013)
18. Arisoy, E., Sethy, A., Ramabhadran, B., et al.: Bidirectional recurrent neural network language models for automatic speech recognition. In: Proceedings of the 2015 Annual Conference of International Speech Communication Association, pp. 5421–5425 (2015)
19. Liang, J., Chai, Y., Yuan, H., et al.: Emotional analysis based on polarity transfer and LSTM recursive network. J. Chin. Inf. Sci. **29**(5), 152–159 (2015)
20. Liu, P., Qiu, X., Chen, X., et al.: Multrtimescale long short-term memory neural network for modelling sentences and documents. In: Proceedings of Conference on Empirical Methods in Natural Language Processing, pp. 2326–2335 (2015)
21. Wang, X., Liu, Y., Sun, C., et al.: Predicting polarities of tweets by composing word embeddings with long short-term memory. In: Proceedings of Meeting of the Association for Computational Linguistics and the International Joint Conference on Natural language Processing, pp. 1343–1353 (2015)
22. Sutskever, I., Vinyals, O., Le, Q.V.: Sequence to sequence learning with neural networks. In: Proceedings of the 20th NIPS, pp. 3104–3112 (2014)
23. Liu, W., Su, Y., Wu, N., et al.: Research on mongolian-chinese machine translation based on LSTM. Comput. Eng. Sci. **40**(10), 1890–1896 (2018)

24. Graves, A., Mohamed, A.R., Hinton, G.: Speech recognition with deep recurrent neural networks. In: Proceedings of IEEE International Conference on Acoustics, vol. 38, pp. 6645–6649 (2013)
25. Wang, D., Nyberg, E.: A long short-term memory model for answer sentence selection in question answering. In: Meeting of the Association for Computational Linguistics and the International Joint Conference on Natural Language Processing, pp. 707–712 (2015)

# Ransomware Detection Based on an Improved Double-Layer Negative Selection Algorithm

Tianliang Lu, Yanhui Du[⊠], Jing Wu, and Yuxuan Bao

People's Public Security University of China, Beijing, China
duyanhui@ppsuc.edu.cn

**Abstract.** The encrypting ransomware using public key cryptography is almost impossible to decrypt, so early detection and prevention is more important. Signature matching technology has low detection rate for unknown or polymorphic ransomware, and some intelligent algorithms have been proposed for solving this problem. Inspired by the Artificial Immune System (AIS), an improved double-layer negative selection algorithm (DL-NSA) was proposed which can reduce the number of holes in NSA and increase the detection rate. To obtain the behavior characteristics (e.g., files read or write, cryptography APIs call and network connection) of ransomware, a Cuckoo sandbox was built to simulate the malicious code running environment. After dynamic analysis, the behavior characteristics of ransomware were encoded to antigens. The improved double-layer negative selection algorithm has two sets of immune detectors. The first layer detectors set was generated by the original negative selection algorithm using $r$-contiguous bits matching. The second layer detectors set was directional generated holes' detectors using $r$-chunk matching with variable matching threshold. Simulation result shows that comparing with NSA this algorithm can achieve high-rate space coverage for non-self, and can increase the detection rate of ransomware.

**Keywords:** Ransomware · Negative selection algorithm · API call sequence · Artificial Immune System · Cuckoo sandbox

## 1 Introduction

Ransomware is one of the most threatening attacks nowadays. In the late 1980s, PC Cyborg known as the first ransomware has been developed. In recent years, ransomware of mobile devices has grown sharply. Ransomware targeting companies or governments is also rising. Wannacry that hit the headline in May 2017, has affected more than 200,000 computers in 150 countries, with total damages ranging from hundreds of millions to billions of dollars [1].

The ransom is usually paid by snail mail, bank transfer or Amazon gift card. With the popular of cryptocurrencies, nowadays ransom commonly paid by bitcoins. From 2013 to mid-2017, the market for ransomware payments has a minimum worth of USD 12,768,536 [2]. In January 2018, a hospital Hancock Health paid out a $55,000 bitcoin ransom following a SamSam infection, because paying up was deemed the quickest

H. Gao et al. (Eds.): TridentCom 2019, LNICST 309, pp. 46–61, 2020.
https://doi.org/10.1007/978-3-030-43215-7_4

way to get systems back online. But sometimes the victims will not get the decryption key even paying the ransom.

The crypto ransomware can be most destructive typically using strong encryption algorithms [3]. Ransomware such as Wannacry utilized combined encryption algorithms of AES and RSA to make the encryption harder to decrypt [4].

The number of ransomware attacks has grown partly because attackers have adopted Ransomware as a Service (RaaS) [5]. RaaS is available over the dark web, and RaaS is enabling even the most technically illiterate cybercriminal to extort payments from victims.

In order to accurately recognize unknown or polymorphic instances, inspired by the biological immune system to eliminate bacteria, a ransomware detection method based on an improved double-layer negative selection algorithm was proposed.

The rest of this paper is organized as follows. Section 2 gives an overview of the related previous work. Section 3 describes the negative selection algorithm and the problem of undetectable holes. Section 4 introduces the framework and details of the improved double-layer negative selection algorithm. Section 5 explains the ransomware analysis environment and the extraction of behavior characteristics. Section 6 evaluates our ransomware detection algorithm through experiments. Section 7 concludes the paper.

## 2  Related Work

### 2.1  Ransomware Detection

In recent years, studies have been carried out on the detection of ransomware attack. The common malware detection methods include static detection and dynamic detection. Some researchers investigate machine learning methods for detecting viruses.

**Static Detection**
Static detection is the analysis of a malware performed without actually executing the program. Antivirus software mainly uses the signature-based detection method. Depending on a large number of virus signatures, antivirus software can detect known viruses, but cannot deal with unknown viruses. Opcodes are widely used for static detection. Santos et al. [6] proposed a method to detect unknown malware families based on the frequency of the appearance of the opcodes sequences. Wang et al. [7] converted the opcodes sequence to an image, and the image is compared with the image generated from the known malware sample. Zhang et al. [8] proposed a classification method of ransomware families with machine learning based on n-gram of opcodes, and *TF-IDF* is calculated to select feature n-grams which exhibit better discrimination between ransomware families.

**Dynamic Detection**
Dynamic detection is the analysis of a malware performed while executing the program. The suspicious program is run in a controlled environment while recording the malicious operations. Information that can be obtained by dynamic analysis is API calls, system calls, instructions traces, registry changes, files changes and network connections.

Ransomware often use packing (such as ASProtect and Themida) and obfuscation techniques to avoid being detected by static analysis tools. Therefore, dynamic analysis is indispensable to understand the main features and functionalities of ransomware [9]. Xu et al. [10] introduced a framework for hardware-assisted malware detection based on monitoring and classifying memory access patterns. Scaife et al. [11] proposed an early-warning detection system for ransomware that checks for file activities and alerts the user in case of suspicious activities.

Monitoring the API function calls can be useful for detecting ransomware attacks. Many researchers agree that ransomware's typical behavior involves the encryption of files and showing a ransom message, which can be identified through the ransomware's use of API function calls [9, 12, 13].

### 2.2 Artificial Immune System

Bioscience has been a source of inspiration for innovative solutions to computer science and engineering problems for many years. The latest research that has attracted widespread attention in this field is the Artificial Immune Systems (AIS). AIS is inspired by biological immunology to solve complex practical problems by simulating the functions, principles and models of the immune system [14]. It's highly distributed, adaptive, and self-organizing nature, together with learning and memory features offer rich metaphors for its artificial counterpart [15].

AIS has been applied in many research areas, especially to solve many computer security problems [16, 17], such as intrusion detection [18], malware detection [19] and spam detection [20].

## 3    Negative Selection Algorithm and the Problem of Holes

### 3.1    Negative Selection Algorithm

Negative selection algorithm [21] first proposed by Forrest, is a computational imitation of self/non-self discrimination. It is modeled off the T-cell maturing process that happens in the thymus. It has been successfully applied to anomaly detection systems. The negative selection algorithm has two phases [21]: generation of detectors set (see Fig. 1) and non-self detection (see Fig. 2).

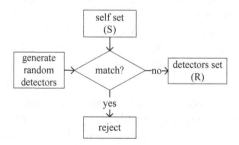

**Fig. 1.** Generation of detectors set

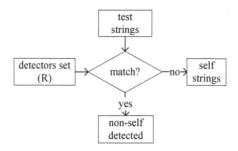

**Fig. 2.** Non-self detection

In NSA, elements including detectors are represented by binary strings. $U = \{0,1\}^L$ represents all binary strings of length $L$. Define shape space $U$, self set $S$ and non-self set $N$, which satisfy $U = N \cup S$ and $N \cap S = \varnothing$.

Some of the most widely used matching rules are Hamming distance, $r$-contiguous bits, $r$-chunk, etc. Take $r$-contiguous bits matching for example. $a = a_1 a_2 \ldots a_L$ and $b = b_1 b_2 \ldots b_L$ are two strings of length $L$, $a$ matches $b$ if and only if $\exists i \leq L - r + 1$ which meets $a_j = b_j, j = i, i+1, \ldots, i + r - 1$.

### 3.2 The Problem of Undetectable Holes

There are a large number of holes exist in anomaly detection system based on negative selection algorithm, which will affect the detection rate of the algorithm. These holes are non-self individuals that cannot be recognized by all possible detectors. Holes (undetectable antigens) also exist in the biological immune system. Hofmeyr [22] proposed to use multiple representations to reduce the number of holes by using the MHC mechanism of the biological immune system. Zhang et al. [23] introduced the $r$-variable detection algorithm to reduce the number of holes by adjusting the matching threshold. However, this method uses a randomly generation mechanism when generating the detectors, which is inefficient for covering holes.

The main reason of holes is the partial matching rules. The matching rules adopted by negative selection algorithm need a matching threshold, which embodies the characteristics of the partial matching rules. The matched two strings do not need to be exactly the same, as long as the degree of similarity is greater than the threshold. Partial matching can be thought as an approximation or generalization.

There are two types of holes in the negative selection algorithm using $r$-contiguous bits matching: crossover holes and length-limit holes [24].

(1) A crossover hole is a "crossover" of certain self strings. The hole $h$ is not in the self set $S$, but string $h$ is the cross combination of certain $r$-step sliding windows of $S$. For instance (see Fig. 3), let $\{S_1, S_2\} = \{1010, 0001\}$ be the self set $S$ with the string length $L = 4$. Define step $r = 2$, $S_1$ generates three substrings $\{10, 01, 10\}$ and $S_2$ generates three substrings $\{00, 00, 01\}$. These six substrings can be combined together into four strings $\{1010, 1001, 0001, 0010\}$ in the direction of the

arrow, in which {1001, 0010} are crossover holes, and the corresponding detectors are impossible to be generated.

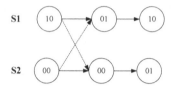

**Fig. 3.** Crossover holes

(2) A length-limit hole is one that has at least one window that does not exist in self strings and has some other windows that will match self strings [24]. For instance, $S = \{010, 011\}$ with string length $L = 3$ and step $r = 2$, in that case string $h = 110$ is a length-limit hole. The detectors for hole $h$ must be generated by the template 11* or *10, where * denotes 0 or 1. But such detectors will not be generated because they match self elements.

# 4   An Improved Double-Layer Negative Selection Algorithm

## 4.1   The Double-Layer Negative Selection Algorithm (DL-NSA)

The double-layer negative selection algorithm contains two matching processes (see Fig. 4), which use the mature detector set $D$ and the hole detector set $D_H$ respectively.

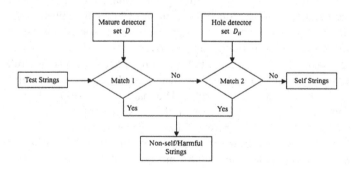

**Fig. 4.** The double-layer negative selection algorithm

**The First Layer Matching**

The set $D$ consists of the mature detectors generated by the original negative selection algorithm, which can identify most of the non-self strings using the $r$-contiguous bits matching.

**The Second Layer Matching**

The set $D_H$ consists of the variable-sized $r$-chunk detectors generated by the algorithm that will be introduced in Sect. 4.2. The hole detector set $D_H$ is mainly used to cover holes and improve the accuracy of detection. The number of hole detectors can also be dynamically adjusted according to the hole coverage requirement.

## 4.2  The Hole Detectors Generation Algorithm

In the biological immune system, holes represent pathogens that cannot be recognized by the immune system, and pathogens usually evolve into holes to avoid detection by the immune system. For computer anomaly detection systems, intrusion behavior and virus programs are also evolving to seem like normal behavior and procedures. Borrowing the principle of crossover holes, the intrusion behavior makes the detection even harder by splicing a series of normal operation segments to complete the attack process. For anomaly detection systems, how to improve coverage of holes is an urgent problem to be solved.

**Variable-Sized $r$-chunk Detectors**

Compared with the NSA proposed by Forrest, this paper introduces variable-sized $r$-chunk matching detectors, which can effectively cover the holes in anomaly detection systems.

The $r$-chunk matching is defined as follows: a detector $d = (i, d_1 d_2 \ldots d_m)$ matches a string $a = a_1 a_2 \ldots a_n (m \leq n)$ under the $r$-chunk matching rule, if and only if $a_j = d_j, j = i, i+1, \ldots, i+r-1 (i \leq m-r+1)$, where $i$ represents the matching starts position.

The $r$-chunk matching indicates that when the detector $d$ and the antigen $a$ match when they have at least $r$ identical contiguous bits from the $i$-th bit position. The $r$-chunk matching reduce the space coverage of detectors by defining start position $i$ and matching length $r$, so as to solve the problem of length-limit holes. For example, the detector $d = \{1, 11\}$ with $r = 2$ can successfully detect the length-limit hole $h = 110$ in Sect. 3.2.

Meanwhile, the variable-sized $r$-chunk detectors can cover the space that $r$-contiguous bits detectors cannot cover. By increasing the matching length $r$, detection range of the detector is further reduced to cover holes that are much closer to self elements. For example, when $r = 3$ the detector $d = \{1,100\}$ and $d = \{1,001\}$ can successfully detect the crossover holes $\{1001, 0010\}$ in Sect. 3.2 respectively.

**Generation Algorithm of Hole Detectors**

Some scholars have proposed methods for discovering holes [25, 26], and we propose an algorithm of generating holes detectors with variable-sized $r$-chunk matching based on the discovered hole set.

Define self set $S = \{s_1, s_2, \cdots, s_N\}$ which has $N$ elements. Define hole set $H = \{h_1, h_2, \cdots, h_M\}$ which has $M$ elements. Define the length of element strings is $L$. Self set is represented by a matrix as follows:

$$S = \begin{bmatrix} s_{1,1} & s_{1,2} & \cdots & s_{1,i} & \cdots & s_{1,L} \\ s_{2,1} & s_{2,2} & \cdots & s_{2,i} & \cdots & s_{2,L} \\ \vdots & & & & & \\ s_{N,1} & s_{N,2} & \cdots & s_{N,i} & \cdots & s_{N,L} \end{bmatrix} \tag{1}$$

According to $r$-contiguous bits, the self set $S$ is divided into $L - r + 1$ sets by the $r$-step sliding window, shown as follows:

$$S = [S_r[1], S_r[2], \cdots, S_r[i], \cdots, S_r[L - r + 1]] \tag{2}$$

$$S_r[i] = \begin{Bmatrix} s_{1,i} & \cdots & s_{1,i+r-1} \\ s_{2,i} & \cdots & s_{2,i+r-1} \\ \vdots & s_{j,i} & \vdots \\ s_{N,i} & \cdots & s_{N,i+r-1} \end{Bmatrix}, i = 1, 2, \cdots, L - r + 1 \tag{3}$$

Similarly, the hole set $H$ can also be divided into $L - r + 1$ sets.

$$H = [H_r[1], H_r[2], \cdots, H_r[i], \cdots, H_r[L - r + 1]] \tag{4}$$

$$H_r[i] = \begin{Bmatrix} h_{1,i} & \cdots & h_{1,i+r-1} \\ h_{2,i} & \cdots & h_{2,i+r-1} \\ \vdots & h_{j,i} & \\ h_{M,i} & \cdots & h_{M,i+r-1} \end{Bmatrix}, i = 1, 2, \cdots, L - r + 1 \tag{5}$$

Calculating the difference set $H_r[i] - S_r[i]$. If exist $H_r[i](j) = h_{j,i}h_{j,i+1} \cdots h_{j,i+r-1}$ that does not appear in the self set $S_r[i]$, then $H_r[i](j)$ can generate $r$-chunk matching detector $d_{r,i} = \{i, h_j\}$ to detect the hole $h_j$.

The hole detectors generation algorithm based on variable-sized $r$-chunk is described as follows:

- Step 1: Define self set $S$ and element length $L$;
- Step 2: Calculate the hole set $H$ according to the EHANDP algorithm [26];
- Step 3: According to the step $r$ of the sliding window, divide $S$ and $H$ into $L - r + 1$ sets respectively, and the initial $r$-chunk matching length is $r = r_0$.
- Step 4: Calculate $D_r[i] = H_r[i] - S_r[i]$, $i = 1, 2 \cdots L - r + 1$. For the non-empty set $D_r[i]$, generate the holes detector set $D_r = \{d_{r,i}\}$ and delete the holes that can be covered by $D_r$ from $H$.
- Step 5: Determine whether there are still some holes in $H$, and if so, increase the matching length $r$ by 1 and the value of $r$ is $r_0, r_1 \cdots$ to maximum $L$ in turn, then go to Step 3; Otherwise, the set of hole detectors $D_H = D_{r_0} \cup D_{r_1} \cup \cdots$ can cover all holes, and the algorithm ends.

The above algorithm is exemplified as follows.

Given a self set $S = \{01001, 00001, 10100, 11101\}$ with $r$-contiguous bits matching where $r = 3$ and $L = 5$. Calculate the hole set $H = \{00000, 01000, 10101, 11100\}$

according to the EHANDP algorithm. Let the initial $r$-chunk matching length $r_0 = 3$, and divide $S$ and $H$ into $L - r_0 + 1 = 3$ sets as follows:

$$S_3[1] = \begin{bmatrix} 010 \\ 000 \\ 101 \\ 111 \end{bmatrix}, S_3[2] = \begin{bmatrix} 100 \\ 000 \\ 010 \\ 110 \end{bmatrix}, S_3[3] = \begin{bmatrix} 001 \\ 001 \\ 100 \\ 101 \end{bmatrix} \tag{6}$$

$$H_3[1] = \begin{bmatrix} 000 \\ 010 \\ 101 \\ 111 \end{bmatrix}, H_3[2] = \begin{bmatrix} 000 \\ 100 \\ 010 \\ 110 \end{bmatrix}, H_3[3] = \begin{bmatrix} 000 \\ 000 \\ 101 \\ 100 \end{bmatrix} \tag{7}$$

$$H_3[1] - S_3[1] = \emptyset \tag{8}$$

$$H_3[2] - S_3[2] = \emptyset \tag{9}$$

$$H_3[3] - S_3[3] = \{000\} \tag{10}$$

$H_3[3] - S_3[3]$ can generate $r$-chunk detector $d = \{3,00000\}$, which can detect holes 00000 and 01000.

Then, there are still two holes in $H = \{10101, 11100\}$. In order to further detect the remaining holes, let $r_1 = r_0 + 1 = 4$, divide $S$ and $H$ into $L - r_1 + 1 = 2$ sets.

$$S_4[1] = \begin{bmatrix} 0100 \\ 0000 \\ 1010 \\ 1110 \end{bmatrix}, S_4[2] = \begin{bmatrix} 1001 \\ 0001 \\ 0100 \\ 1101 \end{bmatrix} \tag{11}$$

$$H_4[1] = \begin{bmatrix} 1010 \\ 1110 \end{bmatrix}, H_4[2] = \begin{bmatrix} 0101 \\ 1100 \end{bmatrix} \tag{12}$$

$$H_4[1] - S_4[1] = \varnothing \tag{13}$$

$$H_4[2] - S_4[2] = \{0101, 1100\} \tag{14}$$

$H_4[2] - S_4[2]$ can generate detectors $d = \{2,10101\}$ and $d = \{2,11100\}$ with matching length $r_1 = 4$, which can detect holes 10101 and 11100. So far all the holes in $H$ can be detected.

## 5    Ransomware Analysis and Feature Extraction

### 5.1    API Call Sequences of Ransomware

The behavior features of ransomware are extracted in a virtual environment named Cuckoo Sandbox that automated the task of analyzing malicious file [13]. In our virtual analyzing environment, some types of fishing files (e.g., jpg, doc, xls, pdf, sql, etc.) are intentionally placed in different directories to trigger the encryption operation of ransomware. Most of the ransomware's implementation of cryptographic algorithm (e.g., RSA and AES) is depended on CryptoAPI that is included in Windows [27].

According to the function of different system calls, we define sixteen categories of API functions. We list some API functions examples of six typical categories that are chosen from the total sixteen categories, shown as Table 1.

**Table 1.** Categories of API functions

| Categories | Description | Examples of API functions |
|---|---|---|
| Crypto | Encryption and decryption of data | CryptEncrypt<br>CryptDecrypt<br>CryptHashData |
| File | File operations, such as read, write, delete, et al. | Writefile<br>MoveFileEx<br>DeleteFile |
| Process | Process and thread operations | NtOpenProcess<br>NtAllocateVirtualMemory<br>NtTerminateProcess |
| Service | Service operations, such as create, start and stop | OpenSCManager<br>OpenService<br>StartService |
| System | System operations | LdrLoadDll<br>NtQuerySystemInformation<br>SetWindowsHookEx |
| Misc | Other miscellaneous operations | GetComputerName<br>GetUserName<br>GetTimeZoneInformation |

### 5.2    *n*-gram Feature Selection

To extract features from API call sequences the *n*-gram model is used. API function names are treated as words of *n*-gram, and extract the *n*-gram features from both the ransomware samples and benign samples [16].

Information gain (*IG*) is used as a feature selection method. Let $x$ be the *n*-gram feature, $y_i \in y$ be one of the $k$ class sample labels (i.e., $k = 2$, ransomware or benign), and the $IG(x)$ be the *IG* weight for feature $x$, calculated as follows [16].

$$IG(x) = H(y) - H(y|x)$$
$$= -\sum_{i=1}^{k} p(y_i) \log(p(y_i))$$
$$+ p(x) \sum_{i=1}^{k} p(y_i|x) \log(p(y_i|x)) \tag{15}$$
$$+ p(\bar{x}) \sum_{i=1}^{k} p(y_i|\bar{x}) \log(p(y_i|\bar{x}))$$

Compute the *IG* value for each *n*-gram feature, and the larger the *IG* value is, the more information the feature contributes for classifying ransomware and benign samples. The feature set $F = \{f_1, f_2, \cdots, f_N\}$ is composed of the top *N* features based on *IG* values.

### 5.3  Feature Vector Encoding

Based on the feature set $F = \{f_1, f_2, \cdots, f_N\}$, each sample will be encoded to a feature vector $v = (v_1, v_2, \cdots, v_N)$, where $v_i$ represents whether the *n*-gram feature $f_i$ appears in the API call sequences of the sample. If $f_i$ appears then $v_i$ is 1, otherwise $v_i$ is 0.

The feature vectors are treated as binary strings in the DL-NSA. The training benign samples are encoded to self set *S*, the training ransomware samples are encoded to antigens which are used for generating mature detector set *D*. The test samples (both benign and ransomware) are encoded to feature vectors and then be distinguished by the detectors of DL-NSA.

## 6  Experimental Design

### 6.1  Collation of Ransomware and Benign Samples

We collect 2,000 ransomware samples of the popular ransomware families, such as CryptoWall, Wannacry, Cerber, etc. We also gather 1,000 benign samples. These two types of samples are both equally divided into two collections: training samples collection is used for immune detectors generation, and test samples collection is used for validating the detection effect.

### 6.2  Experimental Results and Analysis

**Distribution of Hole Detectors**

The training samples collection contains 500 benign samples, and these samples are analyzed in Cuckoo sandbox. All the benign samples are encoded to feature vectors $v = (v_1, v_2, \cdots, v_N)$ which compose the self set, and in our experiment let $N = 30$. For the first layer of DL-NSA using *r*-contiguous bits matching with the matching length *r*, we can obtain all the holes. Then, according to the hole detector generation algorithm we proposed, the second layer variable-sized $r$-chunk hole detectors of DL-NSA are generated. The distribution of different matching threshold of hole detectors is shown as Fig. 5.

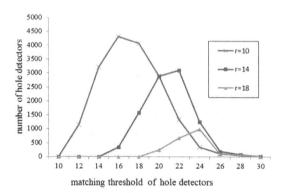

**Fig. 5.** Distribution of hole detectors

We choose three matching length values (i.e. $r = 10, 14, 18$) of the first layer mature detectors. The number of hole detectors is first increased and then decreased along with the increasing of the matching threshold of hole detectors. With the increase of $r$, the total number of hole detectors is decreased, and the peak of the curves shift right. This experiment indicates that the hole detectors of the second layer are affected by the matching length of detectors of the first layer.

### Detectors' Proportion of the Two Layers Affects the Detection Rate

The non-self space is divided into two parts: detectable space and hole space according to whether the elements in non-self space can be detected by the $r$-contiguous bits matching of the first layer. Non-self space coverage includes two aspects: detectable space coverage and hole space coverage. In this part, we will analysis the detectors' proportion of the two layers how to affect the detection rate.

First, we build a non-self space dataset of 2,000 elements, which are the feature vectors extracted from ransomware or random generated. The non-self space dataset contains 1,000 detectable elements and 1,000 hole elements.

The total number of detectors of DL-NSA is $N$, including mature detectors of the first layer and hole detectors of the second layer. Define the percentage of hole detector is $p$. For the first layer, $r$-contiguous bits matching is used with the matching length is 10, and the number of mature detectors is $N_1 = N * (1 - p)$. For the second layer, variable-sized $r$-chunk matching is used, with the initial matching length $r = 10$, and the number of hole detectors is $N_2 = N * p$. If $N_2 > N_H$, that means $N_2$ is greater than the actual total number of holes, then let $N_2 = N_H$ and $N_1 = N - N_H$.

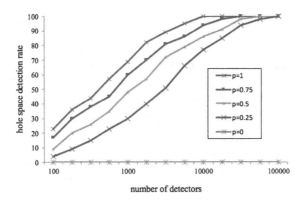

**Fig. 6.** Hole space detection rate

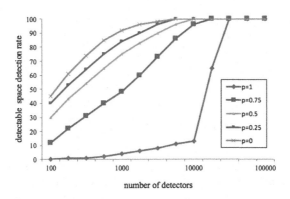

**Fig. 7.** Detectable space detection rate

As shown in Figs. 6 and 7, the detection rate of hole space and detectable space both increase gradually with the increase of the total number of detectors. When the total number of detectors is fixed, the larger $p$ is, the higher detection rate for the hole space and the lower detection rate for the detectable space.

When $p = 0$, DL-NSA degenerates to the original NSA, and the system has a high detection rate for the detectable space, but the hole space detection rate is 0.

When $p = 1$, the first layer detector is generated only when the actual maximum number of hole detectors reaches. As can be seen from Fig. 7, when $p = 1$, the detection rate of detectable space increases slowly in the first half, because only the hole detectors are generated which can cover a small area of detectable space. When $N > N_H$, the detection rate of detectable space increases rapidly.

**Ransomware Detection**

This section compares the ransomware detection performance of NSA proposed by Forrest and $r$-adjustable negative selection algorithm (RA-NSA) [23] with DL-NSA proposed in this paper.

For NSA algorithm, the matching length of detectors is set to 10 and the number of detectors is $N$.

For RA-NSA algorithm, the initial matching length of detector is set to 10, the upper limit of matching length is 25, and the number of detectors is $N$.

For DL-NSA algorithm, the total number of detectors is $N$, and the percentage of hole detectors is $p$. For DL-NSA algorithm, in order to ensure high performance in both detectable space and hole space, $p = 0.1$ is chosen.

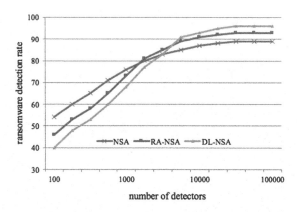

**Fig. 8.** Ransomware detection

As shown in Fig. 8, the detection rate of ransomware shows an upward trend, especially in the initial stage. When the number of detectors is greater than 10,000, the detection rates of the three algorithms tend to be stable. When the number of detectors is small, the coverage space of detectors in NSA algorithm is the largest, so the detection effect of NSA is the best. When the number of detectors is large, DL-NSA algorithm has better coverage of non-self space, especially for hole elements, so the detection effect is the best, up to 96%.

In the practical application of ransomware defense, it is suggested that the combination of NSA and DL-NSA should be used, determined by system requirement of the detection speed and accuracy. If high detection speed is demanded, fewer detectors should be used to achieve more non-self space coverage. At this time, the use of NSA before the intersection of two curves (NSA and DL-NSA) can guarantee the speed while having a higher detection rate. If high detection accuracy is demanded, more detectors should be used, especially to cover the hole space better. At this time, using DL-NSA after the intersection of two curves (NSA and DL-NSA) can achieve a higher detection rate of ransomware.

# 7  Conclusion

Ransomware has attracted wide attention from government, security companies and scientific researchers. In order to effectively identify ransomware, the main work of this paper is as follows.

(1) An API call sequences feature extraction and selection method of ransomware is proposed. The Cuckoo sandbox is used for monitoring the sensitive behaviors such as file reading and writing, data encryption and so on, during the execution of the ransomware.
(2) A method of generating hole detectors with variable-sized $r$-chunk matching is proposed. The original NSA is improved, and a DL-NSA model is constructed by introducing a double-layer detectors.
(3) The improved DL-NSA is applied to the detection of ransomware. By adjusting the proportion of two-layer detectors, better ransomware detection effect of ransomware can be achieved.

Although some ransomware recovery and decryption tools have been released by security companies, most ransomware cannot be cracked in fact. Therefore, in the defense of ransomware, the prevention in advance and file backup are more important. The confrontation between security companies and ransomware writers will continue. The application of cryptographic algorithms will make the confrontation more intense. Higher-strength cryptographic algorithms and more complex combinations of cryptographic algorithms will appear. So we must get prepared, and put forward the method of analysis, detection and protection for ransomware.

**Acknowledgments.** This work was supported by the National Key R&D Program of China (2016YFB0801100), the National Natural Science Foundation of China (61602489), the Fundamental Research Funds for the Central Universities of PPSUC (2019JKF108) and the National Cryptography Development Fund (MMJJ20180108).

# References

1. Muhammad, U.K., Jantan, A.: The age of ransomware: understanding ransomware and its countermeasures. In: Artificial Intelligence and Security Challenges in Emerging Networks, pp. 1–4. IGI Global, Pennsylvania (2019)
2. Masarah, P.C., Bernhard, H., Benoit, D.: Ransomware payments in the bitcoin ecosystem. In: Proceeding of the 17th Annual Workshop on the Economics of Information Security (WEIS), pp. 1–10. Innsbruck (2018)
3. Rehman, H., Yafi, E., Nazir, M., Mustafa, K.: Security assurance against cybercrime Ransomware. In: Vasant, P., Zelinka, I., Weber, G.-W. (eds.) ICO 2018. AISC, vol. 866, pp. 21–34. Springer, Cham (2019). https://doi.org/10.1007/978-3-030-00979-3_3
4. Maigida, A.M., Abdulhamid, S.M., Olalere, M., et al.: Systematic literature review and metadata analysis of ransomware attacks and detection mechanisms. J. Reliable Intell. Environ. 5(2), 67–89 (2019)
5. Hull, G., John, H., Arief, B.: Ransomware deployment methods and analysis: views from a predictive model and human responses. Crime Sci. 8(1), 1–22 (2019)

6. Santos, I., Brezo, F., Ugarte-Pedrero, X., et al.: Opcode sequences as representation of executables for data-mining-based unknown malware detection. Inf. Sci. **231**(9), 203–216 (2013)

7. Wang, T., Xu, N.: Malware variants detection based on opcode image recognition in small training set. In: Proceedings of the 2nd IEEE International Conference on Cloud Computing and Big Data Analysis, pp. 328–332. IEEE, Piscataway (2017)

8. Zhang, H., Xiao, X., Mercaldo, F.: Classification of ransomware families with machine learning based on n-gram of opcodes. Future Gener. Comput. Syst. **90**(2019), 211–221 (2019)

9. Sgandurra, D., Muñoz-González, L., Mohsen, R., et al.: Automated dynamic analysis of ransomware: benefits, limitations and use for detection. arXiv preprint arXiv:1609.03020. Accessed 1 December 2016

10. Xu, Z., Ray, S., Subramanyan, P., et al.: Malware detection using machine learning based analysis of virtual memory access patterns. In: Proceedings of the 2017 Design, Automation & Test in Europe Conference & Exhibition (DATE), pp. 169–174. IEEE, Piscataway (2017)

11. Scaife, N., Carter, H., Traynor, P., et al.: CryptoLock (and drop it): stopping ransomware attacks on user data. In: Proceedings of the 36th International Conference on Distributed Computing Systems, pp. 303–312. IEEE, Piscataway (2016)

12. Hampton, N., Baig, Z., Zeadally, S.: Ransomware behavioural analysis on windows platforms. J. Inf. Secur. Appl. **40**(2018), 44–51 (2018)

13. Lu, T.L., Zhang, L., Wang, S.Y., et al.: Ransomware detection based on V-detector negative selection algorithm. In: Proceedings of the 2017 International Conference on Security, Pattern Analysis, and Cybernetics (SPAC), pp. 531–536. IEEE, Piscataway (2017)

14. Gao, X.Z., Chow, M.Y., Pelta, D., et al.: Theory and applications of artificial immune systems. Neural Comput. Appl. **19**(8), 1101–1102 (2010)

15. Dasgupta, D., Yu, S., Nino, F.: Recent advances in artificial immune systems: models and applications. Appl. Soft Comput. **11**(2011), 1574–1587 (2011)

16. Lu, T.L., Zhang, L., Fu, Y.X.: A novel immune-inspired shellcode detection algorithm based on hyper-ellipsoid detectors. Secur. Commun. Netw. **8**(2018), 1–10 (2018)

17. Tan, Y.: Artificial Immune System: Applications in Computer Security. IEEE Computer Society Press, Piscataway (2016)

18. Hooks, D., Yuan, X., Roy, K., et al.: Applying artificial immune system for intrusion detection. In: Proceedings of IEEE Fourth International Conference on Big Data Computing Service and Applications (BigDataService), pp. 287–292. IEEE, Piscataway (2018)

19. Brown, J., Anwar, M., Dozier, G.: Detection of mobile malware: an artificial immunity approach. In: Proceedings of 2016 IEEE Security and Privacy Workshops (SPW), pp. 74–80. IEEE, Piscataway (2016)

20. Iqbal, M., Abid, M.M., Ahmad, M.: Catching Webspam Traffic with Artificial Immune System (AIS) classification algorithm. In: Proceedings of the 7th IEEE International Conference on Software Engineering and Service Science (ICSESS), pp. 402–405. IEEE, Piscataway (2017)

21. Forrest, S., Perelson, A.S., Allen, L., et al.: Self-nonself discrimination in a computer. In: Proceedings of 1994 IEEE Symposium on Research in Security and Privacy, pp. 202–212. IEEE, Piscataway (1994)

22. Hofmeyr, S.A.: An immunological model of distributed detection and its application to computer security. Department of Computer Sciences, University of New Mexico (1999)

23. Zhang, H., Wu, L.F., Zhang, R.S., et al.: An algorithm of r-adjustable negative selection algorithm and its simulation analysis. Chin. J. Comput. **28**(10), 1614–1619 (2005)

24. Ji, Z., Dasgupta, D.: Revisiting negative selection algorithms. Evol. Comput. **5**(2), 223–251 (2007)

25. Stibor, T., Mohr, P., Timmis, J.: Is negative selection appropriate for anomaly detection. In: Proceedings of Genetic and Evolutionary Computation Conference (GECCO), pp. 321–328. ACM, New York (2005)
26. Liu, X.B., Cai, Z.X.: Properties assessments of holes in anomaly detection systems. J. Cent. South Univ. (Sci. Technol.) **40**(4), 986–992 (2009)
27. Kirda E.: UNVEIL: a large-scale, automated approach to detecting ransomware (Keynote). In: Proceedings of IEEE 24th International Conference on Software Analysis, Evolution and Reengineering (SANER), p. 1. IEEE, Piscataway (2017)

# Genetic Algorithm Based Solution for Large-Scale Topology Mapping

Nada Osman[1(✉)], Mustafa ElNainay[1,2], and Moustafa Youssef[1]

[1] Department of Computer and Systems Engineering,
Alexandria University, Alexandria, Egypt
{nada_s_osman,ymustafa,moustafa}@alexu.edu.eg
[2] Islamic University of Madinah, Medina, Saudi Arabia
melnainay@iu.edu.sa

**Abstract.** Simulating large-scale network experiments requires powerful physical resources. However, partitioning could be used to reduce the required power of the resources and to reduce the simulation time. Topology mapping is a partitioning technique that maps the simulated nodes to different physical nodes based on a set of conditions. In this paper, genetic algorithm-based mapping is proposed to solve the topology mapping problem. The obtained results prove a high reduction in simulation time, in addition to high utilization of the used resources (The number of used resources is minimum).

**Keywords:** Network simulation · Topology mapping · Testbeds · Genetic algorithm

## 1 Introduction

Network simulation is an essential step in designing and validating new networking protocols. The availability of a wide range of network simulators makes it easy for researchers to run simulation experiments on their machines. Nevertheless, simulating large-scale network experiments on a single physical node requires powerful resources to assure time feasibility. Partitioning large-scale network simulation on multiple physical nodes will solve this scalability problem by reducing both the required resources of the used machines and the simulation time.

The partitioning can be done manually based on the number of accessible physical nodes. However, manual partitioning consumes time, and it may not reach an acceptable reduction in simulation time. Another option is the use of an automatic partitioner provided by some online accessible testbed, where the testbed automatically partitions the given experiment based on its available physical nodes.

One of the automatic partitioning techniques is topology mapping, where it maps each simulated node in an experiment to an available physical node. This mapping will partition the traffic of the topology into two parts:

© ICST Institute for Computer Sciences, Social Informatics and Telecommunications Engineering 2020
Published by Springer Nature Switzerland AG 2020. All Rights Reserved
H. Gao et al. (Eds.): TridentCom 2019, LNICST 309, pp. 62–77, 2020.
https://doi.org/10.1007/978-3-030-43215-7_5

- Simulated traffic: The inner traffic between simulated nodes on the same physical machine.
- Emulated traffic: The outer traffic between simulated nodes on different physical nodes, which passes through the real links between the physical nodes.

The main goal of topology mapping is to reduce the simulation time, taking into account the effect of the emulated traffic on the evaluation of the experiment.

Most of the existing topology mapping solutions fix the number of physical nodes and work on finding a load-balanced partitioning over them. But from a testbed viewpoint, it is essential to minimize both the number of occupied physical nodes and their occupation time. Therefore, other topology mapping solutions worked on reducing the used resources by penalizing them with an approximated cost.

In contrast to previous topology mapping solutions that focused on a single topology mapping goal, or needed prior step of cost estimation of the used resources, in this paper, we are proposing a genetic algorithm based solution for the topology mapping problem that achieves all of the following goals, depending only on the developed fitness function:

- Minimizing the number of physical nodes used in the simulation by maximizing their utilization.
- Minimizing the simulation time of the experiment by limiting the amount of simulated traffic on each physical node to the capacity of the node.
- Limiting the amount of emulated traffic passing through real links to the capacity of the links. This is to reduce the effect of using the real network on the evaluation of the experiment.

The evaluation results show that the proposed technique can find mapping solutions that reduce simulation time by more than 90% for different topology sizes while keeping the utilization above 95%, which minimizes the number of used physical nodes.

The paper is organized into six sections. Following the introduction, related work is surveyed in Sect. 2. In Sect. 3, the topology mapping problem is formulated, while the details of the proposed GA approach is explained in Sect. 4. The obtained evaluation results are presented in Sect. 5. Finally, in Sect. 6, conclusion and future works are discussed.

## 2  Related Work

In the topology mapping problem, the used algorithm needs to search the mapping space (between the simulated nodes of a given topology and the available physical nodes to use) for the optimal mapping that minimizes the simulation time while satisfying a set of constraints. Searching for that optimal mapping is an NP-hard problem [1].

A well-known solution for the topology mapping problem is through the use of graph partitioning techniques. The minimum graph cut algorithm is used to partition a given topology on the available workers. Where the load is balanced over the workers, and the traffic on real links is minimized to prevent the physical network from being a bottleneck.

Graph partitioning was used for topology mapping in MaxiNet [2], where Wette et al. used the METIS technique to parallelize the simulation of large software-defined networks [3]. Similarly, Liu et al. applied graph partitioning in [4] and used large realistic network architectures for evaluation. Furthermore, Yocum and Ken et al. compared the minimum graph cut technique to a random partitioning technique, concluding that the minimum graph cut outperforms random partitioning [5].

Other solutions use greedy optimization search to solve the topology mapping problem. In [6], Galvez et al. proposed a randomized mapping technique named GreedyMap. It iterates over tasks, and computes a partial cost of the current mapping state, then chooses the node that minimizes the cost. Another example is [7], where Hoefler et al. applied two greedy approaches: A greedy heuristic approach that worked on integrating heavy traffic on the same physical node. In addition to a graph similarity approach that used the similarity between the simulation experiment topology and the physical network topology to perform the mapping.

The mentioned techniques have two main drawbacks: First, they assume the number of physical nodes to use is fixed and known, without trying to minimize it. Second, they assume homogeneous workers with similar resources and evenly partition the experiment load over them. A generalization is needed to allow the use of heterogeneous physical nodes.

Ricci and Robert et al. proposed a more general solution named *assign* in [8] and [9] using simulated annealing algorithm [10], for the Emulab testbed [11]. The *assign* solution used a cost function that depends on the amount of traffic on the physical network. The cost differs based on the physical resources used, where each resource in the testbed has a fixed approximated cost. Moreover, to minimize the number of physical resources used, the solution penalizes the cost function with the number of physical nodes and physical links used in the mapping.

One drawback of the *assign* solution is the use of fixed approximated costs, which requires manual setting. Furthermore, the solution targets to minimize resources usage, without considering reaching the minimum simulation time.

The proposed genetic algorithm uses a fitness function that depends on analytically computed values of both the utilization of the used resources and the simulation time of the experiment after mapping, where the utilization part of the function controls the number of the used resources. Furthermore, the fitness function takes into account the capacity of each used resource, allowing the use of heterogeneous resources, without the need to fix approximated costs for them. The proposed technique in this paper overcomes the discussed drawbacks, with the privilege of reaching the minimum simulation time and the maximum utilization.

# 3   Topology Mapping Problem Formulation

The topology mapping problem, in this work, is defined as follows: Given a simulation topology of $N$ simulated nodes, and a physical network of $P$ physical nodes, the problem maps each simulated node $n$ to a physical node $p$, such that, the simulation time of the experiment is min, and the utilization of the used resources is max.

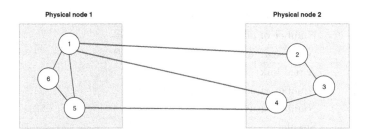

**Fig. 1.** Two physical nodes are used to simulate a topology of six simulated nodes, where the partitioning emulates three links using the topology on the real network interface connecting the two physical nodes.

In Fig. 1, a connected topology of six nodes is simulated on a physical testbed of two physical nodes ($N = 6$ and $P = 2$). As shown in the figure, the mapping partitions the topology links into simulated links inside the physical nodes, and emulated links using the physical network between the physical nodes (Table 1).

Next subsections formulate the topology mapping problem in details.

## 3.1   Simulation Time

As mentioned earlier, there are two types of traffic in the distributed experiment: The emulated traffic, and the simulated traffic. The simulation time differs based on the traffic type.

– **Emulated Traffic:**
Let $L_r^R$ be a set of topology links emulated using the real link $r$. Equation (1) computes the total amount of traffic passing through $r$, and (2) estimates the emulation time of this traffic (in seconds).

$$T_r^R = \sum_{l \in L_r^R} T_l \tag{1}$$

$$\tau_r^R = \frac{T_r^R}{C^R} \tag{2}$$

Where $C^R$ is the capacity of $r$.

**Table 1.** Table of symbols

| Symbol | Definition |
|---|---|
| $N$ | Number of simulated nodes/Number of genes |
| $L$ | Number of simulated links |
| $n$ | A simulated node/A gene, where $n = 1, 2, \ldots, N$ |
| $l$ | A simulated link |
| $T$ | Traffic in Mbps |
| $T_l$ | Traffic on the simulated link $l$, where $l = 1, 2, \ldots, L$ |
| $P$ | Number of all available physical nodes |
| $p$ | A physical node, where $p = 1, 2, \ldots, P$ |
| $r$ | A real link |
| $U_P$ | Number of used physical nodes |
| $U_R$ | Number of used real links |
| $C^S$ | Simulation capacity in MHz |
| $C^R$ | Real traffic capacity in Mbps |
| $C_p^S$ | The simulation capacity of the physical node $p$ |
| $L_p^S$ | Set of simulated links on the physical node $p$ |
| $L_r^R$ | Set of simulated links emulated on the real link $r$ |
| $T_p^S$ | Simulated traffic on the physical node $p$ |
| $T_r^R$ | Real traffic passing through the real link $r$ |
| $\tau$ | Time in seconds |
| $\tau_p^S$ | Time taken to simulate the traffic on the physical node $p$ |
| $\tau_r^R$ | Time taken by real traffic on the real link $r$ |
| $\mu$ | Utilization (%) |
| $\mu_p$ | Utilization of the physical node $p$ |
| $\eta$ | Population size |
| $i$ | An individual in the population, where $i = 1, 2, \ldots, \eta$ |
| $g_n^i$ | The value of the gene $n$ in the individual $i$ |
| $M_I$ | Mutation probability of individuals |
| $M_G$ | Mutation probability of genes |
| $G_\tau$ | Gain in time |
| $D_\mu$ | Drop in utilization |
| $F$ | Fitness value |
| $E$ | Above link capacity error |
| $A, B, C$ | Utilization model Constants |
| $\alpha, \beta, \gamma$ | Scaling parameters |

– **Simulated Traffic:**
Let $L_p^S$ be a set of topology links simulated inside the physical node $p$. Similar
to the emulated traffic, Eq. (3) computes the total amount of traffic running
on $p$.

$$T_p^S = \sum_{l \in L_p^S} T_l \qquad (3)$$

Assuming a discrete-event simulator such as NS3 [12], each bit in the simulated traffic consumes at least two CPU clock events, ignoring the processing
time: A sending event, and a receiving event. Given that, Eq. (4) estimates
the simulation time of this traffic (in seconds).

$$\tau_p^S = \frac{2 \times T_p^S}{C_p^S} \qquad (4)$$

Where $C_p^S$ is the simulation capacity of the physical node $p$.
Figure 2 compares the experimentally measured time and the analytically
computed time using (4). Although the experimental time is longer than the
analytical time, due to ignoring the processing time in the analytical formula,
both times approximately follow the same behavior. Consequently, the analytical time is a valid estimation of the real-time needed to simulate a given
amount of traffic.

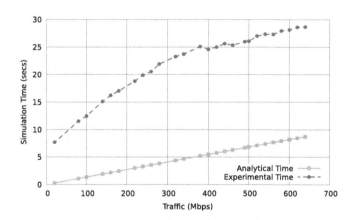

**Fig. 2.** The experimental simulation time measured VS the analytical simulation time
computed using (4)

The total simulation time of an experiment is the maximum time needed by
both the simulated traffic and the emulated traffic, given by (5).

$$\tau(U_P) = Max(\tau_1^S, \tau_2^S, \dots, \tau_{U_P}^S, \\ \tau_1^R, \tau_1^R, \dots, \tau_{U_R}^R) \qquad (5)$$

Where $U_P$ is the number of physical nodes used in the mapping, and $U_R$ is the number of real links used.

## 3.2  Utilization

Figure 3 shows the relation between the amount of traffic running on a physical node and the utilization of the node, which is described by (6). The Constants $A$, $B$, and $C$ were estimated using Regression.

$$\mu_p = A - B \times e^{C \times T_p^S} \tag{6}$$

Where $T_p^S$ is the simulated traffic using the physical node $p$.

The overall utilization is computed using (7), Where $U_P$ is the number of physical machines used in the experiment.

$$\mu(U_P) = Min(\mu_1, \mu_2, \ldots, \mu_{U_P}) \tag{7}$$

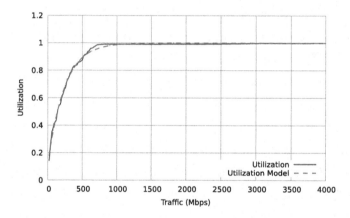

**Fig. 3.** The experimentally measured utilization VS the analytically computed utilization.

## 4  Genetic Algorithm Approach

A genetic algorithm [13] uses the idea of evolution to enhance the searching path of reaching the goal. It starts with an initial population of individuals, where an individual is a chromosome that consists of a set of genes. Each iteration the best individuals in the current generation are elected to produce new ones, supposedly, closer to the goal. The algorithm uses a fitness function to measure how fit is an individual, where the higher the fitness of an individual, the closer it is to the goal and the higher its election probability.

The proposed chromosome in this work is of length $N$, where each gene in the chromosome represents a simulated node. The value of the gene represents the physical node to be used to simulate the corresponding simulated node. Each gene has a value in the range $[1, P]$, where $P$ is the number of available physical nodes in the testbed.

## 4.1 Initial Population

Let the number of individuals in the population to be $\eta$. Initially, $\eta$ individuals are generated by random. For each gene in an individual, a physical node is chosen by random using (8).

$$g_n^i = rand(1, P) \tag{8}$$

Where $g_n^k$ is the gene represents the simulated node $n$ of the individual $i$.

## 4.2 Crossover and Mutation

A new generation consists of $\eta$ new children. To produce a new child, the parents are chosen randomly from the top half of the current population where the population is sorted based on the fitness of the individuals. A child takes half of its genes from one of the parents, and the second half from the other parent.

Genetic algorithm uses mutation to produce new random genes that might lead to better solutions, instead of only depending on inherited genes from parents. In this GA work, a percentage of $M_I\%$ of the produced children are mutated. For each mutated child, $M_G\%$ of its genes are rechosen by random from the set of available physical nodes.

## 4.3 Individual Evaluation and Fitness Function

To measure how fit is an individual (mapping solution), the algorithm needs to compute the following values: The number of physical machines used ($U_P$), the traffic to be simulated on each physical node $p$ ($T_p^S$), and the traffic passing through each real link $r$ ($T_r^R$). The fitness of an individual depends on how much reduction in simulation time it gives, compared to simulating the whole topology on a single physical node, taking into account the reduction in utilization caused by using more physical nodes.

Equation (9) gives the amount of reduction in simulation time, which represents the gain of a given mapping.

$$G_\tau(U_P) = 1 - \frac{\tau(U_P)}{\tau(1)} \tag{9}$$

Where $\tau(1)$ is the time taken to simulate the whole topology on a single physical node ($U_P = 1$).

Equation (10) gives the amount of drop in utilization, which represents the loss of a given mapping.

$$D_\mu(U_P) = 1 - \frac{\mu(U_P)}{\mu(1)} \tag{10}$$

Where $\mu(1)$ is the utilization of simulating the whole topology on a single physical node ($U_P = 1$).

The goal of the algorithm is to maximize the gain and minimize the loss. Many forms of the fitness function were tested, starting from dividing $G_\tau$ by $D_\mu$, passing through many normalization problems. Until reaching the fitness function that gave the best performance in terms of simulation time and utilization. The final fitness function is defined in (11), where $\alpha$ is a scaling parameter that controls the minimization in simulation time against lowering the utilization. $\beta$ is a function that represents a normalization factor between the gain and the loss.

$$F(U_P) = E \times [\alpha \times \beta(U_P) \times G_\tau(U_P) - (1 - \alpha) \times D_\mu(U_P)] \tag{11}$$

For individuals that do not match the maximum link capacity condition, instead of ignoring them, their fitness value is penalized by the amount of exceedance in traffic over the limited capacity as shown in (12), where the $\gamma$ parameter represents the penalization factor. This way, the algorithm can benefit from the infeasible solutions if they can lead to a better feasible solution.

$$E = \gamma \times (1 - \frac{Max(T_1^R, T_2^R, \ldots, T_{U_R}^R) - C^R}{C^R}) \tag{12}$$

### 4.4 Parameters Setting

The value of some parameters such as $\eta$, $M_I$, $M_G$, and $\gamma$, is set using parameter tuning, where the values that achieve the best performance in terms of simulation time and utilization are the values used in the final model. The value of the scaling factor $\alpha$ depends on the following:

- The privileges that are given by the testbed to the user. As a privileged user can use more resources to reduce the simulation time with ($\alpha > 0.5$).
- The cost of the physical nodes used. As ($\alpha < 0.5$) for expensive resources.

For large-scale experiments, the simulation time in seconds (which has no upper limit) is much higher than the utilization (which has a maximum value of 100%). According to (9) and (10), the time gain could be much less than the utilization loss. Hence, the fitness function tends to maximize the utilization more than reducing the time. The normalization parameter $\beta$ described in (13), is used to overcome the dominance of the utilization part.

$$\beta(U_P) = \frac{\tau(U_P)}{\mu(U_P)} \tag{13}$$

## 4.5   Minimum Graph Cut

A simulation topology is a weighted graph, where the traffic passes through a link represents the link's weight. Consequently, the proposed GA-based mapping could benefit from the minimum graph cut technique to enhance the initial population of the algorithm. If there are $P$ available physical nodes, the number of used machines in the final solution $U_p$ is in the range $[1, \ldots, P]$. The algorithm uses the minimum graph cut technique to find a minimum cut for each possible value of $U_p$, then the found solutions are added to the initial population of the GA.

Despite the high complexity of the minimum graph cut algorithm ($O(N^3)$) [14], it can be afforded. The running time of the minimum graph cut is ignored, compared to the high convergence time of the GA.

## 5   Evaluation

This section describes the evaluation procedure and the obtained results of the GA-based mapping compared to other techniques.

### 5.1   Tuning and Testing Procedures

Random topologies are generated for tuning and testing purposes as follows:

- The number of links in the generated topology is in the range $[N-1, \frac{N(N-1)}{20}]$, where $N$ is the number of simulated nodes.
- The traffic passing through each link is in the range $[1, 1000]$ Mbps.

**a- Tuning.** The following procedure is used to tune the parameters:

- Tuning used three categories of topology size: Small topologies of 10 simulated nodes, medium topologies of 50 simulated nodes, and large topologies of 100 simulated nodes. Ten random topologies are generated in each category.
- A set of possible values is defined for each parameter to be tuned.
- For each combination of values of the tuned parameters, the GA-based mapping uses these values to find a solution for the random topologies generated for tuning purpose.
- The final GA-based mapping uses the combination that gives the highest average time gain while minimizing the average utilization loss.

**b- Testing.** For testing, ten random topologies with sizes $\{10, 20, 30, \ldots, 100\}$ simulated nodes, are generated using the same procedure described earlier.

## 5.2   Environment and Parameters Configuration

The proposed GA-based mapping is evaluated using the CRC testbed [15].
Table 2 defines all the used parameters based on the CRC testbed and based
on the performed parameter tuning.

All the computations are performed on the CRC testbed server (Intel(R)
Xeon(R) Silver 4114 CPU @ 2.20 GHz).

**Table 2.** Parameters configuration

| Parameter | Value |
| --- | --- |
| $P$ | 25 physical nodes |
| $C_p^S$ | 4390 MHz |
| $C^R$ | 1000 Mbps |
| $A$ | 1 |
| $B$ | 0.8899 |
| $C$ | 0.004197 |
| $\eta$ | 2000 individuals |
| $M_G$ | 0.5 |
| $M_I$ | 0.05 |
| $\alpha$ | 0.5 |
| $\gamma$ | 0.5 |

## 5.3   Comparing GA-Based Mapping to Single Machine Simulation

The effect of using the GA-based mapping is first compared to not using topology
mapping, and simulating the whole topology on a single node. As shown in Fig. 4,
applying the GA-based mapping reduces the simulation time by more than 90%,
while keeping the utilization above 95%.

## 5.4   Comparing GA-Based Mapping to Other Mapping Techniques

Finally, to evaluate the GA-based mapping approach, the algorithm is compared
to the following:

- The minimum graph cut technique described in Sect. 4.
- A random mapping approach that randomly maps simulated nodes to physical nodes. There are two possible random solutions: 1- The first feasible
  mapping found by the search. 2- The algorithm keeps searching randomly
  for a time equal to the time taken by GA-based mapping to converge, and
  the best mapping found is considered.

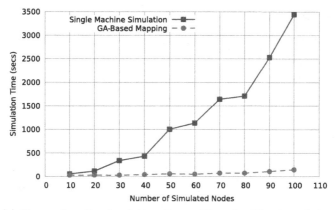

(a) Comparing the simulation time with and without applying the GA-based topology mapping

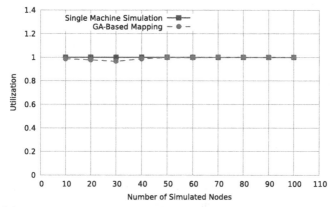

(b) Comparing the utilization with and without applying the GA-based topology mapping

**Fig. 4.** The performance of the proposed GA-based mapping compared to the single machine simulation

Figure 5 illustrates the comparison between the GA-based mapping and the mapping techniques mentioned in four aspects: The simulation time of the experiment, the utilization of the physical nodes, the number of used physical nodes, and the running time of the used technique.

**a- Simulation Time**

Figure 5a shows that the GA-based mapping achieves the lowest simulation time for all topology sizes. On the other hand, the minimum graph cut technique fails to find a feasible mapping for large topologies ($N > 40$), and therefore its simulation time is almost the same as simulating the whole topology on a single node. Thus the number of physical nodes used by the minimum graph cut for large topologies is fixed to one or two nodes only as shown in Fig. 5c.

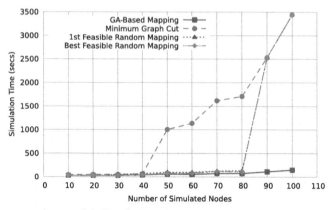

(a) Simulation time comparison

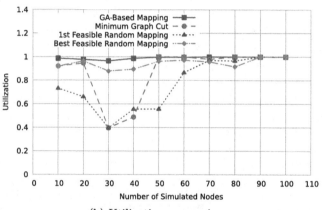

(b) Utilization comparison

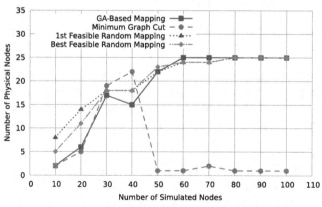

(c) Number of used psychical nodes comparison

**Fig. 5.** A Comparison between the different topology mapping techniques

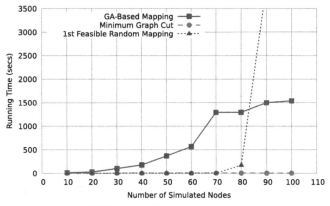

(a) Time to find the mapping

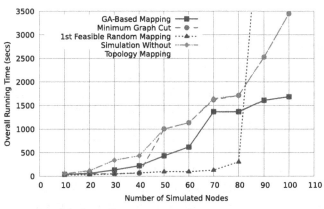

(b) Overall time to run the experiment

**Fig. 6.** Running time comparison

**b- Utilization**

As shown in Fig. 5b, all of used topology mapping techniques gives high utilization for large topologies, and that is due to the limit of the available physical nodes, as they cannot use more nodes. For smaller topology sizes, the GA-based mapping gives the highest utilization.

**c- Number of Physical Nodes**

Ignoring the drop in the minimum graph cut curve caused by its failure to find feasible solutions, Fig. 5c shows that the GA-based mapping approximately uses the minimum number of physical nodes. For large topologies ($N > 70$), all of the techniques almost use all of the available physical nodes. However, the GA-based mapping is better in terms of simulation time and utilization, as shown in Fig. 5a and b.

**d- Running Time**

Figure 6 compares the running time of the three topology mapping techniques. As shown in Fig. 6a, the minimum graph cut technique takes the lowest time to find the mapping for all topology sizes, but running the overall experiment using minimum graph cut takes the longest time, almost the same as running the whole topology on a single physical node without partitioning, as shown in Fig. 6b.

The first feasible solution found by the random search takes low time for small and average topology sizes, but it takes a very long time, or it even might not converge to find a feasible mapping for large topologies.

For the GA-based mapping, it takes higher convergence time than both the minimum graph cut and the random search technique for small topologies, but it achieves the lowest overall time for large topologies. Furthermore, the GA-based mapping finds the mapping that gives the best utilization of the used physical nodes.

# 6    Conclusion and Future Works

This work proposes a genetic algorithm-based solution for the topology mapping problem and designs a fitness function that allows the GA-based technique to find the mapping that minimizes the simulation time and maximizes the utilization. Furthermore, Simulation time and utilization are estimated using new proposed analytical methods, without actually running the simulation.

As shown in the evaluation, GA-based mapping gives the best simulation time and the best utilization for all topology sizes. On the contrary, both the minimum graph cut and random search approach are not able to find a feasible solution for large topologies. Although the GA-based mapping takes a long time to converge for large topologies, the overall experiment time is less than the experiment simulation time on a single machine. Furthermore, Minimizing the simulation time is more important than minimizing the running time, as the testbed server is always available to run the topology mapping search, while the testbed nodes must be reserved to run the simulation. The running time of the GA-based mapping technique can be afforded given the simulation time reduction and the utilization benefits achieved.

Many future works could be done to enhance the proposed GA-based mapping. Improving the fitness function to include more testbed parameters will improve the found solutions; parameters such as the cost of the physical nodes, and the number of concurrent topology mapping requests. Furthermore, developing an advanced method to benefit from infeasible solutions could also improve the performance of the algorithm. Finally, enabling the algorithm to handle parallel topology mapping requests will allow for better time and resources management.

# References

1. Garey, M.R., Johnson, D.S.: Computers and Intractability a Guide to the Theory of NP-Completeness. Freeman and Company, New York (1979)
2. Wette, P., Draxler, M., Schwabe, A.: MaxiNet: distributed emulation of software-defined networks. In: 2014 IFIP Networking Conference (2014)
3. Kreutz, D., Ramos, F.M.V., Verissimo, P.E., Rothenberg, C.E., Azodolmolky, S., Uhlig, S.: Software-defined networking: a comprehensive survey. Proc. IEEE **103**(1), 14–76 (2015)
4. Liu, X., Chien, A.: Realistic large-scale online network simulation. In: Proceedings of the ACM/IEEE SC2004 Conference (2004)
5. Yocum, K., Eade, E., Degesys, J., Becker, D., Chase, J., Vahdat, A.: Toward scaling network emulation using topology partitioning. In: 11th IEEE/ACM International Symposium on Modeling, Analysis and Simulation of Computer Telecommunications Systems, MASCOTS 2003 (2003)
6. Galvez, J.J., Jain, N., Kale, L.V.: Automatic topology mapping of diverse large-scale parallel applications. In: Proceedings of the International Conference on Supercomputing - ICS 2017 (2017)
7. Hoefler, T., Snir, M.: Generic topology mapping strategies for large-scale parallel architectures. In: Proceedings of the International Conference on Supercomputing - ICS 2011 (2011)
8. Ricci, R., Alfeld, C., Lepreau, J.: A solver for the network testbed mapping problem. ACM SIGCOMM Comput. Commun. Rev. **33**(2), 65 (2003)
9. Stoller, M.H.R.R.L., Duerig, J., Guruprasad, S., Stack, T., Webb, K., Lepreau, J.: Large-scale virtualization in the emulab network testbed. In: USENIX Annual Technical Conference, Boston, MA (2008)
10. van Laarhoven, P.J.M., Aarts, E.H.L.: Simulated Annealing: Theory and Applications. D. Reidel, Dordrecht (1988)
11. White, B., et al.: An integrated experimental environment for distributed systems and networks. ACM SIGOPS Oper. Syst. Rev. **36**(SI), 255–270 (2002)
12. Riley, G.F., Henderson, T.R.: The ns-3 network simulator. In: Modeling and Tools for Network Simulation, pp. 15–34 (2010). https://doi.org/10.1007/978-3-642-12331-3_2
13. Davis, L.: Handbook of Genetic Algorithms. International Thomson Computer Press, London (1996)
14. Hagen, L., Kahng, A.: New spectral methods for ratio cut partitioning and clustering. IEEE Trans. Comput.-Aided Des. Integr. Circuits Syst. **11**(9), 1074–1085 (1992)
15. Hanna, S.S., Guirguis, A., Mahdi, M.A., El-Nakieb, Y.A., Eldin, M.A., Saber, D.M.: CRC: collaborative research and teaching testbed for wireless communications and networks. In: Proceedings of the Tenth ACM International Workshop on Wireless Network Testbeds, Experimental Evaluation, and Characterization - WiNTECH 2016 (2016)

# QoS, Reliability, Modeling and Testing

# Formal Modeling and Verification of Software-Defined Networking with Multiple Controllers

Miyoung Kang and Jin-Young Choi[✉]

Center for Information Security Technologies,
Korea University, Seoul 02841, Korea
{mykang, choi}@formal.korea.ac.kr

**Abstract.** Traditional SDN has one controller, but more recent SDN approaches use multiple controllers on one network. However, the multiple controllers need to be synchronized with each other in order to guarantee a consistent network view, and complicated control management and additional control overhead are required. To overcome these limitations, Kandoo [5] has been proposed in which a root controller manages multiple unsynchronized local controllers. However, in this approach, loops can form between the local controllers because they manage different topologies. We propose a method for modeling a hierarchical design to detect loops in the topology and prevent them from occurring using UPPAAL model checker. In addition, the properties of multiple controllers are defined and verified based UPPAAL framework. In particular, we verify the following properties in a multiple controller: (1) elephant flows go through the root controller, (2) all flows go through the switch that is required to maintain security, and (3) they avoid unnecessary switches for energy efficiency.

**Keywords:** SDN · Formal modeling · Formal verification · UPPAAL

## 1 Introduction

Software-defined networking (SDN) [1] and network function virtualization (NFV) are the core technologies for 5G [2]. SDN is used to connect networks of virtual machines (VMs) in 5G. The 5G core network is deployed in a distributed horizontal cloud form. Horizontal distributed cloud based on cloud infrastructure by core network functions to separate control and data transfer functions using SDN and NFV. Each network function can efficiently cope with explosive increases in traffic by appropriately distributing control functions to the central cloud and data transfer functions to the edge cloud. However, in a 5G network using SDN and NFV as core technologies, even if the independent VNFs do not cause any errors in the central cloud when various applications are run, collisions can occur due to rule conflict in the edge cloud. Because this can cause errors across the entire 5G network, verification is necessary.

Our goal is to suggest a formal verification method to ensure the safety and consistency of multiple controllers in SDN. SDN is a technology that separates the network device control component from the data transfer component using open interfaces, such as the OpenFlow protocol. Through the SDN controller, which deals with the control

H. Gao et al. (Eds.): TridentCom 2019, LNICST 309, pp. 81–94, 2020.
https://doi.org/10.1007/978-3-030-43215-7_6

component, forwarding and packet processing rules are determined, and forwarding rules are transferred to the lower SDN switches.

The controller plays an important role in the traffic transfer process. Unfortunately, when network traffic increases rapidly, a single controller cannot handle all of the flow requests due to a limited controller capacity. If a single controller fails, the switch will not be able to plan the routing of newly arrived packets, which will affect communication and applications on the network. As a result, a new modern controller design has been proposed based on multiple controllers.

A flat design [3, 4] for multiple controllers extends the functionality of the control plane, but it requires complex controller management and additional control overhead because the controllers must communicate with each other to ensure a consistent network. To solve this problem, a hierarchical design has been suggested. This typically uses a two-tiered controller system consisting of local controllers and a root controller. A local controller manages switches locally and runs local control applications, while the root controller manages the local controllers and maintains the global network. Kandoo [5] is a typical hierarchical controller structure, in which the root controller communicates with the local controllers to obtain domain information but the local controllers do not communicate with each other.

However, while the root controller manages each local controller, it does not allow communication between local controllers. Therefore, loops can form within a local controller. We propose a method for formal modeling a hierarchical design that identifies loops in the topology and detects them using simulation in the UPPAAL model checker [6]. The properties of the multiple controllers are also defined and verified based this design.

In this paper, we propose a formal modeling and verification framework of three properties:

- elephant flows going through the root controller that is necessary to verify whether the flow has reached the root controller.
- all flows passing the switch required to maintain security that the flows must also be routed to a switch that performs a firewall function for security reasons.
- all flows avoiding unnecessary switches in order to improve energy efficiency. Many users employ data centers during the day. However, the number of users decreases after 10 o'clock in the evening. Therefore, instead of using all of the switches when there are fewer users, the number of switches can be reduced by selecting an optimal path.

This paper is organized as follows. Section 2 introduces Software-Defined Networking, multiple controllers in SDN and UPPAAL Framework. Section 3 presents the formal modeling of a Hierarchical design for SDN controllers. Section 4 addresses the formal verification of three properties. Section 5 reviews related literature. We conclude the paper in Sect. 6.

## 2  Background

### 2.1  Software-Defined Networking

SDN originated with OpenFlow [7], which was developed as a protocol for future internet infrastructure control technology [8]. However, it evolved into the SDN concept centering on the Open Networking Foundation (ONF) [9], which was established in 2011. It is now used as the core technology for 5G networks.

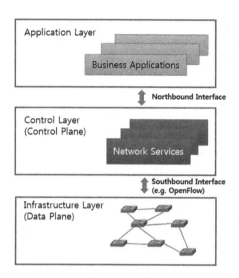

**Fig. 1.** The three-layered SDN architecture

Figure 1 shows the SDN framework, which consists of three layers: the application layer, the control layer, and the infrastructure layer. The application layer includes network applications that can introduce new network features such as security and manageability, provide forwarding schemes, or assist the control layer in the network configuration. The application layer can provide appropriate guidance for the control layer by obtaining an abstracted global view of the network from the controllers. Examples of network applications include network management and traffic engineering, load balancing for application servers, security and network access control, network testing, debugging and verification, inter-domain routing, and network virtualization. The interface between the application layer and the control layer is known as the northbound interface.

In the lower layer, the control plane is found. This is involved in the programming and management of the forwarding plane. In order to achieve this, it uses information provided by the forwarding plane and defines network operations and routing. It consists of one or more software controllers communicating with forwarding network elements through a standardized interface known as a southbound interface. OpenFlow, one of the most commonly used southbound interfaces, primarily considers switches, while other SDN approaches consider other network elements such as routers. The lowest layer is the infrastructure layer, which is also referred to as the data plane. It comprises forwarding network elements. The forwarding plane is primarily responsible for forwarding data, in addition to local information monitoring and statistics collection.

### 2.2  Multiple Controllers in SDN

In this subsection, we will introduce the origin of multiple controllers in SDN using two examples and then summarize two multiple controller architectures: flat and hierarchical.

In one of the earliest SDN designs, a single controller manages the entire network. This is illustrated in Fig. 2. In this design, packets can arrive at a switch where no corresponding rule is installed in the flow table; as a result, the switch cannot forward the packets on its own. The switch then notifies the controller about the packets. The controller identifies the path for the packets and installs appropriate rules in all of the switches along that path. The packets can thus be forwarded to their destination [10].

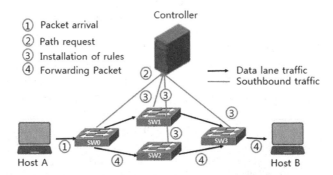

**Fig. 2.** Flow management of a single controller

The controller plays an important role in the traffic transfer process. Unfortunately, when the network traffic is high, a single controller cannot handle all of the flow requests due to limited controller capacity. If a single controller fails, switches will not be able to route newly arriving packets, affecting network communication and applications. As a response to this, the use of multiple controllers was introduced to SDN.

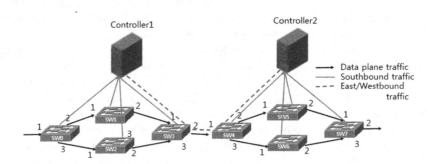

**Fig. 3.** Flat design for multiple controllers

As shown in Fig. 3, a flat design extends the functionality of the control plane but requires complex controller management and additional control overhead for east/westbound traffic. This is because controllers must communicate with each other to ensure a consistent network view. A hierarchical design has been proposed to solve this problem. It typically uses a two-tiered controller known as a root controller, which manages the switches in the local domain, manages local controllers that run local control applications, and maintains a global network view. Kandoo [11] is a typical hierarchical controller structure. In Kandoo, the root controller communicates with the domain controller to obtain domain information, but the local controllers do not contact each other. Figure 4 shows the basic architecture of hierarchical design. In order to redistribute any overload of flow requests at one controller, which is a major issue for single-controller designs, the local controller sends the routing of elephant traffic to the root controller, and the root controller issues the forwarding rules.

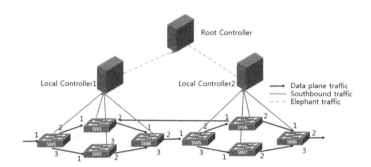

**Fig. 4.** Hierarchical design for multiple controllers

## 2.3   UPPAAL Framework

UPPAAL modeling for multiple controller consists of a root controller, local controllers, switches, and a host. Simulations can be used to confirm that the modeling operates as intended. In particular, the safety and reachability of the system can be verified. As a result of this verification process, users receive either a *satisfied* or *not satisfied* message (Fig. 5). In the paper, the model and its properties are modified through feedback and verification is run again. For details we refer the reader to [6].

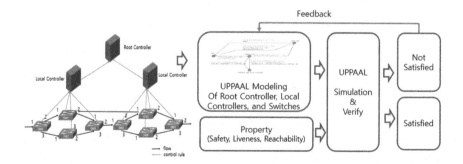

**Fig. 5.** UPPAAL framework

# 3   Modeling of a Hierarchical Design for SDN Controllers

The controllers within a flat design communicate with each other to ensure consistency, which can lead to overloads because of a lot of traffic. To improve this, a hierarchical design has been proposed, in which a logical centralized controller manages the network-wide state without the local controllers communicating with each other. Therefore, a hierarchical design requires considerably less control channel bandwidth compared with normal OpenFlow networks. However, loops can occur in a network-wide topology because the individual local controllers manage their own switches and do not share views with each other. Figure 4 shows that each local controller only manages switches that are linked to them and that only the root controller has the entire logical view. A loop can be created (e.g., Switch 5 -> Switch 1 -> Switch 3 -> Switch 4 -> Switch 5) if the local controller sends a rule that includes a route (Switch 5 -> Switch 1) at a certain time.

Our framework can detect the occurrence of a loop in advance and modify the topology to avoid it. Our framework consists of a host, switches, local controllers, and a root controller. Packets originate from the host. When a flow arrives at the switch, it looks for a matching entry in the flow table of the switch. If a matching entry is found, the actions associated with the specific flow entry are executed. If no match is found, the flow may be forwarded to the local controller. The local controller sends the rule to the switch according to the inquiry. If an elephant flow, which has 1 M pkt-in per second, enters a switch, the flow requests forwarding rules from the root controller via a local controller, and then the root controller determines the action for the elephant flow and sends it to the local controller. The local controller then issues a forwarding rule to the inquiring switch. This process decreases the load on the local and root controllers, preventing the overloading that occurs in a flat design in order to maintain consistency between the controllers.

## 3.1   Host Modeling

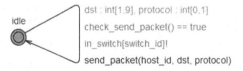

**Fig. 6.**  Model of a host

The host is the starting point for a flow. Each packet in the flow starts with the address of the origin and the address of the destination. The origin is labeled 0 and the destination is randomly labeled between 1 and 9 (dst: int [1,9]). Protocol: int[0,1] sets a normal flow as 0 and an elephant flow as 1 (Fig. 6).

When the host has `check_send_packet ()` `== true`, it sends a packet. When this packet leaves the topology, it sends the next packet. `in_switch [switch_id] !` is a channel that sends packets to a connected switch when the host creates it. Packets are sent to the switch that corresponds to the `switch_id` by synchronizing with the switch's `in_switch [switch_id] ?`. Channel 0 is synchronized first, and the next switch is connected when the host is activated.

```
typedef struct {
  int id;
  int src;
  int dst;
  int protocol;
} PACKET;
```

```
typedef struct {
  int switch_id;
  int src;
  int dst;
  int protocol;
  int action;
}FLOWTABLE;
```

For example, "`host = host (0,0);`" shows that a host with the host ID 0 and the switch ID 0 has been created.

Packets are abstracted and contain information about the packet number, source address, destination address, and protocol. The flow table is abstracted to have a switch ID, a source address, destination address, protocol, and an action.

## 3.2   Switch Modeling

The switch begins in an idle location; after a packet arrives at the switch, it matches the rule to the flow entry of the flow table to determine the forwarding rule for the packet. When the channel is synchronized with `in_switch[switch_id] ?`, it first inquires whether the rule is in the flow table. If there is no rule, it queries the local controller. The controller provides the rule by adding a new flow entry to the switch's flow table (Fig. 7).

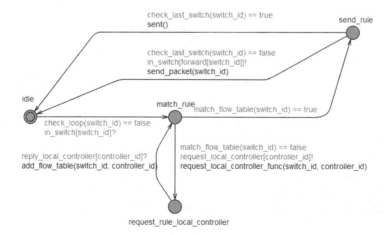

**Fig. 7.** Model of a switch

If the switch checks the flow table and finds a matching field, it looks at the matching flow entry's action and sends the packet to `send_packet(switch_id)` with the next switch. `check_last_switch(switch_id) == false` will send it to the next switch at random if it is not the last switch. For `check_last_switch (switch_id) == true`, no more switches are connected, and the packet leaves the topology.

`Match_flow_table(switch_id) == false` means that, if there is no matching flow entry in the flow table, `request_local_controller [con-troller_id]!` will synchronize with the local controller. `Request_lo-cal_controller_func(switch_id, controller_id)` will query the local controller connected to the switch via `switch_id` and `controller_id`. `add_flow_table(switch_id,controller_id)` adds a forwarding rule to the flow table of the switch through the channel of `reply_local_controller [controller_id]?` in `request_rule_local_controller` location. If `match_flow_table (switch_id) == true, send_packet (switch_id)` is sent according to the action of the rule in the flow table, and the switch becomes idle again.

### 3.3   Local Controller Modeling

If a packet does not match the flow entry of a switch's flow table, it queries the local controller for the rule. This controller has information about the switches. `sw0 : int [0,1]` means that `switch 0` randomly selects 0 or 1. `initialize_con-troller (sw0, sw1, sw2, sw3, sw4, sw5, sw6, sw7)` initializes the state of the switch in the controller. When a query for the forwarding rule comes through the switch channel `local_controller [controller_id]?`, whether it is an ele-phant flow or a normal flow is determined at `Identify_traffic` location (Fig. 8).

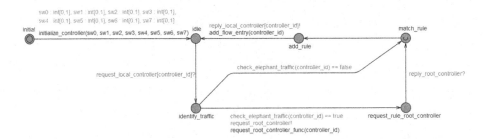

**Fig. 8.** Model of a local controller

If `check_elephant_traffic (controller_id) == true`, the local con-troller again queries the root controller for the rule because an elephant flow has arrived. Conversely, if `check_elephant_traffic (controller_id) == false`, the local controller makes an urgent transition from a `match_rule` location to an `add_rule` location, and than sands `reply_local_controller [con-troller_id]!` channel, and adds a rule to the flow table of the switch via add_flow_entry (controller_id). The reply_local_controller [controller_id]? in the switch and reply_local_controller [controller_id]! transition by synchronizing. Once the local controller has transferred the rule to the switch, it moves to an idle location.

### 3.4    Root Controller Modeling

The root controller handles the path of an elephant flow, so the overloading of the local controllers is reduced. As shown in Fig. 9, after the system starts, initialize_controller (sw0, sw1, sw2, sw3, sw4, sw5, sw6, sw7) initializes the state of the switch in the root controller.

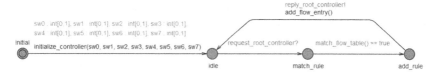

**Fig. 9.** Model of the root controller

When request_root_controller? occurs at an idle location, the root controller searches for the matching rule. If there is a matching rule, it transitions to add_rule location and then adds the rule to add_flow_entry(). In addition, replay_root_controller! synchronizes with the replay_root_controller? of the local controller and then becomes idle.

The root controller can handle elephant flows of more than 1 MB, which not only improves the performance of the system but also distributes a lot of traffic to the SDN controller.

### 3.5    Simulation of Hierarchical Design

After modeling the proposed hierarchical design, we run simulations. Analyzing the results, some problems in the model set-up can be observed. As can be seen in Fig. 10, a loop is created in the simulation and a deadlock occurs.

The destination of an elephant flow can be determined through the root controller. Compared to a normal controller, the root controller is 550 times more bandwidth efficient for control plane loads in an element flow detection scenario. The control plane loads are based on the number of nodes in the network [5]. Therefore, it is necessary to verify whether the flow has reached the root controller. In addition, flows must also be routed to a switch that performs a firewall function for security reasons. It is thus necessary to verify that the flow passes through this switch.

It is also important to verify that a flow does not pass through switches that it does not need to. Many users employ data centers during the day. However, the number of users decreases after 10 o'clock in the evening. Therefore, instead of using all of the switches when there are fewer users, the number of switches can be reduced by selecting an optimal path.

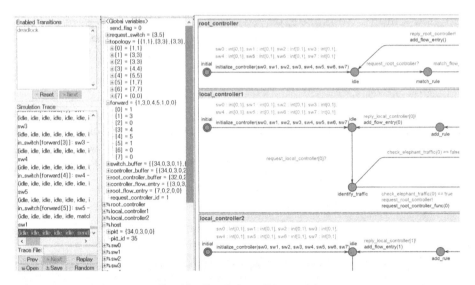

**Fig. 10.** Simulation of the model

The problems we found with the simulation were as follows. First, a loop occurs in the topology and this needs to be avoided in SDN topology. Second, a flow must pass though Switch 1, which functions as a firewall. However, there is a flow that does not pass Switch 1. Third, the fastest route needs to be implemented for energy efficiency. However, during modeling, even though a flow only needs to follow the route Switch 0 -> Switch 1 -> Switch 3 -> Switch 4 -> Switch 5 -> Switch 7, it also passes Switch 2 and Switch 6. We thus revise the topology of the verification framework to avoid these three problems.

```
bool check_loop(int switch_id)
{
    if (switch_buffer[switch_id].time > 10)
        return true;
    else
        return false;
}
```

A loop is found in the simulation and a deadlock occurs (Fig. 10). Therefore, we created a revised topology in which the loop does not occur. The check_loop () function determines whether a loop has occurred by checking switch_buffer [switch_id] .time>10 and, in the improved model, no loop occurs.

In addition, the flow also passes through Switch 1, which it must do for security purposes. In addition, switches that do not need to be included in the route for energy efficiency purposes have been removed from the route.

# 4   Verification of the Hierarchical Design

In our study, the verification framework specifies and verifies each property with TCTL [6]. The query language in TCTL consists of path formulae and state formulae. State formulae describe individual states, whereas path formulae quantify the paths or traces of a model. Path formulae can be classified into reachability and safety [6]. UPPAAL framework that we propose verifies three properties in hierarchical controller: (1) elephant flows go through the root controller using reachability (2) all flows go through the switch that is required to maintain security using safety, and (3) they avoid unnecessary switches for energy efficiency which shows through safety.

## 4.1   Reachability

Reachability properties are often used when designing a model to perform sanity checks and validate the basic behavior of the model [6]. The following formulae verify that the reachability of the root controller is true:

```
E<> (switch_buffer[0].protocol == ELEPHANT_TRAFFIC) &&
      (root_controller.match_rule)
```

They ask whether a given state formula can *possibly* be satisfied by any reachable state, in particular, whether ELEPHANT_TRAFFIC reaches the root_controller.-match_rule state. Figure 11 is verification results which is 'Property is satisfied'. In other words, the elephant traffic reaches the root controller.

**Fig. 11.** Result of reachability verification

## 4.2   Safety

Safety is based on the concept that "something bad will never happen." In UPPAAL, this is formulated positively, e.g., something good is invariantly true. Let P be a state formula. We express that P should be true in all reachable states with the path formula A[] p whereas E[] P says that there should exist a maximal path such that P is always true [6].

Switch 7 must be passed through for security purposes:

```
E[] sw7.idle and sw7.match_rule and sw1.send_rule and sw1.request_rule_
local_controller
```

Packets do not pass through Switches 2 and 6 for energy efficiency purposes:

```
E[] not(sw2.idle and sw2.match_rule and sw2.send_rule and
     sw2.request_rule_local_controller  and  sw2.send_rule)  and  not
(sw6.idle and sw6.match_rule and sw6.request_rule_local_controller and
sw6.send_rule)
```

Figure 12 is verification results which is 'Property is satisfied'. In other words, all flows avoid the Switches 2 and 6 in order to improve energy efficiency.

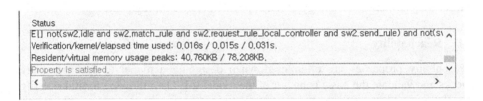

**Fig. 12.** Result of safety verification

## 5   Related Work

Other authors have employed models to verify SDN design. For example, NICE [11] is a model checking tool that uses the symbolic execution of event handlers to identify representation packets that exercise code paths on the controller. NICE detects programming errors such as no forwarding loops, no blackholes, direct paths, and no forgotten packets in testing unmodified controller programs in a NOX controller.

Frenetic [12] is a high-level programming language for OpenFlow applications running on top of NOX. Frenetic allows OpenFlow application developers to express packet processing policies at a higher level than the NOX API. Frenetic also has the network language define the formal semantics for OpenFlow rules and improves NetCore [13] by adding a compiler.

Kazemian *et al.* [14] allows the static checking of network specifications and configurations to identify important classes of failure, such as reachability failure, forwarding loops, and traffic isolation and leakage problems. A framework using formalism, referred to as header space analysis (HSA), looks at the entire packet header as a concatenation of bits. Hassel, which is a library of HSA tools, analyzes a variety of networks and protocols. The model developed by Kazemian *et al.* was the starting point for the Reitblatt *et al.* [15] model.

Reitblatt *et al.* [15] developed a formal model of OpenFlow networks and proved that consistent updates preserve a large class of properties. The formal model is made up of the notion of consistent network updates when transitioning between configurations. The model identified two distinct consistency levels, per-packet and per-flow, and presented general mechanisms for implementing the two levels in SDN using OpenFlow. The verification tool, which is an implemented prototype that reduces the overhead required to perform consistent updates, checks the correctness of the controller software.

Canini *et al.* [16] introduced a formal model describing the interaction between the data plane and a distributed control plane that consists of a collection of fault-prone controllers. In addition, Kang *et al.* [17] introduced a framework in which the consistency between a specification and its implementation is checked by dead-lock detection in the parallel composition of two different pACSR processes generated from two entities in different forms, one in the rule and the other in the OpenFlow table.

Xiao *et al.* [18] introduced the modeling and verification of SDN with multiple controllers to apply Communicating Sequential Processes (CSP). Using the model checker Process Analysis Toolkit (PAT), they verified that the models satisfied three properties: deadlock freeness, consistency, and fault tolerance. They plan to investigate other architectures, such as Kandoo.

Our study differs from the others mentioned above in that our verification and simulation identifies loops generated by the SDN in the hierarchical design of multiple controllers and receives feedback from the UPPAAL framework to remove these loops. It also verifies that elephant flows pass through the switch required to maintain security, that they do not pass through switches that are not required, and finally that they pass through the root controller.

# 6 Conclusion

SDN, a core technology of 5G communication, uses multiple controllers in a single network. However, synchronizing multiple controllers in order to ensure a consistent network view is problematic. Complex controller management and additional control overhead are also an issue. Therefore, a hierarchical controller structure has been proposed to manage asynchronous local controllers with many root controllers. However, when the root controller manages each local controller, loops can form between the local controllers because they manage different topologies.

We have modeled a hierarchical design that can extract loops that occur in these topologies. In addition, the three properties of the multiple controllers are defined and verified based on a simplified version of TCTL. The properties that must be validated in the multiple controllers are identified, including that elephant flows go through the root controller, pass through the security switch, and avoid unnecessary switches to improve energy efficiency. We also explained how reachability and safety can be verified.

Future research should focus on systems that automatically detect loops in a hierarchical design, and modeling and verification should be applied for the occurrence of collisions between rules in VNFs for the 5G core technologies SDN and NFV.

**Acknowledgments.** This research was supported by Basic Science Research Program through the National Research Foundation of Korea (NRF) funded by the Ministry of Education (2018R1A6A3A01012955) and supported by Basic Science Research Program through the National Research Foundation of Korea (NRF) funded by the Ministry of Education (2018R1A2B6009122).

# References

1. KcKeown, N., et al.: OpenFlow: enabling innovation in campus networks. ACM SIGCOMM Comput. Commun. Rev. **28**, 69–74 (2008)
2. Hawilo, H., Shami, A., Mirahmadi, M., Asal, R.: NFV: state of the art, challenges and implementation in next generation mobile networks (vEPC). IEEE Netw. Mag. **28**, 18–26 (2014)
3. Dotan, D., Pinter, R.Y.: HyperFlow: an integrated visual query and dataflow language for end-user information analysis. In: IEEE Symposium Visual Languages and Human-Centric Computing (VL/HCC), pp. 27–34 (2005)
4. Shtykh, R.Y., Suzuki, T.: Distributed data stream processing with Onix. In: IEEE 4th International Conference on Big Data Cloud Computing, pp. 267–268 (2014)
5. Yegabeh, S.H., Ganjali, Y.: Kandoo: a framework for efficient and scalable offloading of control applications. In: HotSDN 2012, Helsinki, Finland (2012)
6. Behrmann, G., David, A., Larsen, K.G.: A tutorial on UPPAAL. In: Bernardo, M., Corradini, F. (eds.) SFM-RT 2004. LNCS, vol. 3185, pp. 200–236. Springer, Heidelberg (2004). https://doi.org/10.1007/978-3-540-30080-9_7
7. OpenFlow Switch Specification. https://www.opennetworking.org/software-defined-standards/specifications/. Accessed 26 Aug 2019
8. SDN. https://www.opennetworking.org/sdn-definition/. Accessed 18 Jan 2019
9. ONF. https://www.opennetworking.org/. Accessed 25 July 2018
10. Braun, W., Menth, M.: Software-defined networking using OpenFlow: protocols, applications and architectural design choices. Future Internet **6**, 302–3363 (2014)
11. Canini, M., Venzano, D., Peresini, P., Kostic, D., Rexford, J.: A NICE way to test OpenFlow applications. In: NSDI (2012)
12. Foster, N., Harrison, R., Meola, M.L., Freedman, M.J., Rexford, M.J.J., Walker, D.: Frenetic: a high-level language for OpenFlow networks. In: Proceedings on PRESTO 2010 (2011)
13. Monsanto, C., Foster, N., Harrison, R., Walker, D.: A compiler and run-time system for network programming languages. In: POPL (2012)
14. Kazemian, P., Varghese, G., McKeown, N.: Header space analysis: static checking for networks. In: NSDI (2012)
15. Reitblatt, M., Foster, N., Rexford, J., Schlesinger, C., Walker, D.: Abstraction for network update. In: SIGCOMM (2012)
16. Canini, M., Kuznetsov, P., Levin, D., Schmid, S.: Distributed and robust SDN control plane for transactional network updates. In: INFOCOM 2015 (2015)
17. Kang, M., Choi, J., Kang, I., Kwak, H., Ahn, S., Shin, M.: A verification method of SDN firewall applications. IEICE Trans. Commun. **E99-B**(7), 1408–1415 (2016)
18. Xiao, L., Xiang, S., Zhu, H.: Modeling and verifying SDN with multiple controllers. In: Proceedings of SAC 2018: Symposium on Applied Computing (2018)

# Modified-Energy Management of Multiple Microgrid

Yi Zhao[1,2(✉)] and Jilai Yu[1]

[1] School of Electrical Engineering and Automation,
Harbin Institute of Technology, Harbin 150001, Heilongjiang, China
reef614@163.com
[2] School of Electric Power, Shenyang Institute of Engineering, Shenyang, China

**Abstract.** This paper presented an energy management model for managing an active distribution network (ADN) consisting of multiple microgrids. The distribution system operator (DSO) of the ADN needs to coordinate the microgrids to achieve optimal energy management. This paper formulated the energy management of ADN with multiple microgrids as a mixed integer second-order cone programming (MISOCP), which considered network reconfiguration, on-load tap changer (OLTC) and static Var compensators (SVC). A case study on a modified IEEE 33-bus distribution network demonstrates the effectiveness of the proposed method.

**Keywords:** Active power distribution network · Energy management · Multiple microgrids

## 1 Introduction

Driven by the rapid development and integration of distributed energy resources (DERs), the distribution network is evolving towards active distribution network (ADN). Microgrid technology has been widely recognized as an effective means of integrating distributed generation, energy storage such that it is friendly and controllable to the distribution network [1]. DERs clustered in a microgrid include non-controllable renewable generators, controllable conventional generators, energy storage devices, etc. Each microgrid has a central controller which has two-way communication with the DERs and controls their operation as well as the power exchange between microgrid and externa utility grid. Networked microgrids can supply their local power demands not only by their on-site resources but also by the external supply from the remaining part of the ADN [2]. These networked microgrids can also provide ancillary services to the ADN [3, 4].

In the ADN, the MGCCs and DSO are different parities seeking for their own individual interests. The energy management in ADNs involves multi-party decision making, forming a complex optimization problem. Each decision maker has separate observability and controllability in the whole distribution network [5]. Traditionally, centralized optimization models are used for the energy management of DSO to coordinate the operations of microgrids and the ADN. In this context, the DSO needs to have full observability and controllability on all of the DERs in microgrids. However,

H. Gao et al. (Eds.): TridentCom 2019, LNICST 309, pp. 95–106, 2020.
https://doi.org/10.1007/978-3-030-43215-7_7

the centralized fashion is facing new challenges [6, 7]. The MGCCs and DSO are independent parties with different interests so that they may not be willing to share private or sensitive information with each other [8, 9]. In addition, with integrating all the DERs in microgrids into the centralized model of DSO, the complexity and problem size will increase dramatically, making the model much more complicated and difficult to solve. Therefore, we need to consider the coordination between the DSO and MGCCs in the energy management for ADNs to overcome these challenges and meanwhile retain the same quality of optimal solutions [10, 11].

The most prominent appearance of high permeability of multiple microgrids is that it brings greater variability and uncertainty to the site selection, constant capacity and real-time output of microgrid, increasing the risk of congestion of active power flow and uneven distribution of reactive power flow in distribution network. The high degree of autonomy of the cast and cast behavior in the normal and accident conditions of the multiple microgrids aggravates the uncertainty and risk. Due to the unidirectivity of protection configuration, the distribution network should have the characteristics of closed-loop design and open-loop operation. This paper proposed an optimal energy management framework for AND based on MISOCP, consisting of multiple networked microgrids. It aimed at achieving energy management in an ADN while comprehensively considering the security constraint, advanced control strategies, such as OLTC, SVC, network reconfiguration, etc.

## 2   Energy Management in Active Distribution Network with Multiple Microgrids

A MISOCP-based security-constrained economic dispatch model is proposed for the energy management of active distribution networks with multiple microgrids. Here the single-period operation [12] of an ADN is considered. The energy management of the DSO and MGCCs is shown in Fig. 1.

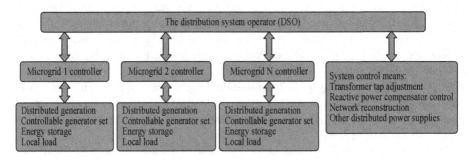

**Fig. 1.** Energy management of multiple microgrids in ADNs.

## 2.1   Power Flow Model of ADN with Network Reconfiguration

The distribution network usually has a radial topology, for which DistFlow model was proposed in [12] to simplify the conventional full AC power flow model. According to the DistFlow model, the line flow and node injections related to node m can be written as:

$$P_{I,m} = p_{mn_1} + p_{mn_2} - (p_{km} - r_{km}l_{km}) \tag{1}$$

$$Q_{I,m} = q_{mn_1} + q_{mn_2} - (q_{km} - x_{km}l_{km}) \tag{2}$$

$$v_k - v_m = 2(r_{km}p_{km} + x_{km}q_{km}) - (r_{km}^2 + x_{km}^2)l_{km} \tag{3}$$

$$p_{km}^2 + q_{km}^2 = v_k l_{km} \tag{4}$$

In the above model, Eqs. (1) and (2) are the nodal balance equations for active and reactive power at node m, respectively. Equation (3) describes the voltage drop equation between the two end nodes of the distribution line. Equation (4) describes the relationship among voltage, current, active power and reactive power.

To convexify Eq. (4), SOC relaxation is applied and Eq. (4) is converted into the following SOC form.

$$p_{km}^2 + q_{km}^2 \leq v_k l_{km} \tag{5}$$

Equation (5) is a rotated quadratic cone. The exactness of this SOC relaxation has been proved.

## 2.2   On-load Tap Changer (OLTC)

On-load tap changer (OLTC) is an important means in distribution network to regulate the voltage. The DSO can adjust the tap position of the transformers to control the voltage over the network. In this paper, we introduce a dummy bus named as k' and add into the bus set $\Omega$. Then the transformer can be modeled as a distribution line kk' and added into the distribution line set $\Psi_{NS}$ and a series connected tap changer k'm included in the transformer set $\Psi_T$. At each line representing the transformer, we have the following equation regarding the two nodal voltages.

$$v_{k'} = \eta_{km}^2 v_m, \ \forall(k',m) \in \Psi_T \tag{6}$$

where the tap changing ratio is represented by:

$$\eta_{km} = \underline{\eta}_{km} + \kappa_{km}T_{km}, \ \forall(k',m) \in \Psi_T \tag{7}$$

and the tap position can be modeled as an integer:

$$0 \leq \kappa_{km} \leq \frac{\bar{\eta}_{km} - \underline{\eta}_{km}}{T_{km}}, \quad \forall (k', m) \in \mathbf{\Psi}_{\mathrm{T}} \tag{8}$$

Using binary expansion, we can further represent the tap position by the following equation.

$$\kappa_{km} = \sum_{h=0}^{H_{km}} 2^h \alpha_{km,h}, \quad \forall (k', m) \in \mathbf{\Psi}_{\mathrm{T}} \tag{9}$$

The value $H_{km}$ can be determined by Eq. (10).

$$\sum_{h=0}^{H_{km}-1} 2^h < \frac{\bar{\eta}_{km} - \underline{\eta}_{km}}{T_{km}} \leq \sum_{h=0}^{H_{km}} 2^h, \quad \forall (k', m) \in \mathbf{\Psi}_{\mathrm{T}} \tag{10}$$

It can be observed that, by substituting (6) and (7), Eq. (9) will contain a number of products of continuous and binary variables, which is highly non-linear and will increase the computational complexity significantly. To address this issue, we introduce auxiliary variables $\alpha_{km,h}$, $\beta_{km,h}$, and $\gamma_{km,h}$ to replace the nonlinear terms, and then the following set of equations [12] are written in (11a–11f), which is equivalent to Eq. (6).

$$v_{k'} = \underline{\eta}_{km} \delta_{km} + T_{km} \sum_{h=0}^{H_{km}} 2^h \gamma_{km,h}, \quad \forall (k', m) \in \mathbf{\Psi}_{\mathrm{T}} \tag{11a}$$

$$\delta_{km} = \underline{\eta}_{km} v_m + T_{km} \sum_{h=0}^{H_{km}} 2^h \beta_{km,h}, \quad \forall (k', m) \in \mathbf{\Psi}_{\mathrm{T}} \tag{11b}$$

$$0 \leq v_{m,t} - \beta_{km,h} \leq \bar{v}_m (1 - \alpha_{km,h}), \quad \forall h, \forall (k', m) \in \mathbf{\Psi}_{\mathrm{T}} \tag{11c}$$

$$0 \leq \beta_{km,h} \leq \bar{v}_m \alpha_{km,h}, \quad \forall h, \forall (k', m) \in \mathbf{\Psi}_{\mathrm{T}} \tag{11d}$$

$$0 \leq \delta_{km} - \gamma_{km,h} \leq \bar{v}_m \bar{\eta}_{km} (1 - \alpha_{km,h}), \quad \forall h, \forall (k', m) \in \mathbf{\Psi}_{\mathrm{T}} \tag{11e}$$

$$0 \leq \gamma_{km,h} \leq \bar{v}_m \bar{\eta}_{km} \alpha_{km,h}, \quad \forall h, \forall (k', m) \in \mathbf{\Psi}_{\mathrm{T}} \tag{11f}$$

where $\delta_{km}$ is an auxiliary variable representing voltage magnitude.

## 3 Energy Management Model of Active Distribution Network with Multiple Microgrids

The network energy management of active power distribution with multiple microgrids can be divided into two layers. The upper layer is the energy management of the active distribution network. The lower layer considers the power exchange with the distribution network for each sub-microgrid and performs optimal scheduling of local power generation resources and loads.

## 3.1    Energy Management of DSO

The active and reactive power exchange between the networked microgrids and the ADN need to meet the constraints as follows.

$$P_{I,m} = P_{X,m}, \quad Q_{I,m} = Q_{X,m}, \quad \forall m \in \Omega_M \tag{12}$$

$$\underline{P}_{X,m} \leq P_{X,m} \leq \bar{P}_{X,m}, \quad \underline{Q}_{X,m} \leq Q_{X,m} \leq \bar{Q}_{X,m}, \quad \forall m \in \Omega_M \tag{13}$$

Equation (12) defines the active and reactive power flows from the microgrids to the ADN. Equation (13) enforces the lower and upper limits of the power exchange. The load curtailments at non-microgrid nodes are subject to the constraints below.

$$0 \leq P_{LS,m} \leq P_{D,m}, \quad \forall m \in \Omega \backslash \Omega_M \tag{14}$$

$$P_{LS,m} Q_{D,m} = Q_{LS,m} P_{D,m}, \quad \forall m \in \Omega \backslash \Omega_M \tag{15}$$

Equation (14) represent the limit of active power demand curtailment at non-microgrid buses. Equation (15) is representing that the curtailment of load demand will not affect the power factor at this node.

According to the above model, the net power injections at each non-microgrid bus in the ADN can be formulated as follows.

$$P_{I,m} = P_{B,m} - P_{D,m} + P_{LS,m}, \quad \forall m \in \Omega_B \tag{16}$$

$$P_{I,m} = -P_{D,m}, \quad \forall m \in \Omega \backslash \{\Omega_B \cup \Omega_M\} \tag{17}$$

$$Q_{I,m} = Q_{B,m} - Q_{D,m} + Q_{LS,m}, \quad \forall m \in \Omega_B \tag{18}$$

$$Q_{I,m} = Q_{S,m} - Q_{D,m} + Q_{LS,m}, \quad \forall m \in \Omega_S \tag{19}$$

$$\underline{Q}_{S,m} \leq Q_{S,m} \leq \bar{Q}_{S,m}, \quad \forall m \in \Omega_S \tag{20}$$

$$Q_{I,m} = -Q_{D,m} + Q_{LS,m}, \quad \forall m \in \Omega \backslash \{\Omega_M \cup \Omega_S \cup \Omega_B\} \tag{21}$$

Equations (16) and (18) represent active and reactive power injections at the buses on the boundary; Eq. (17) shows the injected active power at the buses that are neither the external transmission network nor a microgrid and has no distributed energy resources; Eq. (19) indicates the injected reactive power at the buses with SVCs. Equation (27) represents the models of SVS with continuous adjustment of reactive power output; (21) represents reactive power injection at the buses without SVCs.

The operation costs of networked microgrids $C_{mg}$, including power exchange and production, are calculated by the MGCCs. The DSO will consider the following costs of buying power from transmission power grid $C_{imp}$ and load shedding $C_{shed}$.

$$C_{imp} = \sum_{m \in \Omega_B} \rho_{E,m} P_{B,m} \tag{22}$$

$$C_{shed} = \sum_{m \in \Omega \backslash \Omega_M} \rho_{LS} P_{LS,m} \tag{23}$$

It is noted that load curtailment is the last action that the DSO makes to maintain supply-demand balance, so $\rho_{LS}$ is set to be a value that is much larger than $\rho_{E,m} (\forall m \in \Omega_B)$.

The operational security constraints including line flow and voltage limits are shown as follows.

$$p_{km}^2 + q_{km}^2 \leq S_{km}^2, \quad \forall (k,m) \in \Psi \tag{24}$$

$$\underline{v}_m \leq v_m \leq \bar{v}_m, \quad \forall m \in \Omega \backslash \Omega_B \tag{25}$$

$$v_m = \tilde{v}_m, \quad \forall m \in \Omega_B \tag{26}$$

Equation (24) indicates the line flow capacity limits. Equation (25) is the voltage limit on each node and Eq. (26) enforces that the voltage magnitude of substation nodes are equal to preset values.

To minimize the voltage deviation from the nominal voltage, a penalty term is included to represent the cost of accumulated deviations.

$$C_{vol} = \rho_V \sum_{m \in \Omega} \upsilon_m \tag{27}$$

where $\upsilon_m$ is defined as

$$\upsilon_m = |v_m - \tilde{v}_m|, \quad \forall m \in \Omega \tag{28}$$

In addition, Eq. (28) can be converted to the following two constraints by eliminating the absolute value operator.

$$\upsilon_m \geq v_m - \tilde{v}_m, \quad \forall m \in \Omega \tag{29}$$

$$\upsilon_m \geq \tilde{v}_m - v_m, \quad \forall m \in \Omega \tag{30}$$

### 3.2   Energy Management of Individual Microgrids

The microgrids operate a number of dispatchable generation resources to serve their local load demands and exchange power with ADN. The central controller of the microgrid, MGCC, will conduct energy management based on the operational characteristics of its disputable distributed energy resources. The renewable-based and dispatchable generators are modelled as follows.

$$\underline{P}_{G,g} \leq P_{G,g} \leq \bar{P}_{G,g}, \quad \forall g \in \mathbf{\Pi}_{C,m} \tag{31}$$

$$P_{G,g} = \tilde{P}_{G,g}, \quad \forall g \in \mathbf{\Pi}_{R,m} \tag{32}$$

Equation (31) enforces upper and lower generation limits on dispatchable units. To maximize the utilization of renewable generation, Eq. (32) sets the active power output of the renewable generators to be the forecasted values.

In the microgrid, energy storage system is used to smooth the variations of active power consumption and renewable power generation by discharging and charging management, which can be modelled as follows.

$$-\bar{P}_{E,e} \leq P_{Ch,e} - P_{Dch,e} \leq \bar{P}_{E,e}, \quad \forall e \in \mathbf{\Lambda}_m \tag{33}$$

$$\underline{E}_e \leq \tilde{E}_e + \xi_e P_{Ch,e} - \frac{1}{\zeta_e} P_{Dch,e} \leq \bar{E}_e, \quad \forall e \in \mathbf{\Lambda}_m \tag{34}$$

$$P_{Ch,e} \geq 0, P_{Dch,e} \geq 0, \quad \forall e \in \mathbf{\Lambda}_m \tag{35}$$

Equation (33) indicates the maximum charging and discharging power limits. Equation (34) describes that the energy remained in the energy storage should respect the upper and lower limits. Equation (35) enforces the charging and discharging power to be non-negative.

In addition, the controllable units can provide reactive power by smart inverters. The reactive power output constraint is expressed as.

$$\underline{Q}_{G,m} \leq Q_{G,m} \leq \bar{Q}_{G,m} \tag{36}$$

where $Q_{G,m}$ is the reactive power output of the generator m, $\underline{Q}_{G,m}$ and $\underline{Q}_{G,m}$ is the lower and upper limits.

Part of the load demand in the microgrid is interruptible or adjustable, so we consider load curtailment in the energy management of MGCC, expressed as the following equtions.

$$0 \leq P_{LS,m} \leq P_{D,m} \tag{37}$$

$$P_{LS,m} Q_{D,m} = Q_{LS,m} P_{D,m} \tag{38}$$

Equation (38) indicates that the curtailment of active and reactive power load demands will not affect the power factor.

The active and reactive power balances in the microgrid need to be maintain by the MGCC, shown in Eq. (39) and (40) respectively.

$$\sum_{g \in \mathbf{\Pi}_m} P_{G,g} + \sum_{e \in \mathbf{\Lambda}_m} \left( P_{Dch,e} - P_{Ch,e} \right) = P_{X,m} + P_{D,m} - P_{LS,m} \tag{39}$$

$$\sum_{g\in\Pi_m} Q_{G,g} = Q_{X,m} + Q_{D,m} - Q_{LS,m} \tag{40}$$

The operation costs of a microgrid includes the generation cost of controllable generator, load curtailment cost and deprecation cost of energy storage while assuming that the generation cost of renewable generator is close to zero. The generation cost curve of a controllable generator is modelled in a quadratic function.

$$C_{gen,m} = \sum_{g\in\Pi_{C,m}} \left( a_g P_{G,g}^2 + b_g P_{G,g} + c_g \right) \tag{41}$$

The load curtailment cost is expressed as

$$C_{shed,m} = \rho_{LS} P_{LS,m} \tag{42}$$

The charging and discharging of energy storage will cause the depreciation of energy storage and impact its lifetime. The depreciation cost of energy storage devices are modelled as

$$C_{deg,m} = \sum_{e\in\Lambda_m} a_e \left[ \left(P_{Ch,e}\right)^2 + \left(P_{Dch,e}\right)^2 \right] \tag{43}$$

The above capacity degradation coset model is a quadratic function that has been verified in [7] using experimental data.

### 3.3 Energy Management of ADN with Multiple Microgrids

In summary, the optimization model of the energy management of the DSO and multiple MGCCs is formulated as an MISOCP problem as follows. The DSO will solve the optimization model to make optimal decisions in the ADN and the MGCCs of the microgrids will follow the DSO's commands in order to collaborate with each other to achieve the overall optimal operation of the ADN:

$$\min C_{imp} + C_{shed} + C_{vol} + C_{mg} \tag{44}$$

$$\text{s.t. } C_{mg} = \sum_{m\in\Omega_M} \left( C_{gen,m} + C_{shed,m} + C_{deg,m} \right) \tag{45}$$

In this model, the objective aims at minimizing the total operation cost of the ADN with considerations of the physical and operational constraints of the ADN and microgrids.

## 4  Case Studies

In this section, the case study is carried out on a modified IEEE 33-bus distribution system. The proposed model and algorithm are implemented in MATLAB 2016a with the commercial solver MOSEK 8.1 on a personal computer with 2.4 GHz CPU and 12G RAM. In the mixed integer programming, the relative optimality gap is set at 0.01% by default.

### 4.1  System Description

A modified IEEE 33-node distribution system is used to test the proposed model [12]. The operational data of the dispatchable generators and energy storage devices in the microgrids are listed in Tables 1 and 2. The data of renewable power generation, load demand and reactive power generation in each microgrid are given in Table 3. The base-case network topology is given in Fig. 2 and the three microgrids are located at node 13, 18 and 30, respectively. Two SVCs are at node 12 and 28, repetively [13, 14].

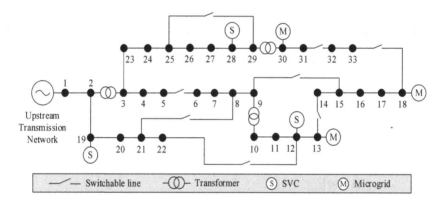

**Fig. 2.** Test power distribution system in the base case.

**Table 1.** Controllable generation units in the three microgrids.

| Bus | Technical parameters | | Cost coefficients | | |
|-----|---------------------|-----------------|-------------------|-----------|---------|
|     | Min output (kW) | Max output (kW) | a ($/(MW)2 h) | b ($/MWh) | c ($/h) |
| 13  | 50  | 300 | 0.5 | 10 | 5 |
| 18  | 100 | 500 | 1.2 | 15 | 3 |
| 30  | 100 | 500 | 0.8 | 12 | 4 |

**Table 2.** Energy storage devices in the three microgrids.

| Bus | Max power (kW) | Energy level (kWh) | | |
|---|---|---|---|---|
| | | Min | Max | Initial |
| 13 | 50 | 50 | 200 | 100 |
| 18 | 100 | 100 | 300 | 100 |
| 30 | 100 | 100 | 300 | 200 |

**Table 3.** Onsite load and resources in the three microgrids.

| Bus | Power demand | | Renewable resource (kW) |
|---|---|---|---|
| | Real (kW) | Reactive (kVar) | |
| 13 | 350 | 200 | 0.9/0.9 |
| 18 | 400 | 300 | 0.9/0.9 |
| 30 | 500 | 800 | 0.85/0.85 |

## 4.2   Results

The optimal power exchange schedules of the three micgrogrids in ADN under 10 different scenarios with different load levels by the proposed model are shown in Fig. 3, and the total cost is given in Fig. 4.

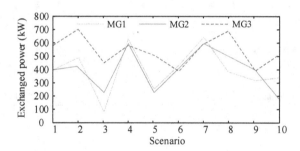

**Fig. 3.** Optimal power exchange schedules of the three microgrids (MG 1–3) in AND under different scenarios.

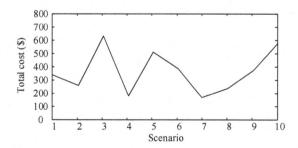

**Fig. 4.** Total cost of the three microgrids (MG 1–3) in AND under different scenarios.

Then we study the impact of exchange limit of microgrid on the optimal exchange schedules. By changing the exchange limit from 500 kVA to 100 kVA, Fig. 5 shows the variations of the microgrid tie-line flow schedules and Fig. 6 gives the total cost.

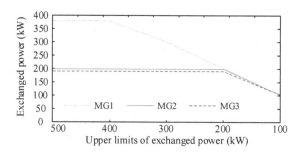

**Fig. 5.** Optimal power exchange schedules of the three microgrids (MG 1–3) in ADN under different exchange limits of microgrids.

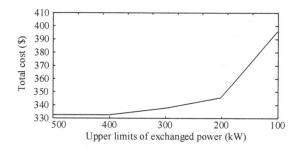

**Fig. 6.** Total cost of the three microgrids (MG 1–3) in AND under different exchange limits of microgrids.

It can be observed from Fig. 6 that with the decrease of the microgrid exchange limit, the total cost increases. When the limit is decreased to 300 kVA, the microgrid exchange power will be limited by these constraints and capped at the maximum exchange limit.

## 5 Conclusion

In this paper, the connection switch of the transfer line is used to realize the network reconstruction under the radial structure of the distribution network so as to reduce the line loss and eliminate the line obstruction. The influence of ADN reconstruction and OLTC transformer operation is considered, and the model realizes the highly autonomous cooperative optimal operation domain control between the microgrids and the distribution network. IEEE 33 bus example shows that the strategy can effectively realize the economic operation in the distribution network.

# References

1. Feng, C., Li, Z., Shahidehpour, M., Wen, F., Liu, W., Wang, X.: Decentralized short-term voltage control in active power distribution systems. IEEE Trans. Smart Grid **9**, 4566–4576 (2017)
2. Koutsoukis, N.C., Siagkas, Di.O., Georgilakis, P.S., Hatziargyriou, N.D.: Online reconfiguration of active distribution networks for maximum integration of distributed generation. IEEE Trans. Autom. Sci. Eng. **14**(2), 437–448 (2017)
3. Li, Z., Shahidehpour, M., Aminifar, F., Alabdulwahab, A., Al-Turki, Y.: Networked microgrids for enhancing the power system resilience. Proc. IEEE **105**(7), 1289–1310 (2017)
4. Wang, H., Huang, J.: Incentivizing energy trading for interconnected microgrids. IEEE Trans. Smart Grid **9**, 2647–2657 (2016)
5. Ma, W.-J., Wang, J., Gupta, V., Chen, C.: Distributed energy management for networked microgrids using online alternating direction method of multipliers with regret. IEEE Trans. Smart Grid **9**, 847–856 (2016)
6. Liu, T., et al.: Energy management of cooperative microgrids: a distributed optimization approach. Int. J. Electr. Power Energy Syst. **96**, 335–346 (2018)
7. Liu, Y., et al.: Distributed robust energy management of a multi-microgrid system in the real-time energy market. IEEE Trans. Sustain. Energy **10**, 396–406 (2017)
8. Malekpour, A.R., Pahwa, A.: Stochastic networked microgrid energy management with correlated wind generators. IEEE Trans. Power Syst. **32**(5), 3681–3693 (2017)
9. Qi, C., et al.: A decentralized optimal operation of AC/DC hybrid distribution grids. IEEE Trans. Smart Grid **9**, 6095–6105 (2017)
10. Wu, L.: A transformation-based multi-area dynamic economic dispatch approach for preserving information privacy of individual areas. IEEE Trans. Smart Grid **10**, 722–731 (2017)
11. Gregoratti, D., Matamoros, J.: Distributed energy trading: the multiple-microgrid case. IEEE Trans. Ind. Electron. **62**(4), 2551–2559 (2015)
12. Baran, M.E., Wu, F.F.: Network reconfiguration in distribution systems for loss reduction and load balancing. IEEE Trans. Power Deliv. **4**(2), 1401–1407 (1989)
13. Setiasih, Suyatno, T.: The effect of product mix and lifestyle toward the amount money spent mediated by marketing strategy. Int. J. Adv. Sci. Technol. **120**, 97–110 (2018)
14. Chen, Y., Tang, Z.: Speaker recognition of noisy short utterance based on speech frame quality discrimination and three-stage classification model. Int. J. Control Autom. **8**(3), 135–146 (2015)

# Bivariate Fisher–Snedecor $\mathcal{F}$ Distribution with Arbitrary Fading Parameters

Weijun Cheng[✉], Xianmeng Xu, Xiaoting Wang, and Xiaohan Liu

School of Information Engineering, Minzu University of China, Beijing,
People's Republic of China
weijuncheng@muc.edu.cn

**Abstract.** A bivariate Fisher–Snedecor $\mathcal{F}$ composite distribution with arbitrary fading parameters (not necessary identical) is presented in this paper. We derive novel theoretical formulations of the statistical characteristics for the correlated $\mathcal{F}$ composite fading model, which include the joint probability density function, the joint cumulative distribution function, the joint moments and the power correlation coefficient. Capitalizing on the joint cumulative distribution function, the bit error rate for binary digital modulation systems and the outage probability of a correlated dual-branch selection diversity system, and the level crossing rate and the average fade duration of a sampled Fisher-Snedecor $\mathcal{F}$ composited fading envelope are obtained, respectively. Finally, we employ numerical and simulation results to demonstrate the validity of the theoretical analysis under various correlated fading and shadowing scenarios.

**Keywords:** Fisher–Snedecor $\mathcal{F}$ distribution · Correlated composite fading · Selection diversity · Second-order statistics

## 1 Introduction

More recently, the Fisher-Snedecor $\mathcal{F}$ fading channel model has been paid great attention in the performance evaluation of wireless digital communication systems [1–9]. This channel model was firstly presented in [1]. It accurately describes the composite impacts of both shadowing components and multipath components on the faded signal, where shadowing components follow inverse Nakagami-m distribution and multipath components follow Nakagami-m distribution. Compared to generalized-K (Nakagami-Gamma) composite fading model, the authors in [1] showed that under non-LOS (NLOS) and line-of-sight (LOS) environments the Fisher composite fading model has a better fit to experimental channel measurements, such as wireless body area networks and device-to-device (D2D) communications. Furthermore, this fading model can reduce to one-sided Gaussian, Rayleigh and Nakagami-m as special cases in the absence of shadowing components. In addition, its other advantage is that the closed-form expressions of its statistical characteristics are more tractable and simpler than those of generalized-K distribution.

The authors in [2] gave the theoretical formulations of the sum of independent and non-identically distributed (i.n.i.d.) random variables (RVs) following Fisher-Snedecor $\mathcal{F}$ distribution and applied them in maximal ratio combining (MRC) receivers. The

H. Gao et al. (Eds.): TridentCom 2019, LNICST 309, pp. 107–119, 2020.
https://doi.org/10.1007/978-3-030-43215-7_8

performance of physical layer security was investigated over $\mathcal{F}$ composite fading channels in [3]. The authors in [1] further studied the achievable channel capacity and energy detection-based spectrum sensing in Fisher-Snedecor $\mathcal{F}$ fading in [4] and [5], respectively. In [6], the performance of the selection combining (SC) scheme with i.n.i. d branches over $\mathcal{F}$ composite fading channels was analyzed. Authors in [7] considered the ergodic capacity of several adaptive transmission strategies and obtained asymptotic and exact representations in Fisher–Snedecor $\mathcal{F}$ fading channels. The effective rate (ER) analysis of multiple-input single-output (MISO) systems was presented in i.n. i.d. and i.i.d. Fisher-Snedecor $\mathcal{F}$ fading channels in [8]. In [9], the symbol error rate (SER) of M-ary quadrature amplitude modulation (M-QAM) and M-ary pulse amplitude modulation (M-PAM), and the average capacity were derived and evaluated in Fisher-Snedecor $\mathcal{F}$ fading channels.

Although the MRC and SC systems over Fisher-Snedecor $\mathcal{F}$ composite fading channel have been investigated in [2] and [6], the authors only considered the i.n.i.d. fading environments. When the distance between antennas is less than $0.38\lambda$ in a diversity system, the received signals could cause correlated each other and lead to a decrease of the diversity gain, where $\lambda$ is the wavelength of the carrier. To be specific, this signal correlation usually occurs in relatively small size mobile equipment because the space between their diversity branches can be too close to keep the received signals independent. Thus, the correlated analysis of the received signals are crucial in the performance evaluation of the diversity received systems. Up to now, the correlated distribution in wireless communication diversity systems has been studied extensively in the open research works. Nevertheless, most of them only considered either the correlated small scale fading or the correlated shadowing, such as [10, 11]. For correlated multipath and shadowing composite distributions, only a few papers have been involved. Based on a gamma shadowing distribution, the correlated K distribution (Rayleigh-Gamma) and generalized-K distribution were investigated in [12] and [13], respectively. In [14] and [15], the outage probability of SC receivers was studied over correlated Weibull-gamma fading channels with identical and non-identical fading conditions, respectively. By using an inverse Gaussian shadowing model, bivariate $\mathcal{G}$ (Rayleigh-inverse Gaussian) fading distribution has been proposed and employed to the dual-branch SC and MRC diversity receivers in [16]. In [17], the authors obtained the statistical properties of bivariate Nakagami-lognormal distribution and discussed the correlation properties under micro- and macro-diversity environments.

To the best of the authors' knowledge, the correlated (bivariate) Fisher–Snedecor $\mathcal{F}$ channel model has not been considered in the published research works. Motivated by the above observation, we study the bivariate Fisher–Snedecor $\mathcal{F}$ composite distribution with not necessary identical fading parameters and its applications in this paper. The statistical characteristics of correlated Fisher–Snedecor $\mathcal{F}$ composite distribution including the bivariate probability density function (PDF), the bivariate cumulative distribution function (CDF) and the joint moments are derived. Capitalizing on the joint CDF, the bit error rate (BER) of binary digital modulation schemes and the outage probability (OP) for a correlated dual-branch SC receiver, the average fade duration (AFD) and level crossing rate (LCR) of a sampled Fisher-Snedecor $\mathcal{F}$ composited fading envelope are also given, respectively. Finally, we evaluate the validity of the performance analysis by using numerical analysis and simulation under various correlated fading and shadowing scenarios.

The remainder of this paper is organized as follows: the closed-form expressions of statistical characteristics of the bivariate Fisher–Snedecor $\mathcal{F}$ composite distribution are derived in Sect. 2. The performance analysis of a correlated dual-branch SC receiver is presented in Sect. 3, and Sect. 4 gives the second-order statistics of a sampled composited fading envelope. Numerical and simulation analysis are shown and discussed in Sects. 5 and 6 outlines the main conclusions.

## 2 Statistical Characteristics

Let $X_i$ ($i = 1, 2$) be the channel fading envelopes of Nakagami-$m$ processes, and the bivariate (joint) PDF between $X_1$ and $X_2$ given from [10, eq. (12)] as

$$
\begin{aligned}
f_{X_1,X_2}(x_1,x_2) = {} & 4(1-\rho_N)^{m_2} \sum_{k=0}^{\infty} \frac{(m_1)_k \rho_N^k}{k!} {}_1F_1\left[m_2 - m_1, m_2 + k; \frac{\rho_N m_2 x_2^2}{Y_2(1-\rho_N)}\right] \\
& \times \prod_{i=1}^{2} \left[\frac{m_i}{Y_i(1-\rho_N)}\right]^{m_i+k} \frac{x_i^{2(m_i+k)-1}}{\Gamma(m_i+k)} \exp\left[-\frac{m_i x_i^2}{(1-\rho_N)Y_i}\right]
\end{aligned}
\tag{1}
$$

where $m_2 > m_1 \geq 1/2$ is the Nakagami-$m$ shaping parameter, $Y_i$ is the average fading power $Y_i = \mathbb{E}[X_i^2]$ with $\mathbb{E}[\cdot]$ denoting expectation, and $\rho_N$ denotes the power correlation coefficient between $X_1^2$ and $X_2^2$. Furthermore, ${}_1F_1(\cdot; \cdot; \cdot)$ is the confluent hypergeometric function defined in [18, eq. (9.210/1)], $(x)p$ is the Pochhammer's symbol defined in [18, p. xliii], $(x)_p = \Gamma(x+p)/\Gamma(x)$, with $p \in \mathbb{N}$, and $\Gamma(\cdot)$ is the gamma function in [18, eq. (8.310/1)].

In composite fading environments, $Y_i$ slowly varies when small scale fading is superimposed on shadowing, and its root-mean-square (rms) can be considered as a random variable following the inverse Nakagami-m distribution. Based on the proposed signal model in [1], $Y_i = w_i^2 \Omega_i$, where $w_i$ is inverse Nakagami-m random variable, $\Omega_i = \mathbb{E}[R_i^2]$ denotes the mean power of the composite signal envelope $R_i$, then the PDF in (1) is conditioned on $w_i$. To model the inverse Nakagami-m distribution, we let the parameter $w_i = 1/r_i$, where $r_i$ follows Nakagami-m distribution defined in [10, eq. (12)]. By utilizing a change of random variables, the joint PDF of inverse Nakagami-m distribution can be obtained as

$$
\begin{aligned}
f_{W_1,W_2}(w_1,w_2) = {} & 4(1-\rho_G)^{n_2} \sum_{l=0}^{\infty} \frac{(n_1)_l \rho_G^l}{l!} {}_1F_1\left[n_2 - n_1, n_2 + l; \frac{\rho_G n_2 w_2^{-2}}{1-\rho_G}\right] \\
& \times \prod_{j=1}^{2} \left[\frac{n_j}{1-\rho_G}\right]^{n_j+l} \frac{w_j^{-2(n_j+l)-1}}{\Gamma(n_j+l)} \exp\left[-\frac{n_j w_j^{-2}}{1-\rho_G}\right]
\end{aligned}
\tag{2}
$$

where $n_2 > n_1 \geq 1/2$ is the inverse Nakagami-$m$ shaping parameter, $\rho_G$ denotes the power correlation coefficient between $w_1^2$ and $w_2^2$. In this paper, we set scale parameter, $\Omega_s$, equal to unity.

In [1], the PDF of Fisher–Snedecor $\mathcal{F}$ composite envelopes is obtained by averaging the conditional PDF of the Nakagami-$m$ process over the random variation of the rms signal power. Therefore, the joint PDF of bivariate Fisher–Snedecor $\mathcal{F}$ composite distribution is written as

$$f_{R_1,R_2}(r_1, r_2) = \int_0^\infty \int_0^\infty f_{Y_1|W_1,Y_2|W_2}(r_1|w_1, r_2|w_2) f_{W_1,W_2}(w_1, w_2) dw_1 dw_2 \tag{3}$$

By substituting (1) and (2) in (3), and using [19, eq. (55)], the joint PDF of bivariate Fisher–Snedecor $\mathcal{F}$ distribution can be derived, after some algebraic manipulations, as

$$
\begin{aligned}
f_{R_1,R_2}(r_1, r_2) = \sum_{k=0}^\infty \sum_{l=0}^\infty & \frac{4(m_1)_k \rho_N^k (n_1)_l \Theta \rho_G^l}{k!l!B(m_1+k, n_1+l)B(m_2+k, n_2+l)} \\
& \times \frac{\beta_1^{m_1+k} \beta_2^{m_2+k} r_1^{2(m_1+k)-1} r_2^{2(m_2+k)-1}}{(1+\beta_1 r_1^2)^{\lambda_1}(1+\beta_2 r_2^2)^{-\lambda_2}} \\
& \times F_2\left[\lambda_2; m_2-m_1, n_2-n_1; m_2+k, n_2+l; \frac{\rho_N \beta_2 r_2^2}{\beta_2 r_2^2+1}, \frac{\rho_G}{\beta_2 r_2^2+1}\right]
\end{aligned}
\tag{4}
$$

where $\beta_i = m_i(1-\rho_G)/(n_i(1-\rho_N)\Omega_i)$, $(i = 1, 2)$, $B(\cdot, \cdot)$ is the Beta function defined in [18, eq. (8.384.1)], $F_2[\cdot]$ is the Appell Hypergeometric function defined in [18, eq. (9.180.2)], $\lambda_1 = m_1+k+n_1+l$, $\lambda_2 = m_2+k+n_2+l$, $\Theta = (1-\rho_N)^{m_2}(1-\rho_G)^{n_2}$.

To achieve a closed-form representation of joint CDF, we use the infinite series expressions of the Appell's function in [18, eq. (9.180.2)]. Based on (4), the corresponding joint CDF of $R_1$ and $R_2$ can be given by

$$
\begin{aligned}
F_{R_1,R_2}(r_1, r_2) &= \int_0^{r_1} \int_0^{r_2} f_{R_1,R_2}(r_1, r_2) dr_1 dr_2 \\
&= \sum_{k=0}^\infty \sum_{l=0}^\infty \sum_{i=0}^\infty \sum_{j=0}^\infty \frac{\rho_N^{k+i} \rho_G^{l+j} \Theta \beta_1^{m_1+k} \beta_2^{m_2+k+i}}{i!j!k!l!\Gamma(m_1)\Gamma(n_1)} \\
&\quad \times \frac{(m_2-m_1)_i (n_2-n_1)_j \Gamma(\lambda_1) r_1^{2(m_1+k)} r_2^{2(m_2+k+i)}}{B(m_2+k+i, n_2+l+j)(m_1+k)(m_2+k+i)} \\
&\quad \times {}_2F_1[\lambda_1, m_1+k; m_1+k+1; -\beta_1 r_1^2] \\
&\quad \times {}_2F_1[\lambda_2+i+j, m_2+k+i; m_2+k+i+1; -\beta_2 r_2^2]
\end{aligned}
\tag{5}
$$

where ${}_2F_1[\cdot]$ is the Gauss hypergeometric function in [18, eq. (9.100)].

The joint central moments of the bivariate Fisher–Snedecor $\mathcal{F}$ composite distribution can be obtained as

$$
\begin{aligned}
\mu_{R_1,R_2}(q_1,q_2) &= E[r_1^{q_1} r_2^{q_2}] \\
&= \int_0^\infty \int_0^\infty r_1^{q_1} r_2^{q_2} f_{R_1,R_2}(r_1,r_2)\,dr_1\,dr_2
\end{aligned}
\tag{6}
$$

By substituting (4) into (6), and employing [18, eq. (3.194.3)] and the identities [18, eqs. (9.180.1) and (9.182.11)], after some mathematical manipulations, we have

$$
\begin{aligned}
\mu_{R_1,R_2}(q_1,q_2) =\ & \frac{B(m_1 + {}^{q_1}\!/_2, n_1 - {}^{q_1}\!/_2)\, {}_2F_1[-{}^{q_2}\!/_2, -{}^{q_1}\!/_2; m_2; \rho_N]}{(B(m_2 + {}^{q_2}\!/_2, n_2 - {}^{q_2}\!/_2)\, {}_2F_1[{}^{q_2}\!/_2, {}^{q_1}\!/_2; n_2; \rho_G])^{-1}} \\
& \times \frac{(n_1\Omega_1/m_1)^{q_1/2}(n_2\Omega_2/m_2)^{q_1/2}}{B(m_1,n_1)B(m_2,n_2)}
\end{aligned}
\tag{7}
$$

By definition, the power correlation coefficient of $R_1^2$ and $R_2^2$ can be expressed as

$$
\rho \triangleq \frac{\mathrm{cov}(r_1^2, r_2^2)}{\sqrt{\mathrm{var}(r_1^2)}\sqrt{\mathrm{var}(r_2^2)}} = \frac{E[r_1^2 r_2^2] - E[r_1^2]E[r_2^2]}{\sqrt{E[r_1^4] - E^2[r_1^2]}\sqrt{E[r_2^4] - E^2[r_2^2]}}
\tag{8}
$$

where $E(r_i^q) = \frac{B(m_i + q/2, n_i - q/2)}{B(m_i, n_i)(m_i/n_i\Omega_i)^{q/2}}$ is given in [1], $i = 1, 2$.

Then, substituting (7) into (8) and after some straightforward simplifications, the correlation coefficient can be yielded as

$$
\rho \triangleq \frac{{}_2F_1(-1,-1; m_2; \rho_G)\, {}_2F_1(1,1; n_2; \rho_N) - 1}{\sqrt{\frac{(m_1 + n_1 - 1)(m_2 + n_2 - 1)}{m_1 m_2 (n_1 - 2)(n_2 - 2)}}}
\tag{9}
$$

## 3  Dual-Branch SC Diversity Receiver

In this paper, we consider a correlated dual-branch SC receiver over Fisher–Snedecor $\mathcal{F}$ composite environments. Its equivalent baseband received signal at the $i$th ($i = 1, 2$) antenna can be given by $r_i = ag_i + n_i$, in which $a$ denotes the complex transmitted symbol with average energy $E_a = \mathbb{E}[|a|^2]$, $n_i$ denotes the complex AWGN (additive white Gaussian noise) with $N_0$ (single sided power spectral density) which is supposed identical and uncorrelated to two branches, and $g_i$ denotes the complex channel gain with its magnitude $R_i = |g_i|$ following a Fisher–Snedecor $\mathcal{F}$ distribution. Furthermore, the general assumptions are made that only the channel fading magnitude has effects on the received signal and the phase can be accurately estimated, similar as in [13]. The instantaneous SNR (signal-to-noise ratio) per received symbol is written as $\gamma_i = R_i^2 E_a/N_0$, its average SNR can be given as $\bar{\gamma}_i = \mathbb{E}[R_i^2]E_a/N_0 = \Omega_i E_a/N_0$. In the following, we will give the OP and the BER analysis of the correlated dual-branch SC diversity system over Fisher–Snedecor $\mathcal{F}$ composite fading, respectively.

### 3.1   Outage Probability

For a SC receiver, the instantaneous output SNR can be expressed $\gamma_{SC} = \max(\gamma_1, \gamma_2)$, its corresponding CDF can be written as $F_{\gamma_{SC}}(\gamma) = F_{\gamma_1,\gamma_2}(\gamma,\gamma)$ in [20]. By making use of (5) and this equation, and carrying out a simple transformation of variables, we obtain the close-form expressions of $F_{\gamma_{SC}}(\gamma)$ over correlated Fisher–Snedecor $\mathcal{F}$ composite fading as follows

$$
\begin{aligned}
F_{\gamma_{SC}}(\gamma) = \sum_{k=0}^{\infty}\sum_{l=0}^{\infty}\sum_{i=0}^{\infty}\sum_{j=0}^{\infty} & \frac{\rho_N^{k+i}\rho_G^{l+j}\Theta\alpha_1^{m_1+k}\alpha_2^{m_2+k+i}}{k!l!i!j!\Gamma(m_1)\Gamma(n_1)} \\
\times\ & \frac{(m_2-m_1)_i(n_2-n_1)_j\Gamma(\lambda_1)\gamma^{\lambda_3}}{B(m_2+k+i,n_2+l+j)(m_1+k)(m_2+k+i)} \\
\times\ & {}_2F_1[\lambda_1,m_1+k;m_1+k+1;-\alpha_1\gamma] \\
\times\ & {}_2F_1[\lambda_2+i+j,m_2+k+i;m_2+k+i+1;-\alpha_2\gamma]
\end{aligned}
\tag{10}
$$

where $\alpha_i = m_i(1-\rho_G)/n_i(1-\rho_N)\bar{\gamma}_i$, $\lambda_3 = m_1 + 2k + m_2 + i$.

The OP is the probability that the instantaneous output SNR of SC falls below a given outage threshold $\gamma_{th}$ in [20]. Utilizing (10), we can obtain the OP by using $\gamma_{th}$ instead of $\gamma$ as Pout $= F_{\gamma_{SC}}(\gamma_{th})$.

### 3.2   Bit Error Rate

By using (10) and the Eq. (12) in [21], we can obtain the average BER as follows

$$
\bar{P}_e = \frac{q^p}{2\Gamma(p)}\int_0^{\infty} \exp(-q\gamma_{SC})\gamma_{SC}^{p-1}F_{\gamma_{SC}}(\gamma_{SC})d\gamma_{SC}
\tag{11}
$$

where the parameters $p$ and $q$ for different digital modulation systems has been given in [22]. Specifically, $p = 1$, $q = 1$ for DPSK (differential phase shift keying), $p = 0.5$, $q = 1$ for BPSK (binary phase shift keying) and BFSK (binary frequency shift keying) is represented by $p = 0.5$ and $q = 0.5$.

Substituting (10) into (11), and using [23, eqs. (12) and (9)] along with some mathematical manipulations, (11) can be rewritten as

$$P_e = \sum_{k=0}^{\infty} \sum_{l=0}^{\infty} \sum_{i=0}^{\infty} \sum_{j=0}^{\infty} \frac{q^p \rho_N^{k+i} \rho_G^{l+j} \Theta \alpha_1^{m_1+k} \alpha_2^{m_2+k+i}}{2\Gamma(p) i! j! k! l! q^{\lambda_3+p}}$$

$$\times \frac{(m_2-m_1)_i (n_2-n_1)_j}{\Gamma(m_1)\Gamma(n_1)\Gamma(m_2+k+i)\Gamma(n_2+l+j)} \quad (12)$$

$$\times \ G_{1,0:2,2:2,2}^{0,1:1,2:1,2} \left[ \begin{matrix} 0.5-\lambda_3 \\ - \end{matrix} \middle| \begin{matrix} 1-\lambda_1, 1-(m_1+k) \\ 0, -(m_1+k) \end{matrix} \middle| \begin{matrix} 1-\lambda_2+i+j, 1-(m_2+k+i) \\ 0, -(m_2+k+i) \end{matrix} \middle| \begin{matrix} \alpha_1 \\ q \end{matrix}, \begin{matrix} \alpha_2 \\ q \end{matrix} \right]$$

where $G[\cdot|\cdot| \cdot |\cdot, \cdot]$ is a bivariate Merjer G-function which is used in [23]. Noted that a Mathematical code that is provided in [23] is available to calculate it.

## 4 Level Crossing Rate and Average Fade Duration

As two important examples, The LCR and AFD are often applied to characterize higher-order statistics of the received signal envelope in small scale multipath and/or large scale shadowing environments. They are very helpful to design and select error control techniques and diversity systems since they can provide useful information about the burst error statistics. The former denotes the expected rate at which the fading envelope crosses a specified threshold level in a positive (or negative) direction, while the latter is defined as the average period of time which the envelope stays below this threshold level. Traditionally, the joint PDF of the continuous fading envelop and its time derivative has been employed to calculate them. In [24], the authors proposed an alternative analytical approach that the AFD and the LCR can be obtained based on the CDF and the bivariate CDF of a sampled random envelope. Recently this approach has been used to evaluate the LCR and the AFD in a Rician shadowed fading channel in [25]. In [24], the LCR of a sampled random envelope is written as

$$LCR(\mu) = \frac{\Pr\{R_1 < \mu, R_2 > \mu\}}{T_s} \quad (13)$$

where $R_1 \triangleq R(t)$ and $R_2 \triangleq R(t+Ts)$ are correlated and identical random variables, $R(t)$ is the continuous time envelope, $\mu$ is a specified threshold level and $Ts$ denotes the sampling period. Moreover, the CDF of $R_1$ and $R_2$ is given as $F_R(x) \triangleq F_{R_1}(x) \triangleq F_{R_2}(x)$. Therefore, we can express the compact form of the LCR by using the bivariate CDF of $R_1$ and $R_2$ and the marginal CDF of $R_1$ as follows

$$LCR(\mu) = \frac{F_{R_1}(\mu) - F_{R_1,R_2}(\mu,\mu)}{T_s} \quad (14)$$

where $F_{R_1}(\mu)$ can been found in [1]. Substituting (5) into (14), the LCR can be obtained as

$$
\begin{aligned}
LCR(\mu) = {} & \frac{m_1^{m_1-1}\mu^{2m_1}}{B(m_1,n_1)(n_1\Omega_1)^{m_1}T_s}{}_2F_1[m_1+n_1,m_1;m_1+1;-\frac{m_1\mu^2}{n_1\Omega_1}] \\
& -\sum_{k=0}^{\infty}\sum_{l=0}^{\infty}\sum_{i=0}^{\infty}\sum_{j=0}^{\infty}\frac{\rho_N^{k+i}\rho_G^{l+j}\Theta\beta_1^{m_1+k}\beta_2^{m_2+k+i}}{i!j!k!l!\Gamma(m_1)\Gamma(n_1)T_s} \\
& \times \frac{(m_2-m_1)_i(n_2-n_1)_j\Gamma(\lambda_1)\mu^{2\lambda_3}}{B(m_2+k+i,n_2+l+j)(m_1+k)(m_2+k+i)} \\
& \times {}_2F_1[\lambda_1,m_1+k;m_1+k+1;-\beta_1\mu^2] \\
& \times {}_2F_1[\lambda_2+i+j,m_2+k+i;m_2+k+i+1;-\beta_2\mu^2]
\end{aligned}
\tag{15}
$$

Based on the definition of the AFD in [24], we have the expression of AFD as

$$
AFD(\mu) = \frac{\Pr(R_1 < \mu)}{LCR(\mu)} = \frac{T_s F_{R_1}(\mu)}{F_{R_1}(\mu) - F_{R_1,R_2}(\mu,\mu)}
\tag{16}
$$

Similar as (15), (16) can be calculated.

## 5 Numerical Results and Discussion

In this section, we will present various numerical and simulation results under different correlated Fisher–Snedecor $\mathcal{F}$ fading and shadowing scenarios based on the previous derived analytical expressions. In simulation, we adopted the simulation method described in [26] to generate two correlated Nakagami-$m$ variables and their inverse variables with arbitrary fading parameters. The simulations that are obtained via generating $10^6$ iterations are compared with the analytical results. Simulation results matched well with the numerical analysis and verify the accuracy of our derivations. In these figures, the lines represent the numerical analysis and the circle marks stand for the simulated results.

Firstly, we show the OP as a function of the average SNR with the outage threshold $\gamma_{th} = 3$ dB over correlated $\mathcal{F}$ composite fading channels in Fig. 1. In numerical analysis and simulation, seven different combinations of the multipath parameters ($m_1$ and $m_2$), the shadowing parameters ($n_1$ and $n_2$) and the correlation coefficients ($\rho_G$ and $\rho_N$) are considered. It can be seen from Fig. 1 that the OP gets better as the $m$-parameters increases with the same shadowing parameters ($n_1 = 5, n_2 = 6$) and the same correlation coefficients ($\rho_G = \rho_N = 0.5$) by comparing the red line (where the dash line denotes $m_1 = 0.5$ and $m_2 = 0.8$, the dot line denotes $m_1 = 2$ and $m_2 = 3$) with the black line ($m_1 = 1.2$ and $m_2 = 1.5$ as a benchmark). It is because the small scale fading has impact on the slope of the OP performance, namely, the lager the value of $m$, the lager the curve slope. On the other hand, the shadowing parameters and the correlation coefficients have impact on the coding gain of the OP performance in high SNR region, where the coding gain is considered as the shift degree of OP or bit (symbol) error rate line to the left versus SNR in a log-log scale. When the shadowing parameter $n$ gets larger from heavy shadowing to light shadowing, the code gain

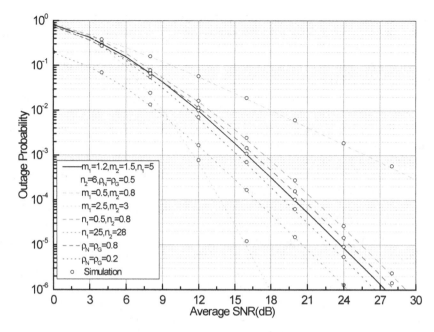

**Fig. 1.** Outage probability of the dual-branch SC system as a function of the average SNR with $\gamma_{th} = 3$ dB over correlated $\mathcal{F}$ composite fading channels (Color figure online)

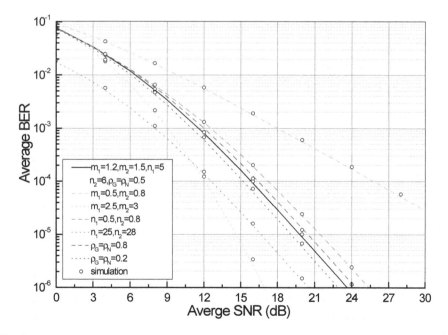

**Fig. 2.** Average BER of DPSK of the dual-branch SC system as a function of the average SNR over correlated $\mathcal{F}$ composite fading channels (Color figure online)

increases by comparing the green line (where the dash line denotes $n_1 = 0.5$ and $n_2 = 0.8$, the dot line denotes $n_1 = 25$ and $n_2 = 28$) with the black line ($n_1 = 5$ and $n_2 = 6$ as a benchmark), where the other parameters keep the same as those of the benchmark line. However, the code gain changes less as the correlation coefficients decrease by comparing the blue line (where the dash line denotes $\rho_G = \rho_N = 0.2$, the dot line denotes $\rho_G = \rho_N = 0.8$) with the black line ($\rho_G = \rho_N = 0.5$ as a benchmark) in Fig. 1.

Secondly, in Fig. 2, we illustrate the average BER of DPSK as a function of the average SNR with the same parameters as those used in Fig. 1. As expected, this figure also confirms our results that is shown in Fig. 1.

Thirdly, Fig. 3 demonstrates the LCR · $Ts$ as a function of the specified lever $\mu$ with $\Omega_i = 1 (i = 1, 2)$ in the moderate shadowing scenarios. As it was expected, when the value of $m$ increases, the LCR decreases by comparing the green line with the black line (as a benchmark) in Fig. 3, which shows that fades take place less frequently. Moreover, the shape of LCR gets narrower and falls rapidly on both sides as the value of $m$ increases. This is because $m$ characterizes the fast fading of the instantaneous signal envelope. On the contrary, the correlation coefficients show less effect on the LCR at lower threshold levels whereas the LCR decreases as the correlation coefficients grows at higher threshold levels. In Fig. 4, the ADF/$Ts$ is plotted under the same scenarios as Fig. 3. Since LCR and AFD are inversely proportional, some similar conclusions can be also obtained. It is interesting that these curves show a floor effect at lower threshold levels.

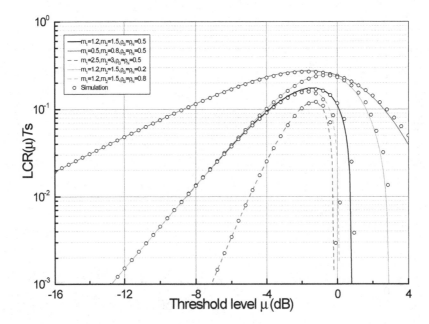

**Fig. 3.** LCR · $Ts$ of the sampled correlated $\mathcal{F}$ composite fading envelope as a function the specified threshold lever $\mu$ with $\Omega_i = 1, n_1 = 5, n_2 = 6$ (Color figure online)

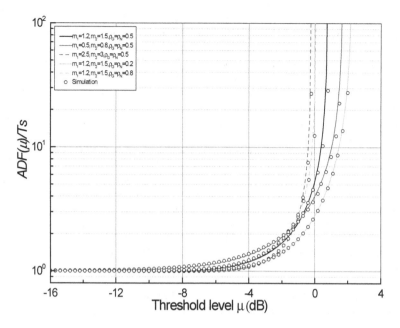

**Fig. 4.** ADF/*Ts* of the sampled correlated $\mathcal{F}$ composite fading envelope as a function the threshold lever u with $\Omega_i = 1, n_1 = 5, n_2 = 6$ (Color figure online)

## 6   Conclusions

In this paper, we investigated a correlated Fisher–Snedecor $\mathcal{F}$ composite distribution with arbitrary fading parameters. The novel theoretical representations including the bivariate PDF, the bivariate CDF, the joint moments and the power correlation coefficient for this distribution were derived. Based on the bivariate CDF, we analyzed the OP and the BER of different binary digital modulation schemes for a correlated dual-branch selection diversity receiver and evaluated the LCR and the AFD of a sampled Fisher-Snedecor $\mathcal{F}$ composited fading envelope. Simulation results matched well with the numerical analysis and verified the validity of the theoretical expressions under various correlated fading and shadowing scenarios.

## References

1. Yoo, S.K., Cotton, S.L., Sofotasios, P.C., Matthaiou, M., Valkama, M., Karagiannidis, G.K.: The Fisher-Snedecor $\mathcal{F}$ distribution: a simple and accurate composite fading model. IEEE Commun. Lett. **21**(7), 1661–1664 (2017)
2. Badarneh, O.S., da Costa, D.B., Sofotasios, P.C., Muhaidat, S., Cotton, S.L.: On the sum of Fisher-Snedecor $\mathcal{F}$ variates and its application to maximal-ratio combining. IEEE Wirel. Commun. Lett. **7**(6), 966–969(2018)
3. Kong, L., Kaddoum, G.: On physical layer security over the Fisher-Snedecor $\mathcal{F}$ wiretap fading channels. IEEE Access **6**, 39466–39472 (2018)

4. Yoo, S.K, Sofotasios, P.C., Cotton, S.L., et al.: A comprehensive analysis of the achievable channel capacity in $\mathcal{F}$ composite fading channels. IEEE Access **7**, 34078–34094 (2019)

5. Yoo, S.K., Sofotasios, P.C., Cotton, S.L., Muhaidat, S., Badarneh, O.S., Karagiannidis, G. K.: Entropy and energy detection-based spectrum sensing over $\mathcal{F}$-composite fading channels. IEEE Trans. Commun. **67**(7), 4641–4653 (2019)

6. Al-Hmood, H., Al-Raweshidy, H.S.: Selection combining scheme over non-identically distributed Fisher-Snedecor $\mathcal{F}$ fading channels. arXiv:1905.05595 (2019)

7. Zhao, H., Yang, L., Salem, A.S., Alouini, M.: Ergodic capacity under power adaption over Fisher-Snedecor $\mathcal{F}$ fading channels. IEEE Commun. Lett. **23**(3), 546–549 (2019)

8. Chen, S., Zhang, J., Karagiannidis, G.K., Ai, B.: Effective rate of MISO systems over Fisher-Snedecor $\mathcal{F}$ fading channels. IEEE Commun. Lett. **22**(12), 2619–2622 (2018)

9. Aldalgamouni, T., Ilter, M.C., Badarneh, O.S., Yanikomeroglu, H.: Performance analysis of Fisher-Snedecor $\mathcal{F}$ composite fading channels. In: 2018 IEEE Middle East and North Africa Communications Conference (MENACOMM), pp. 1–5, IEEE, Jounieh (2018)

10. Reig, J., Rubio, L., Cardona, N.: Bivariate Nakagami-m distribution with arbitrary fading parameters. Electron. Lett. **38**(25), 1715–1717 (2002)

11. Zhang, R., Wei, J., Michelson, D.G., Leung, V.C.M.: Outage probability of MRC diversity over correlated shadowed fading channels. IEEE Wirel. Commun. Lett. **1**(5), 516–519 (2012)

12. Bithas, P.S., Sagias, N.C., Mathiopoulos, P.T., Kotsopoulos, S.A., Maras, A.M.: On the correlated K-distribution with arbitrary fading parameters. IEEE Sig. Process Lett. **15**, 541–544 (2008)

13. Bithas, P.S., Sagias, N.C., Mathiopoulos, P.T.: The bivariate generalized-K ($K_G$) distribution and its application to diversity receivers. IEEE Trans. Commun. **57**(9), 2655–2662 (2009)

14. Reddy, T., Subadar, R., Sahu, P.R.: Outage probability of selection combiner over exponentially correlated Weibull-gamma fading channels for arbitrary number of branches. In: 2010 National Conference on Communications, pp. 1–5, IEEE, Madras (2010)

15. Ni, Z., Zhang, X., Liu, X., Yang, D.: Bivariate Weibull-gamma composite distribution with arbitrary fading parameters. Electron. Lett. **48**(18), 1165–1167 (2012)

16. Trigui, I., Laourine, A., Affes, S., Stéphenne, A.: Bivariate $\mathcal{G}$ distribution with arbitrary fading parameters. In: 2009 3rd International Conference on Signals, Circuits and Systems (SCS), pp. 1–5, IEEE, Medenine (2009)

17. Reig, J., Rubio, L., Rodrigo-Peñarrocha, V.M.: On the bivariate Nakagami-lognormal distribution and its correlation properties. Int. J. Antennas Propag. **2014**, 1–8 (2014)

18. Gradshteyn, I., Ryzhik, I.: Table of Integrals, Series, and Products, 8th edn. Academic Press, London (2007)

19. Chun, Y.J., Cotton, S.L., Dhillon, H.S., Lopez-Martinez, F.J., Paris, J.F., Yoo, S.K.: A comprehensive analysis of 5G heterogeneous cellular systems operating over $\kappa - \mu$ shadowed fading channels. IEEE Trans. Wirel. Commun. **16**(11), 6995–7010 (2017)

20. Simon, M.K., Alouni, M.-S.: Digital Communication over Fading Channels, 2nd edn. Wiley, New York (2005)

21. Ansari, I.S., Al-Ahmadi, S., Yilmaz, F., Alouini, M., Yanikomeroglu, H.: A new formula for the BER of binary modulations with dual-branch selection over generalized-K composite fading channels. IEEE Trans. Commun. **59**(10), 2654–2658 (2011)

22. Wojnar, A.H.: Unknown bounds on performance in Nakagami channels. IEEE Trans. Commun. **34**(1), 22–24 (1986)

23. García-Corrales, C., Canete, F.J., Paris, J.F.: Capacity of $\kappa - \mu$ shadowed fading channels. Int. J. Antennas Propag. **2014**, 1–8 (2014)

24. López-Martínez, F.J., Martos-Naya, E., Paris, J.F., Fernández-Plazaola, U.: Higher order statistics of sampled fading channels with applications. IEEE Trans. Veh. Technol. **61**(7), 3342–3346 (2012)
25. López-Fernández, J., Paris, J.F., Martos-Naya, E.: Bivariate Rician shadowed fading model. IEEE Trans. Veh. Technol. **67**(1), 378–384 (2018)
26. Reig, J., Martinez-Amoraga, M.A., Rubio, L.: Generation of bivariate Nakagami-m fading envelopes with arbitrary not necessary identical fading parameters. Wirel. Commun. Mob. Comput. **2007**(7), 531–537 (2007)

# PLDetect: A Testbed for Middlebox Detection Using PlanetLab

Paul Kirth[1] and Vahab Pournaghshband[2(✉)]

[1] California State University, Northridge, Los Angeles, USA
paul.kirth.155@my.csu.edu
[2] University of San Francisco, San Francisco, USA
vahab.p@usfca.edu

**Abstract.** Designing, coordinating and deploying repeatable experiments outside of a fully controlled environment pose a serious challenge when conducting network research. In particular, it can be difficult to correctly schedule experiments that collect bulk data using a shared resource. To address this problem, we introduce PLDetect, a simple testbed built on top of PlanetLab which simplifies configuring, scheduling, and deploying large scale Internet experiments for evaluating middlebox detection methods.

**Keywords:** Middlebox · Detection method · Active measurements · Testbed · PlanetLab

## 1 Introduction

When conducting network research, it becomes clear that performing live Internet experiments presents a significant challenge: these networks use non-deterministic paths, are subject to a variety of competing administrative policies, and are mostly out of the researcher's control. After overcoming these obstacles, researchers must still provide sound methodologies and test infrastructure to validate their measurements. Overtime, these methodologies and testing practices should become commonplace, widely adopted, and, in some cases, standardized. In practice, researchers often do not have the opportunity to reuse the infrastructure or testing practices described in prior work, even if they wish to use the same methods and verification process. This can be due to several factors, such as the author's not releasing their test infrastructure, lack of sufficient detail in the original work, or an unmaintained codebase. Regardless of the reason, research efforts are becoming increasingly sophisticated, and their tools and methodologies must evolve to keep pace. Reinventing tools and infrastructure that perform similar function is a net loss for the research community, and even within industry the emergence of Dev-Ops has highlighted the need to reduce repeated efforts.

In the past, formalized research testbeds, such as PlanetLab, have provided researchers with superior methods of conducting network research. Previous

© ICST Institute for Computer Sciences, Social Informatics and Telecommunications Engineering 2020
Published by Springer Nature Switzerland AG 2020. All Rights Reserved
H. Gao et al. (Eds.): TridentCom 2019, LNICST 309, pp. 120–130, 2020.
https://doi.org/10.1007/978-3-030-43215-7_9

work often sought to simplify deploying experiments using PlanetLab [2,5], but few, if any, are still maintained. As a result, using PlanetLab is still as challenging as when these works were initially conceived, a state that is further complicated by the nearly decade old Linux distribution on which PlanetLab is based [1]. This environment makes running modern software a challenge, and means that researchers must take infrastructure idiosyncrasies into account when designing their experiments. Even after addressing these limitations, a researcher is often forced to use a custom solution to deploy and manage their data collection activities across their PlanetLab slice.[1] We contend that few researchers should need to implement their own methods for interacting with a research tool as popular as PlanetLab, and furthermore that most should not need to create new infrastructure to deploy proven experimental configuration and validation experiments.

Consider, NetPolice [16], PackSen [15], and ChkDiff [11], three middlebox detection tools that employ similar detection methodologies and were validated using PlanetLab. In each work, the author spent non-trivial effort to implement and validate their detection infrastructure without the opportunity to easily reuse an existing test infrastructure. We point this issue out, not to highlight any fault on behalf of these authors, whose work is exemplary, but rather to illuminate a problem of culture and focus for the larger research community. Many other engineering fields have standardized testing methods for researchers to follow, and, even within Computer Science, test suites, such as SPEC [7], are widely used when validating research efforts. These formalized test suites and methodologies not only simplify the work of the researcher by providing previously vetted and validated tools, but also provide a common language and frame of reference for readers.

To address these challenges, we present PLDetect: a testbed for validating middlebox detection tools on PlanetLab that provides a vetted and well explored set of default configurations for conducting data collection and validation measurements for new middlebox detection tools. PLDetect is a simple framework that uses a combination of Python, Shell scripts, and configuration files to provide support for long duration experiments that must avoid overlapping measurements to maintain correctness. These can be important criteria for middlebox detection tools, as concurrent measurements can skew results for many experimental configurations. Furthermore, remote system administration tools, such as Ansible, do not yet properly manage temporal accesses with sufficient guarantees for research purposes. Throughout this work we will use the term *middlebox detection experiments* to refer to experiments designed to *validate* middlebox detection tools, rather than those that are trying to detect and map middlebox on the open Internet. This is an important distinction in PLDetect's intended application and typical usage.

The testbed consists of two major components, a configuration utility, that can setup remote PlanetLab nodes, and a central dispatcher responsible for

---

[1] A slice is a set of allocated PlanetLab resources to which users can add PlanetLab nodes, and through which they are granted access to the nodes in their slice.

initiating experiments and ensuring that they did not exceed their allotted time. This dispatcher controls access to the test server, and will not initiate a new data collection event until the previous measurement has either successfully completed or has been terminated for exceeding its maximum allowed duration. It has, thus far, improved our ability to deploy new middlebox detection experiments across a PlanetLab slice and preserve the timing and scheduling constraints discussed in Sect. 2. PLDetect is freely available open source software, and its source code can be found on Github: https://github.com/ilovepi/PL-Detect.

The remainder of this work is organized as follows: in Sect. 2 we discuss the design, implementation, and use of PLDetect; Sect. 3 describes our evaluation of the testbed, our experimental configuration, and the results of our experiment; Sect. 4 discuses related work; Sect. 5 outlines the future direction of PLDetect; and Sect. 6 concludes this paper.

## 2    Testbed

PLDetect was created to allow researchers to quickly deploy middlebox detection experiments across their PlanetLab slices, and provide simple ways to configure the frequency and duration of data collection. In part, this tool was born out of necessity, because we found no prior solutions that addressed our particular needs for test administration, scheduling, and deployment. While simplicity is one of our driving goals, PLDetect must also support potentially complex experimental configurations and requirements. As a result, the bulk of this Section is focused on providing details on how PLDetect can be used to configure, deploy, and manage middlebox detection experiments across a PlanetLab slice.

### 2.1    Design

PLDetect is designed with three goals in mind: (1) to simplify the deployment of middlebox detection experiments across PlanetLab, (2) to prevent undesired overlap between experiments, and (3) to be easily extensible. To this end, a combination of Python and Shell scripts have been used to strike a balance between expressiveness and maintainability. We favor simple, direct code and interfaces to ease future development, and when possible we try to accomplish tasks using Shell scripts to better integrate with PlanetLab. In general, we use Shell scripts for managing tasks that are best handled directly via *NIX commands, and Python for more complex tasks and calculations.

### 2.2    Configuration

The PLDetect experimental testbed consists of a set of PlanetLab nodes, a set of Python and Shell scripts, and a set of configuration files. Configuring the testbed requires editing several configuration files prior to deploying the experiment across a PlanetLab slice. The user must configure:

1. Experiment folder: contains all the test scripts, program executable files, and data required to run the experiment on the remote node, including any logging scripts or scripts used to connect to remote databases.
2. `target_ip.conf`: a list of PlanetLab node IP addresses.
3. `install.sh`: an install script that installs the required packages on each PlanetLab node and copies the experimental folder.
4. `schedule.conf`: controls the experimental dates, period, and duration of measurements.
5. `start_experiment.sh`: a Shell script responsible for starting the experiment on the remote host.
6. `sqlinsert.conf`: configures the remote MySQL database.
7. `sqlinsert.sh`: a Shell script used to connect to a remote MySQL database and add experimental results.
8. `functions.sh`: contains a list of user defined functions used during the experimental execution, such as generating experimental parameters or recording metadata.

## 2.3   Node Configuration

**Node Selection.** The first file a user should configure is the `target_ip.conf` file. This file allows the user to select a set of PlanetLab nodes available to their PlanetLab slice for use in the experiment. The configuration format for this file is simple: each line of the file should contain only one of the IP addresses of the PlanetLab nodes that should be configured to run the experiment. This list of IP addresses will be consulted by the install script, `install.sh`, that is responsible for configuring the software environment on each PlanetLab node for the experiment to complete, and used in later phases to generate a schedule of data collection events for each PlanetLab node.

**Experiment Folder.** The next item to configure is the experiment folder, which should contain all of the executables and scripts needed to successfully run the experiment on the remote PlanetLab node. The use of this folder is an important design choice for the testbed. PlanetLab discourages its users from conducting compilation activities on their nodes, and recommends that the users compile their software outside of PlanetLab with an appropriate 32-bit Linux target. For most applications this is favorable because it allows them to compile their projects using a modern compiler with features that will likely not be found on a PlanetLab node. Additionally, most PlanetLab nodes have limited software selections unless the user is comfortable adding updated repositories to all of their PlanetLab nodes. Peterson et al. [9] advise users to create an experimental directory that can be copied to the PlanetLab node using `parallel-rsync`. By moving all of the necessary test materials into a single folder, updating each experimental node becomes a single invocation of `parallel-rsync`, and avoids difficulties with the often outdated software packages available on PlanetLab. The experimental directory can be updated and resynchronized using the install script or by using `parallel-rsync` directly.

## 2.4   Test Scheduling

After each node has been configured, the user will then select the testing schedule by editing the `schedule.conf` file and running a Python script to create a test schedule. The scheduling script, `ScheduleManager.py`, is used to generate a schedule for each data collection event, and does not allow these events to overlap. It works by consulting a tab delimited configuration file, `schedule.conf`. This file specifies the dates the experiment should run, the frequency of tests, and the commands to be executed at each time the experiment begins.

The output of the scheduling script is a file where each line associates the PlanetLab node IP, the time when a test should run, and the command or script to be run at that time. For example, `experiment.sh` might be scheduled to run at March 15, 2016 to `some.pl.node.edu`. The user can create the `experiment.sh` script that defines how the experiment should run, and have the local operating system invoke that script at the correct time. This script is invoked locally by default, but can be configured to run as a command on the targeted PlanetLab node instead.

By default, the `ScheduleManager.py` creates a schedule where a PlanetLab node takes one measurement per hour for every hour of the day for the entire duration (in days) of the experiment. These parameters can be configured directly in the invoking script, via the command line, or in the `schedule.conf` file. The schedules are created using the `at` command to accommodate irregular and singleton tasks rather than using other facilities, like `cron`.

## 2.5   Running Experiments

When it is time for an experiment to run, the scheduling machine will `ssh` into the PlanetLab node and invoke the command or script set in the scheduling configuration. The maximum duration for each test is used to set a timeout on each of the measurements to ensure that no two tests will overlap. Once the test program is invoked, the test scripts collect test metadata from the PlanetLab node and invoking context, and write the experimental results to a temporary results file.

## 2.6   Collecting Experimental Results

After the experiment is complete, the test script on the PlanetLab node logs into the remote MySQL database and records the results of the test along with test metadata by using the `sqlinsert.sh` and `sqlinsert.conf`. Note that the maximum test duration specified in `schedule.conf` should also include the time needed to report experimental results.

## 2.7   Verifying the Experimental Configuration

For testing purposes the user should provide the scheduling scripts with a single PlanetLab IP and ensure that their experiment and scripts are running as expected before deploying them across the entire list of PlanetLab nodes.

## 2.8   Limitations

Our testbed is not intended to be a general solution for deploying all types of network measurements on PlanetLab, but is instead focused on correctly scheduling independent measurements at a single site. PLDetect was built for a specific class of experimental configuration, in which measurements are conducted at a site that the researcher controls. For middlebox detection, this will often be a switch, or another routing element, that the researcher is trying to detect, and whose behavior they can alter. In this configuration (Fig. 1) each PlanetLab node connects to a target IP behind the middlebox, and data is collected from each of the configured PlanetLab nodes. We further assume that each data collection event should be completely independent from one another, so that traffic from one measurement does not interfere with another. This does not preclude an experiment from using several sources of traffic for each measurement, but will require additional configuration steps when creating the test scripts described in this Section. Additionally, we do not support managing access to multiple test sites, or coordinating multiple experiments at the same site.

## 3   Evaluation

In this Section, we present the details of our evaluation: the middlebox detection method used, our experimental configuration, and our results. One of PLDetect's goals is to offer a premade validation platform for researchers conducting middlebox detection experiments, and the evaluation experiment discussed in this Section was designed with this use case in mind. Moreover, this experiment provides an example of the testbed's expected use in conducting experiments to validate middlebox detection tools. The goal of these measurements is to infer the behavior of the middlebox based on the detection methodology presented in Sect. 3.1. While we discuss the detection method and describe a typical experiment for evaluating the compression detection tool used in our experiments, we want to stress that the analysis of the data collected is not significant to the evaluation of the testbed itself. Rather, this data serves to demonstrate PLDetect's ability to correctly configure, schedule, and execute data collection activities in the desired manner, regardless of the success of the detection method.

### 3.1   Detection

To validate PLDetect we used a tool for detecting network compression based on the *relative discrimination technique* [15] to infer the presence of a compression link. The tool detects network compression based on significant differences in loss and delay between a *base* flow composed of low entropy data (all bytes are zeros), and a *discrimination* flow composed of high entropy data (all bytes are random). This is congruent with prior work in Pournaghshband et al. [10] that leveraged the difference in processing times for high and low entropy packets for detecting compression links.

## 3.2   Experimental Configuration

To validate the compression detection tool, we designed an experiment to take independent measurements from several different sites, each trying to connect a test server that was under our control. This allowed us to position the test server behind a middlebox capable of operating as either a compression link or a normal switch so that we could enable and disable the middlebox behavior (compression) as we desired. This topology appears in several prior works aimed at detecting middleboxes [10,15], and is an important part of PLDetect's expected configuration for supporting validation efforts. Figure 1 illustrates an example of our experimental configuration, and highlights the portion of it that are fully within our control.

The testbed in this experiment consisted of five PlanetLab nodes, a middlebox capable of operating as a compression link, and a test server. Each of the PlanetLab nodes tried to correctly infer the presence of a compression link along the transmission path to the test server using the detection method discussed in Sect. 3.1. We selected a geographically distributed set of PlanetLab nodes to capture a wide variety of transmission paths and network conditions. Each node in the PlanetLab slice was configured using PLDetect's install procedure, as outlined in the Sect. 2.3. Our experiment executed one measurement every hour for each of the five PlanetLab nodes in our slice over a period of 30 h. Each measurement had a maximum duration of one minute, and recorded the number of packet losses and transmission latency for each stream, along with a complete packet trace of the measurement. These results are then recorded to the remote database for future analysis. Part of our validation strategy uses bulk data to alleviate any undue influence normal fluctuations in network conditions might have on our measurements.

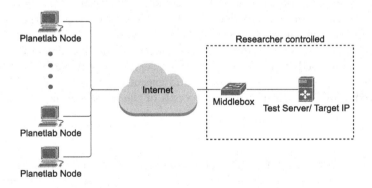

**Fig. 1.** PLDetect network topology.

## 3.3  Experimental Results

We collected data using five planet lab nodes, taking measurements once per hour at each site, over a period of 30 h. The entire deployment was configured, scheduled, and recorded using `PLDetect`. Figure 2 contains a plot of the relative differences in transmission times between the base and discrimination flows. We can see that each PlanetLab node recorded its measurements once per hour over the entire 30 h duration, and that the detection tool was able to record significant differences in the loss rates between the base and discrimination flows. By contrast, without a compression link there is virtually no difference between the loss rates or transmission times of the two flows. This large, persistent difference meets the criteria of our detection methodology, and shows the tool's ability to identify the compression link in our configuration. We again stress that what these measurements show is not important, rather they appear here to highlight our ability to manage an experiment and schedule our data collection with `PLDetect` using the procedures outlined in Sect. 2.

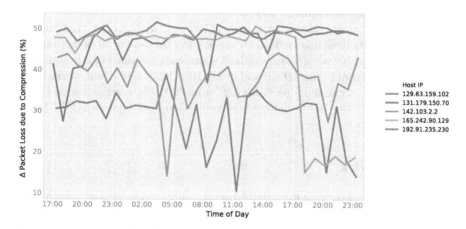

**Fig. 2.** Percentage of discrimination packets lost when compression is enabled

## 4  Related Work

`PLDetect` is a network testbed built on top of PlanetLab, and in that regard, it is not unique. Many past works, like Stork [5] and Plush [2], were built to simplify how users create and deploy their experiments on PlanetLab, and while these tools have proved useful, many of them are either no longer maintained or were not made public. `PLDetect` separates itself form these prior efforts in its narrow focus on providing a simple solution for deploying a specific type of measurement, and is made from freely available tools that have thus far performed well on PlanetLab slices. For other platforms, such as GENI [4], the GEE [3] provides an abstraction layer in which the authors facilitate the rapid prototyping, management, and administration of GENI experiments. Our solution does not try to provide the same level of abstraction to PlanetLab as GEE applies to GENI. GENI's resources also are more friendly towards virtualization and the use of containerized environments which plays a key role in GEE's IaaS design. Our tools, by contrast, are much simpler: each script or configuration file plays a limited role in how experiments are conducted and maintained, and we provide relatively primitive forms of configuration management.

Recently, Wachs et al. [14] presented GPLMT, a general purpose testbed framework for managing experiments on PlanetLab. This work does an excellent job of generalizing experimental configuration and abstracting the complicated aspects of managing large scale experiments. However, `PLDetect` and GPLMT have fundamentally different goals and philosophies. GPLMT is a general purpose tool, suitable for managing many types of experiment, while `PLDetect` is focused on supporting middlebox detection with a well known methodology and experimental configuration in addition to managing the experiment. Where `PLDetect` distinguishes itself from existing testbeds, is in its focus on supporting one class of network experiment very well.

While it may seem odd to contrast `PLDetect` with works that are not testbeds, most of its design is focused on supporting the testing of detection tools and methodologies. In particular, we adapt significant portions of our configuration and methods from Pournaghshband et al. [10]. Other significant works in this area, `Packsen` [15], `Tracebox` [6], `NANO` [12], and `POPI` [8], each provided insight and inspiration for the methodology and validation techniques that PLDetect tries to encapsulate.

## 5    Future Work

Ansible [13] is a popular tool for administering remote systems, and provides two important benefits to its users: simple YAML based configuration and an easy way to share and distribute automation tasks. While YAML based configuration is a superior solution to our simple configuration files, Ansible's main draw is the large repository of community made solutions available through Ansible-Galaxy. As one of `PLDetect`'s design goals is to simplify configuration and automation, we believe that allowing users to easily reuse these existing solutions is the right choice. However, incorporating Ansible into our design will require some care to ensure that our scheduling requirements can still be met. We can integrate Ansible by modifying how we generate scheduling commands, to instead use Ansible playbooks, or by modifying `PLDetect`'s design to provide a new queuing phase for measurements.

As GENI [4] matures, it is becoming an important platform for conducting network research. Future versions of `PLDetect` should incorporate support for the GENI platform, and integration with the more modern services available outside of PlanetLab, such as support for virtual machines and docker containers.

# 6    Conclusion

In this paper we presented PLDetect: a testbed for middlebox detection, discussed its design and intended use, and demonstrated its usefulness as a research tool through an example experiment. To our knowledge it is the only research testbed focused on middlebox detection, and we believe its focus on providing a specialized network research infrastructure can provide a valuable blueprint for others to follow.

# References

1. Releases/8/schedule - FedoraProject. https://fedoraproject.org/wiki/Releases/8/Schedule
2. Albrecht, J., Tuttle, C., Snoeren, A.C., Vahdat, A.: PlanetLab application management using plush. ACM SIGOPS Oper. Syst. Rev. **40**(1), 33–40 (2006)
3. Bavier, A., et al.: The GENI experiment engine. ACM
4. Berman, M., et al.: GENI: a federated testbed for innovative network experiments. Comput. Netw. **61**, 5–23 (2014)
5. Cappos, J., et al.: Stork: package management for distributed VM environments. In: LISA, vol. 7, pp. 1–16
6. Detal, G., Hesmans, B., Bonaventure, O., Vanaubel, Y., Donnet, B.: Revealing middlebox interference with tracebox. In: Proceedings of the 2013 Conference on Internet Measurement Conference, IMC 2013, pp. 1–8. ACM (2013)
7. Henning, J.L.: SPEC CPU2006 benchmark descriptions. SIGARCH Comput. Archit. News **34**(4), 1–17 (2006). https://doi.org/10.1145/1186736.1186737
8. Lu, G., Chen, Y., Birrer, S., Bustamante, F., Cheung, C.Y., Li, X.: End-to-end inference of router packet forwarding priority. In: IEEE INFOCOM 2007, 26th IEEE International Conference on Computer Communications, pp. 1784–1792 (2007)
9. Peterson, L.L., Bavier, A.C.: Using PlanetLab for network research: Myths, realities, and best practices. In: WORLDS
10. Pournaghshband, V., Afanasyev, A., Reiher, P.: End-to-end detection of compression of traffic flows by intermediaries. In: 2014 IEEE Network Operations and Management Symposium (NOMS), pp. 1–8 (2014)
11. Ravaioli, R., Urvoy-Keller, G., Barakat, C.: Towards a general solution for detecting traffic differentiation at the internet access. In: 2015 27th International Teletraffic Congress (ITC 27), pp. 1–9 (2015)
12. Tariq, M.B., Motiwala, M., Feamster, N., Ammar, M.: Detecting network neutrality violations with causal inference. In: Proceedings of the 5th International Conference on Emerging Networking Experiments and Technologies, CoNEXT 2009, pp. 289–300. ACM (2009)
13. Venezia, P.: Review: ansible orchestration is a veteran Unix admin's dream; ansible and AnsibleWorks AWX bring simplicity and power to Linux and Unix server automation. http://www.infoworld.com/article/2612397/data-center/review-ansible-orchestration-is-a-veteran-unix-admin-s-dream.html
14. Wachs, M., Herold, N., Posselt, S.-A., Dold, F., Carle, G.: GPLMT: a lightweight experimentation and testbed management framework. In: Karagiannis, T., Dimitropoulos, X. (eds.) PAM 2016. LNCS, vol. 9631, pp. 165–176. Springer, Cham (2016). https://doi.org/10.1007/978-3-319-30505-9_13

15. Weinsberg, U., Soule, A., Massoulie, L.: Inferring traffic shaping and policy parameters using end host measurements. In: 2011 Proceedings IEEE INFOCOM, pp. 151–155 (2011)
16. Zhang, Y., Mao, Z.M., Zhang, M.: Detecting traffic differentiation in backbone ISPs with NetPolice. In: Proceedings of the 9th ACM SIGCOMM Conference on Internet Measurement Conference, IMC 2009, pp. 103–115. ACM (2009)

# EuWireless RAN Architecture and Slicing Framework for Virtual Testbeds

Jarno Pinola[1]([✉])(iD), Ilkka Harjula[1], Adam Flizikowski[2], Maria Safianowska[2], Arslan Ahmad[2], and Suvidha Sudhakar Mhatre[2]

[1] VTT Technical Research Centre of Finland, Kaitoväylä 1, 90571 Oulu, Finland
{jarno.pinola,ilkka.harjula}@vtt.fi
[2] IS-Wireless, Pulawska Plaza, ul. Pulawska 45b, 05-500 Piaseczno, Poland
{a.flizikowski,m.safianowska,a.ahmad,s.mhatre}@is-wireless.com

**Abstract.** The most recent evolutionary steps in the development of mobile communication network architectures have introduced the concepts of virtualisation and slicing also into the Radio Access Network (RAN) part of the overall infrastructure. This trend has made RANs more flexible than ever before, facilitating resource sharing concepts which go far beyond the traditional infrastructure and RAN sharing schemes between commercial Mobile Network Operators (MNO). This paper introduces the EuWireless concept for a pan-European mobile network operator for research and presents its vision for RAN slicing and network resource sharing between the infrastructures of the EuWireless operator, commercial MNOs and research organisations around Europe. The EuWireless approach is to offer virtual large-scale testbeds, i.e., EuWireless experimentation slices, to European mobile network researchers by combining the experimental technologies from the local small-scale research testbeds with the commercial MNO resources such as licensed spectrum. The combined resources are configured and managed through the distributed EuWireless architecture based on interconnected local installations, so-called Points of Presences (PoP).

**Keywords:** Virtual testbed · Radio access network · Network resource sharing · Slicing · Virtualisation

## 1 Introduction

The Radio Access Network (RAN) architecture specified by the 3rd Generation Partnership Project (3GPP) has evolved from the metro-site topology, where all base station functionality is integrated into proprietary hardware at the cell site, towards more flexible deployments with the 3G and 4G technologies. An important step has been the separation of the radio front-end and the baseband

This work is funded by the European Union's Horizon 2020 research and innovation programme, grant agreement No. 777517 (EuWireless project).

H. Gao et al. (Eds.): TridentCom 2019, LNICST 309, pp. 131–149, 2020.
https://doi.org/10.1007/978-3-030-43215-7_10

processing units, which has made it possible to split the base station functionality into several network components inter-connected with optical fibre. Centralised RAN (C-RAN) [10] is a RAN architecture which takes advantage of this functional split and the concept of virtualisation to cope with the challenge of flexible resource provisioning for RANs.

In C-RAN, the base station functionality is divided into two RAN elements, i.e., the Baseband Unit (BBU) and the Remote Radio Head (RRH). All functionality related to baseband processing and protocols on the Physical Layer (PHY) and above is provided by the BBU. The RRH handles the radio functionalities. The C-RAN approach centralises multiple BBUs in one location (i.e., Centralised RAN) and can further enhance the flexibility of the architecture by virtualising some functions of the BBUs in a common resource pool (a.k.a Cloud-RAN). The additional steps of BBU resource virtualisation and pooling in the Cloud-RAN approach enable the use of Commercial Off-the-Shelf (COTS) servers for processing the majority of the BBU routines and utilisation of data centres to host the required equipment [9].

The latest evolutionary steps in mobile network architectures go even further in the virtualisation of the network functions. The 3GPP system architecture evolution for 5G with its Service Based Architecture (SBA) approach relies on a fully virtualised 5G Core Network (5GC) [22]. 5G supports also the virtualisation of the radio access nodes, i.e., 5G NodeBs (gNB), with new functional split defined for the Next Generation RAN (NG-RAN) [8]. The ability to built a full 5G network by utilising Virtual Network Functions (VNF) enables flexible end-to-end slicing for mobile networks. This in turn facilitates the sharing and joint management of network resources between Mobile Network Operators (MNO) and other stakeholders in the future. The widespread adoption of open standardised interfaces, a feature seen by the MNOs as one of the key enablers for flexible deployment of future networks, would further open up the mobile network infrastructures for a variety of new sharing scenarios and business cases.

The EuWireless project is focusing on a design of a pan-European mobile network operator for research. The EuWireless concept includes both the system architecture and the operation model for the EuWireless operator. The main objective behind the project is to provision a European level mobile network that facilitates open large-scale experimentation. This is achieved by combining research stage technology components from local small-scale testbed with commercial equipment and resources from MNO networks into a single virtual testbed [25]. The configuration, management and orchestration of the shared resources can be performed by the EuWireless experimenter using the virtual testbed through the provided online portal.

This paper introduces the key components of the EuWireless concept and architecture focusing on the virtualisation and sharing of RAN resources. The overall EuWireless architecture and the technology enablers for resource sharing in the RAN domain are reviewed. In addition, the plans to introduce virtualised RAN functions into the utilised virtualisation architecture as well as the foreseen usage scenarios and configurations for the RAN part of the EuWireless virtual testbeds are presented. As at the time of writing the EuWireless project is still in its first phase finalising the overall concept and architecture design, this paper also discusses some challenges regarding the large-scale implementations planned for the second phase of the project.

The rest of the paper is organised as follows. Section 2 reviews the related work in the field of large-scale wireless testbeds, whereas Sect. 3 introduces the EuWireless concept in more detail. Section 4 presents the RAN virtualisation and slicing techniques required to bring the EuWireless concept into life and Sect. 5 discusses the challenges related to their implementation. Finally, Sect. 6 concludes the paper.

## 2 Related Work

Several testbed initiatives and projects already offer possibilities for researchers and telecommunication engineers to experiment in real mobile network infrastructures. Different approaches ranging from infrastructures fully owned and operated by the projects to Virtual Mobile Network Operator (vMNO) models relying on commercial MNO infrastructures have been taken to provide these experimentation platforms to the research community.

The 5G Infrastructure Public Private Partnership (5G-PPP) initiative launched three large-scale end-to-end 5G test facilities as part of the European Horizon 2020 programme in 2018. These facilities and their infrastructure is developed, operated and owned by dedicated projects called 5GENESIS, 5G EVE and 5G-VINNI. For example, 5GENESIS [20] comprises of five interconnected large-scale local sites in different European countries which together provide a pan-European test platform addressing multiple vertical use cases. 5G EVE and 5G-VINNI have similar approaches with different sites and vertical industry focus areas. The RAN part of these facilities is based on commercial 5G equipment, but the coverage is limited to the local sites.

Another set of inter-connected test facilities in Europe are made available to the researchers by the Future Internet Research and Experimentation (FIRE) initiative, which provides technology laboratories equipped with components to perform experimental research also in mobile networks. However, the experiments must usually be executed inside the laboratories where the RAN part of the infrastructure is simulated or offered as local amendments to the wired infrastructure in pre-defined local sites as in the 5GINFIRE [36] project.

The Global Environment for Network Innovations (GENI) program offers large-scale Internet testbeds for researchers in the US. The SciWiNet [7] project has added support for wireless networking systems research into the platform based on the vMNO model. SciWiNet offers cellular connectivity via Sprint's 3G, WiMAX, and LTE networks. Consequently, SciWiNet is able to provide a test facility for a variety of mobile network services and vertical industry use cases. However, the underlying RAN infrastructure is not under full control of the testbed provider and the testbed user.

EuWireless extends these existing test infrastructure concepts by introducing the possibility to share and combine resources of the existing research testbeds with those of commercial MNO networks. Integration with MNO networks offers enhanced coverage for large-scale field tests and better access to scarce regulated resources such as licensed spectrum. In order to avoid the CAPEX/OPEX challenges related to fully owned network infrastructures and the limited possibilities to manage the network infrastructure as a vMNO, EuWireless combines the advantages of both by relying on a virtualisation concept. The selected approach allows the creation of generic connectivity slices as the baseline infrastructure for a virtual testbed. The desired network and service functionality can then be built on top of the baseline virtual infrastructure with additional slices defined by the EuWireless user.

In the European Horizon 2020 Research and Innovation programme, a variety of projects have also studied the reference architectures and technology enablers for 5G systems. Majority of these projects have been executed under the coordination of 5G-PPP, which has managed the jointly funded 5G project portfolio in Europe since 2015. EuWireless have studied the key results of the projects from 5G-PPP Phase 1 and Phase 2. The final concept, architecture and utilised technologies for the European mobile network operator for research will be defined to be in line with the 5G vision of the European research community and the telecommunications industry.

## 3    EuWireless Concept

The implementation of the EuWireless architecture should consider its own resources, MNO resources and the resources from local small-scale research testbeds. Typical MNO resources enabling large-scale testing in realistic operational environments are the licensed spectrum and the physical locations to install new functionality or equipment to the access, core and transport networks. Typical resources from local small-scale research testbeds include experimental network functions and all the equipment necessary to perform the experiments of the EuWireless user.

The sharing and combining of resources from these different domains is approached from two different angles in the EuWireless project. First, an overall architecture enabling flexible resource sharing is defined, including the required functionalities and interfaces to enable smooth interaction between resources from different network domains. Second, the sharing options for the network resources in the radio access, core and transport networks are specified in conjunction with the requirements for the virtualisation of different network functions and network slicing.

### 3.1    Overall Architecture

The EuWireless architecture follows the network slicing approach for the creation of virtual large-scale testbeds, combining resources from the EuWireless infrastructure, commercial MNO networks and local research testbeds as shown in Fig. 1. EuWireless operator offers the required interfaces for the users of the infrastructure, i.e., the EuWireless experimenters, to create and control their virtual testbeds through an online portal. Application Programming Interfaces (API) are used to directly interact with the virtual testbeds and the EuWireless infrastructure. The other considered design options and the rationale behind the choices made to define the EuWireless architecture are described in [32].

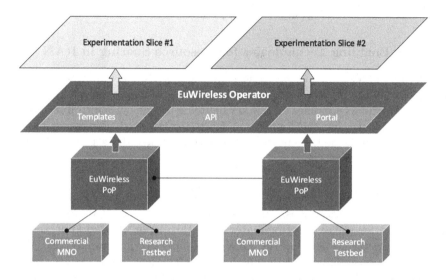

**Fig. 1.** EuWireless overall architecture.

The EuWireless slicing approach is supported by a flexible virtualisation platform provided by the GÉANT Testbeds Service (GTS) [14] and its Generic Virtualisation Model (GVM) architecture. GTS allows the creation of raw connectivity slices on top of the pan-European GÉANT backbone network infrastructure and additional sub-slices which can be used to build the required experimentation functionality on top of the raw connectivity slice. EuWireless operator will create and provide to the EuWireless experimenters a generic main slice template and, based on the main template, several sub-templates, which will fit the requirements of specific experimentation use cases. After the slice is defined with the provided templates, the required resources will be reserved from the available infrastructure. When the resources have been reserved, the slice will be instantiated and control handed over to the EuWireless experimenters. They can then perform their experiments with absolute control of the virtual testbed, i.e., the EuWireless experimentation slice, assigned to their use.

The EuWireless owned infrastructure resources will be deployed into Points of Presences (PoP). PoP is a core object in the EuWireless overall architecture and acts as an intermediate component between the MNO network resources and the local research testbed resources. PoPs consist of selected network functions capable of configuring and managing the end-to-end slices created for the experiments. A single PoP can be run as an independent node or as a part of a network of PoPs. That is, PoPs must be able to independently provide services in a certain geographical or logical area, but also to interconnect in a seamless and decentralised way in order to guarantee scalability. Based on PoPs as the leading design principle, the EuWireless infrastructure can be built as a flexible and incremental deployment. This means that the EuWireless owned resources can be added or relocated according to the needs of the EuWireless experimenters or the availability of funding.

### 3.2 Key Enabling Technologies for Resource Sharing in RAN

In order for EuWireless to go beyond traditional RAN sharing when combining resources from the EuWireless, MNO and local research testbed infrastructures, the overall architecture relies on few key enabling technologies introduced below. These technologies lay the foundation for the centralised management of the combined resources in the end-to-end experimentation slices provided for the EuWireless experimenters.

**Spectrum Sharing.** In the EuWireless project, the sharing of radio spectrum is studied from two perspectives. First approach is to view the RAN functions and their cooperative use as described later on in this paper. Second approach is to share radio spectrum between the EuWireless operator and commercial MNOs with dynamic spectrum access techniques. Dynamic spectrum access, in the form of spectrum sharing, is seen as one of the key enablers for the 5G and beyond systems [37]. Currently, there are two prevailing methods for shared access to the licensed frequency bands, i.e., Licensed Shared Access (LSA) in Europe and Spectrum Access System (SAS) in the US. LSA overcomes the inefficiencies of the generic TV White Space (TVWS) communication system approach with a defined economy flow between the Incumbents and the LSA Licensees. Incumbent is the primary user of the shared spectrum resource, whereas LSA Licensees are operating their wireless systems under a sharing agreement. LSA provides guaranteed quality of service in a given geographical area, frequency band and time period [26].

From the point of view of dynamic spectrum management, EuWireless needs to provide the experimenters a unified interface from which suitable frequency bands can be reserved for research purposes. The negotiations of the spectrum access for a certain geographical area and time window must follow the national regulations and laws. The required negotiations are to be carried out by the EuWireless operator locally with the MNOs. Depending on the size of the experiments being carried out by the EuWireless experimenter, the need for licensed spectrum resources might vary greatly. The experiments can concern only a limited area of a few cells or even only a single base station, or require the same frequency bands to be available across multiple EuWireless PoPs located in several countries. For the former case, the RAN slicing methods discussed in Sect. 4 can be utilised. The latter case is out of scope of this paper.

**Network Slicing.** 5G network slicing, as introduced in [27], allows the creation of multiple isolated logical networks on top of a single shared physical infrastructure by relying on virtualisation techniques. This slicing concept enables the EuWireless operator to offer each experimenter a virtual testbed composed of shared resources. An abstraction layer distributes those resources to the virtual testbeds and maintains their isolation. One key advantage of network slicing is that the same abstraction and sharing principles can be applied to resources that are not owned by the entity providing the service to the end users [6]. This approach is the essence of the EuWireless concept and offers the EuWireless operator the opportunity to extend the functionality and services included in the experimentation slices by entering into agreements with commercial MNOs providing key resources such as licensed spectrum.

The 5G network slices are identified and differentiated by using a Single Network Slice Selection Assistance Information (S-NSSAI) parameter, which is used as a unique slice ID in all control signalling [4]. The S-NSSAI parameter not only identifies a network slice, but it also contains information on the service type provided or supported by the slice in question. Hence, it provides the basic means for the separation of the slices and traffic handling on per-slice basis also in the RAN. Currently, the 3GPP Release 15 specifications lay down the high-level basic functionalities required to enable slicing of the NG-RAN resources [3].

**Network Functions Virtualisation and Software-Defined Networking.** Virtualisation and programmability of the network functions and services offer the required flexibility and act as the key enablers for network slicing. The NFV framework, as defined by the European Telecommunications Standards Institute (ETSI), offers the means to realise previously proprietary hardware-based Physical Network Functions (PNF) as virtual software-based components on top of a COTS cloud computing platform [12]. The NFV framework defines the architecture and interfaces to arrange the VNFs, the underlying NFV Infrastructure (NFVI) and the required Management & Orchestration (MANO) functionality. As a result, the desired network functions can be flexibly chained to provide the overall functionality and performance fulfilling the requirements of a given use case or service.

Software-Defined Networking (SDN) provides the required programmability to the networking fabric by separating the control and data planes. This separation facilitates the end-to-end centralised control for SDN-enabled network domains [21]. The SDN controller is a key component in the network and can be made to play a central role in the management of 5G network slicing and/or NFV. The complementary nature of the functionalities provided by network slicing, NFV and SDN has resulted into numerous approaches to utilise them in parallel when creating and maintaining virtual networks [13,30,31]. In order to better support the specific performance requirements of some RAN and legacy system components, most of them allow a mix of VNFs and PNFs to be used in a single service function chain.

**3GPP Service Based Architecture.** Building on the key enabling technologies introduced above, 3GPP Release 15 defines an SBA for 5G networks. Essentially, SBA integrates spectrum sharing, NFV and SDN principles into the RAN and core networks so that flexible 5G network slicing is enabled end-to-end. In SBA, the interconnections between network functions are no longer defined with reference points between individual network functions. In the earlier generations of mobile communication networks this approach resulted in fixed multi-hop signalling paths in the core network [17]. Instead, network functions in the SBA provide and consume services following the REpresentational State Transfer (REST) architecture design [23]. This approach based on RESTful APIs and a set of principles on how to create and deploy distributed services enables direct interactions between network functions and facilitates flexible service function chaining and slicing in 5G networks.

The new network functions in the centre of the SBA are the Network Repository Function (NRF) and the Network Exposure Function (NEF). The creation of virtual networks and service function chains in the SBA is performed through the NRF and RESTful APIs following a three step procedure. In the service registration phase, a network function registers with the NRF the services it provides to the other network functions. In the service discovery phase, a network function queries the NRF for the services it requires and the NRF responses with a list of other network functions that are able to provide these services. In the session establishment phase, an interconnection is established between two network functions for direct interaction. By repeating this procedure between network functions, a service function chain providing the required overall network functionality can be created. NEF, on the other hand, enables service discovery from the SBA for external 3rd parties such as vertical industries. NEF exposes the properties of the network functions in the SBA towards the 3rd party services via a northbound RESTful API.

## 4    RAN Functions Virtualisation and Slicing Framework

In order to enable sharing of the physical and virtual RAN functions in the EuWireless, MNO and local research testbed infrastructures, the project follows the advancements in the virtualisation of RAN functions from different forums. As 3GPP specifications define the technologies deployed in commercial mobile networks worldwide, the baseline RAN architecture for EuWireless is based on 3GPP Release 15 NG-RAN. 3GPP studied a variety of different options for a cloud-based RAN architecture in its study item for New Radio Access Technology [1], where different options to split the Evolved NodeB (eNB) and gNB functionalities were analysed.

After the assessment of the advantages and disadvantages of different split options, the Higher Layer Split (HLS) Option 2 was chosen as the main functional split for 3GPP Release 15 NG-RAN [8]. The main advantage of the HLS Option 2 is the increased flexibility in the implementation and deployment of NG-RANs as a mix of VNFs and PNFs. In addition, the HLS Option 2 benefitted from the already existing 3GPP specifications on Long Term Evolution (LTE) Dual Connectivity (DC) functionality.

In HLS Option 2, the Central Unit (CU) contains the Radio Resource Control (RRC), Packet Data Convergence Protocol (PDCP) and Service Data Application Protocol (SDAP) functionalities. The Distributed Unit (DU) contains the Radio Link Control (RLC), Medium Access Control (MAC) and PHY functionalities. DU can be further divided into the DU and the Radio Unit (RU). RU can contain either the low-PHY and the Radio Frontend (RF) functionalities corresponding to the Lower Layer Split (LLS) Option 7 [1], or only the RF functionality as in LLS Option 8 and in traditional C-RAN architectures.

A simplified representation of the resulting NG-RAN architecture is depicted in Fig. 2. The logical interfaces inter-connecting the RAN functions are the NG interface between the 5GC and the CU, the F1 interface between the CU and the DU, and the so called F2 interface between the DU and the RU. The F2 interface is not defined in 3GPP Release 15, but it is currently used to represent the interface between the DU and the RU, e.g., in several industry forums. The 5G air interface is called the Uu interface.

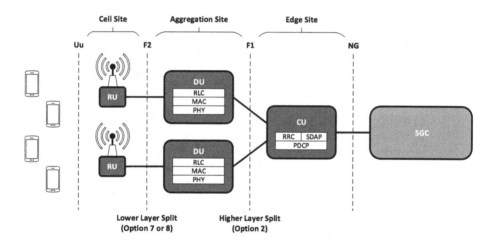

**Fig. 2.** 3GPP Release 15 NG-RAN architecture.

The different CU-DU-RU configurations and deployment options as well as the additional interfaces interconnecting the different logical entities can be found from the 3GPP Release 15 RAN specifications [2,3] and from [28]. They are also further discussed in the following subsections focusing on the EuWireless studies on RAN virtualisation and slicing.

## 4.1 RAN Functions Virtualisation

As already mentioned above, the baseline RAN architecture for EuWireless studies is NG-RAN. In addition to the division of the NG-RAN functionalities into the CU, DU and RU as shown in Fig. 2, the Control Plane (CP) and User Plane (UP) functionalities are also separated allowing centralised control for the RAN functions.

There are three main deployment scenarios defined for the 3GPP Release 15 NG-RAN [28]. The first scenario represents a basic case where both the CP and UP functionalities are centralised in the CU as in Fig. 3. This approach enables the installation of all CU functionality near the 5GC services and applications. The CU can reside, e.g., in the MNO's data centre, facilitating the cooperation and management of the overall network. However, if the data centre hosting the CUs is far away from the DUs, the transport latencies can cause RAN performance issues in very demanding use cases. This first deployment scenario is the most interesting one from the EuWireless perspective as it provides the means to centrally coordinate both CP and UP in case of a shared infrastructure with a commercial MNO. It also facilitates the deployment and testing of more elaborate communication schemes in the RAN part of the overall architecture, e.g., with coordinated use of Multiple Radio Access Technologies (multi-RAT) or multi-RAT scheduling.

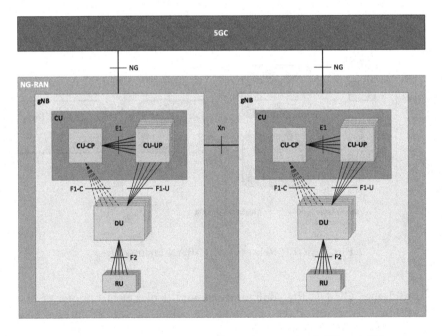

**Fig. 3.** NG-RAN functional split with centralised CP and UP.

The second and third deployment scenarios allow optimisation either for the control signalling or user data, respectively. In the second scenario, the CP functionality is distributed to the DUs and the UP functionality is centralised in the CU. This approach enables low latency control signalling between the network and the User Equipment (UE). It also decreases the amount of CP traffic in the transport network. In the third scenario, the CP functionality is centralised to the CU and the UP functionality is distributed to the DUs. This allows extremely low latency access to the user specific service and application data, which is cached at the network edge.

Another important reference for future RAN architectures comes from the industry-led O-RAN Alliance, which is currently working on a number of specifications for open and intelligent virtualised RAN architectures [29]. The O-RAN Alliance Reference Architecture is compliant with the 3GPP NG-RAN specifications and extends it with additional open interfaces and design for an intelligent RAN controller entity. The 5G-PPP view on 5G architecture [5] also provides enhancements to the baseline NG-RAN architecture. The main addition in the 5G-PPP RAN architecture is the controller layer, which interfaces with the CUs and adds programmability to CP functionality.

Based on the current consensus in the industry, the virtualisation of the non-real-time part of the gNBs is the natural first step towards fully virtualised RANs. Following the current trends, the O-RAN Alliance Reference Architecture provides a good starting point for EuWireless RAN virtualisation studies and validation tests on top of the GTS platform. Starting from the CU functions, the project will define the virtual object configuration and the related Resource Control Agent (RCA) functionality needed to run RRC, SDAP and PDCP as virtualised resources in GTS.

In the end, atomisation and orchestration of the radio resources between the EuWireless operator and commercial MNOs is needed across multiple cells, administrative domains and heterogeneous operational environments. In addition, the different domains can contain 4G, 5G, WiFi and other wireless access technologies. Consequently, analysis of the possibilities to virtualise the DU functions are performed based on both the nominal performance of the utilised virtualisation and networking technologies, and the measured performance of the GTS architecture and EuWireless PoPs. The final aim is to be able to support as many of the functional split options from [1] as the performance limits of the EuWireless virtualisation framework allow.

## 4.2   RAN Functions Chaining Scenarios

Flexible distribution and chaining of the virtualised and physical RAN functions open up new possibilities for RAN sharing between EuWireless, MNOs and local research testbeds. Depending on which RAN functions are selected from which infrastructures, the combined virtual testbed/experimentation slice will enable the EuWireless user to do different things. A few example scenarios for the chaining of the RAN functions in EuWireless experimentation slices have been defined for the purpose of Proof of Concept (PoC) testing in the second phase of the project.

The first Service Function Chaining (SFC) [24] example is presented in Fig. 4. In the first simple example, the EuWireless experimenter wants to deploy a large-scale virtual testbed with a simple spectrum sharing scenario based on the selection of RUs from different infrastructures. The RUs are all operating on different frequency bands, but supporting the same Radio Access Technology (RAT). Hence, based on the temporal availability of bandwidth at the different frequencies, the EuWireless experimenter can utilise the RU providing largest amount of free resources on its frequency band at any given time. The actual selection process can be based on historical spectrum occupancy data, real-time measurements or a combination of databases and sensing at different frequency bands.

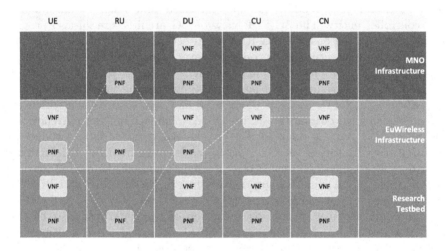

**Fig. 4.** SFC example between EuWireless, MNO and local research testbed resources.

In order to get the desired functionality into the virtual testbed in this example, the EuWireless experimenter combines the Core Network (CN) and CU VNFs from an EuWireless PoP as the baseline architecture. Similar services would have been available for chaining also from the MNO infrastructure as well as from the local small-scale research testbed either as VNFs or PNFs. In order to reach higher performance in the air interface, the EuWireless experimenter selects the DU PNF from the EuWireless PoP. He/she interconnects it with RU PNFs residing in the same geographical area from the EuWireless PoP, MNO infrastructure and local research testbed. The UE utilised in the tests is a smartphone equipped with an EuWireless SIM card.

The second example scenario is based on the sharing of both the DUs and RUs between the EuWireless PoP, MNO infrastructure and a local research testbed. By following a similar approach for the CN and CU as in the first example shown in Fig. 4, but selecting several DUs and RUs from different network domains, the EuWireless experimenter can deploy a virtual testbed that supports, e.g., multi-RAT and coordinated transmission schemes in the shared RAN.

In the third example scenario, the virtual testbed comprises of shared CUs, DUs and RUs. By extending the sharing of resources to the CU, a more global picture of the shared RAN is available for the EuWireless experimenter, who can now deploy test cases including, e.g., proactive Quality of Service (QoS)/Quality of Experience (QoE) assurance or load balancing between the different network domains.

All of the presented example scenarios require interworking interfaces between the chained VNFs and PNFs. This means that all of the utilised CUs, DUs and RUs should support open standardised interfaces or be from the same vendor if proprietary interface and protocol implementations are utilised. The latter can be the case when legacy RAN components or special functionalities related to smart antennas are desired to be tested as part of the virtual testbed.

## 4.3   RAN Slicing Implementation Options

Depending on the selected resource sharing and SFC scenarios, the implementation of the virtual testbed, i.e., the experimentation slice, in the RAN can differ from various perspectives. The definition of a RAN slice can be a simplified realisation either with a dedicated RU and frequency band for the EuWireless traffic or with traffic prioritisation using 5G QoS flows [22]. These options provide a straightforward way to implement at least rudimentary slicing in the RAN, but both of them have limitations. When slicing is based on dedicated frequency bands for each slice, the isolation between the RAN slices is good, but the end result is inflexible and uses radio resources inefficiently. On the other hand, when slicing is based only on QoS flows, the setup is flexible and multiplexing of several slices on the same frequency band is possible, but the isolation between the RAN slices is poor.

As already mentioned before, network slicing in the 3GPP Release 15 networks is based on the S-NSSAI parameter, which identifies a network slice and contains information on the service type provided and/or supported by the slice in question. Hence, the provided slicing framework for 5G networks offers a lot more options to find the best compromise between slicing flexibility, efficiency and isolation. The authors in [11] analyse the impact of the high-level functional requirements for RAN slicing in 5G networks from the RAN protocol architecture, network function and management framework design perspectives. The authors in [15] extend the analysis to the level of specific protocol functionalities, messages and parameters at different gNB protocol layers. They propose a solution to implement the slice configuration and management functionality into the NG-RAN protocol stack. They also present simulation results demonstrating the different levels of isolation achieved between RAN slices, depending on the configuration of the shared and dedicated resources at different protocol layers of the RAN slices.

Regarding the different options to implement slicing in the RAN, the authors in [35] analyse four different approaches from the traffic (e.g., overload situations) and radio-electrical (e.g., mutual interference) isolation perspectives. The analysed RAN slicing approaches are based on spectrum planning, Inter-Cell Interference Coordination (ICIC), packet scheduling and admission control functionalities. These approaches are hierarchical in the sense that if resource slicing is performed at the highest spectrum planning level, the configuration of ICIC, packet scheduling and admission control functionalities can be customised for each slice. Similarly, if slicing is implemented utilising ICIC, the packet scheduling and admission control functionalities can be configured slice-by-slice, and so on. The higher in the hierarchy the slicing approach is, the larger is the area and the longer the time window it covers, and the better is the traffic and radio-electrical isolation that can be achieved. On the other hand, the RAN slicing options lower down in the hierarchy, especially the ICIC and packet scheduling-based approaches, offer higher granularity for reconfigurations. Hence, they offer more flexibility and adaptability for dynamic slice management than RAN slicing implemented with high-level spectrum planning.

From the EuWireless perspective, the main RAN slicing feature should be the guaranteed isolation between the MNO resources used for commercial operations and the resources shared with the EuWireless operator. From this starting point, the network functionalities and the level of runtime control over the shared resources offered for the EuWireless experimenter are defined. Hence, for EuWireless, the default option to realise RAN slicing is on the spectrum planning level, e.g., with dynamic spectrum sharing methods. RAN slicing realised with joint packet scheduling between network domains offers an interesting possibility for EuWireless in the future. When the development of commercial network infrastructures continues towards fully virtualised, open and programmable RANs, more and more possibilities for the use of shared resources from different domains with guaranteed isolation become available.

## 5    Implementation Challenges and Future Work

In the end of the first phase of the EuWireless project, the concept and architecture design for the European mobile network operator for research is finished. With the set of selected key technologies and the initial PoP implementation in Malaga, Spain, the next step in the realisation of the pan-European EuWireless operator is a pilot implementation comprising of multiple PoPs around Europe. With the pilot implementations, feasibility studies for different components of the EuWireless design will be performed on top of the GTS infrastructure. Some high-level challenges and test cases for the next phase of the EuWireless project are introduced below.

**RAN Controller Design.** One of the key challenges in the creation of virtual testbeds is the design of the RAN controllers and their placement in the overall architecture. When following an SDN-like approach [5,13], the dynamic nature of the wireless medium and the mobile network architecture complicate the task distribution process and information sharing between different controller entities [18]. Additional challenges come from the heterogeneity of the interfaces and protocols used especially in legacy RANs. In addition, the support for the mobile network control functionalities in the current SDN protocols is still missing [34].

The RAN controller architecture also plays an important role in network reliability, scalability, and security. A centralised controller architecture may provide a global network view and facilitate network programmability, but it may cause a single point of failure leading to less reliability. The centralised controller architecture also has scalability issues. Increase in the amount of network devices may limit the performance of the controller since a single controller needs to perform all network control routines requiring large computing resources. On the other hand, a distributed controller architecture overcomes the scalability, reliability and security limitations of the centralised controller at the cost of the global network view and the ease of the MANO implementation. Hence, a hybrid controller architecture can provide a fine trade-off between the centralised and distributed architectures. However, the components and functionalities to be centralised and distributed still need to be defined based on the end user requirements, which in turn may vary greatly between individual use cases, services and applications [33]. Figure 5 shows an example of a hybrid RAN controller architecture.

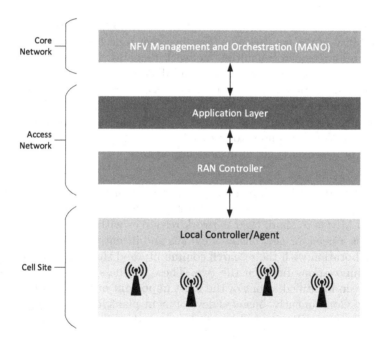

**Fig. 5.** Hybrid architecture for a software-defined RAN controller.

**Virtual RAN Performance.** Complex virtualised systems contain a variety of potential performance bottlenecks if not designed and implemented properly. The softwarisation of the RAN requires splitting of the CP and UP functionalities based on the SDN concept, which in turns requires splitting of the 3GPP radio protocol stack. Many protocol functionalities are sensitive to signalling delays and a number of the foreseen 5G use cases rely on high data rates and low end-to-end latencies. Consequently, issues such as excess delay and jitter caused by the SDN CP [19] or by the location and required amount of virtualised RAN functions in the overall architecture become crucial [16]. Poor isolation between the RAN slices can also result in performance issues in the shared infrastructure [31].

**Southbound and Northbound Interfaces.** The split of the radio protocol stack and the introduction of the RAN controller requires new implementations or at least functional extensions to the current state-of-the-art southbound interfaces between the CP and UP. Since the radio protocol stack and the control functionalities of the cellular network are completely different than the normal computer network protocols/functionalities, new southbound and northbound interface specifications are required for performance-oriented network management and monitoring [18].

**Multi-domain Orchestration and Interoperability.** Orchestration and interoperability of the network functions becomes a necessity when sharing and combining resources across multiple network domains. First problem in multi-domain orchestration is the availability and dissemination of the required information on configuration and state of the network functions between the different domains. Second problem is the amount and timely processing of the information when it is made available. Related to both, the methods to describe the information so that it is understood by all involved parties [16] and to automate the related processes [31] are of utmost importance.

**Cooperation with MNOs.** From a non-technical perspective, an essential enabler for the realisation of the EuWireless concept is the willingness of the commercial MNOs to share their network resources with the EuWireless operator. There is a need for new business models and incentives for the MNOs to do closer collaboration with the research community and share both the infrastructures and innovations between the two. These business models and incentives have also been identified as one of the most important outcomes of the EuWireless project. Consequently, business development plans for the EuWireless operator will be prepared to complement the created architecture and technology definitions.

## 6    Conclusion

This paper briefly introduced the overall concept and architecture for the EuWireless pan-European mobile network operator for research, focusing especially on the RAN. The key enabling technologies to realise the EuWireless vision of virtual large-scale testbeds available everywhere in Europe were reviewed and the designed RAN function virtualisation and slicing framework was presented.

By combining the key resources and assets from the local research testbeds and commercial MNO infrastructures, the EuWireless experimenter is able to pick and choose the functionalities required to deploy the virtual testbed for his/her specific testing needs. The EuWireless PoPs provide a set of selected network resources and all the required interfaces for the EuWireless experimenter to find, reserve and manage the resources belonging to their virtual testbed. As the first phase of the EuWireless project draws to an end with a complete architecture design and individual technology PoC implementations, the second phase will take the presented concept into the large-scale piloting and validation stage.

# References

1. 3rd Generation Partnership Project: Study on new radio access technology: radio access architecture and interfaces. 3GPP TR 38.801 V14.0.0 (2017)
2. 3rd Generation Partnership Project: NG-RAN; Architecture description. 3GPP TS 38.401 V15.1.0 (2018)
3. 3rd Generation Partnership Project: NR; NR and NG-RAN Overall Description; Stage 2. 3GPP TS 38.300 V15.1.0 (2018)
4. 3rd Generation Partnership Project: System Architecture for the 5G System; Stage 2. 3GPP TS 23.501 V15.1.0 (2018)
5. 5G-PPP Architecture Working Group: View on 5G architecture. Version 3.0 (2019)
6. Afolabi, I., Taleb, T., Samdanis, K., Ksentini, A., Flinck, H.: Network slicing and softwarization: a survey on principles, enabling technologies, and solutions. IEEE Commun. Surv. Tutor. **20**(3), 2429–2453 (2018). https://doi.org/10.1109/COMST.2018.2815638
7. Berman, M., et al.: GENI: a federated testbed for innovative network experiments. Comput. Netw. **61**(2014), 5–23 (2014). https://doi.org/10.1016/j.bjp.2013.12.037
8. Bertenyi, B., Burbidge, R., Masini, G., Sirotkin, S., Gao, Y.: NG Radio Access Network (NG-RAN). J. ICT Stand. **6**(1), 59–76 (2018). https://doi.org/10.13052/jicts2245-800x.614
9. Checko, A., et al.: Cloud RAN for mobile networks - a technology overview. IEEE Commun. Surv. Tutor. **17**(1), 405–426 (2015). https://doi.org/10.1109/COMST.2014.2355255
10. China Mobile Research Institute: C-RAN: The Road Towards Green RAN (2011)
11. Da Silva, I., et al.: Impact of network slicing on 5G Radio Access Networks. In: European Conference on Networks and Communications, EUCNC 2016, pp. 153–157 (2016). https://doi.org/10.1109/EuCNC.2016.7561023
12. European Telecommunications Standards Institute: Network Functions Virtualisation (NFV); Architectural Framework. ETSI GS NFV 002 - V1.2.1 (2014)
13. European Telecommunications Standards Institute: Network Functions Virtualisation (NFV); Ecosystem; Report on SDN Usage in NFV Architectural Framework. ETSI GS NFV-EVE 005 V1.1.1 (2015)
14. Farina, F., Szegedi, P., Sobieski, J.: GÉANT world testbed facility: federated and distributed testbeds as a service facility of GÉANT. In: 2014 26th International Teletraffic Congress, ITC 2014, Karlskrona, pp. 1–6. IEEE (2014). https://doi.org/10.1109/ITC.2014.6932972
15. Ferrús, R., Sallent, O., Pérez-Romero, J., Agustí, R.: On 5G radio access network slicing: radio interface protocol features and configuration. IEEE Commun. Mag. **56**(5), 184–192 (2018). https://doi.org/10.1109/MCOM.2017.1700268

16. Foukas, X., Patounas, G., Elmokashfi, A., Marina, M.K.: Network slicing in 5G: survey and challenges. IEEE Commun. Mag. **55**(5), 94–100 (2017). https://doi. org/10.1109/MCOM.2017.1600951
17. Guttman, E., Ali, I.: Path to 5G: a control plane perspective. J. ICT Stand. **6**(1), 87–100 (2018). https://doi.org/10.13052/jicts2245-800x.616
18. Haque, I.T., Abu-Ghazaleh, N.: Wireless software defined networking: a survey and taxonomy. IEEE Commun. Surv. Tutor. **18**(4), 2713–2737 (2016). https://doi.org/ 10.1109/COMST.2016.2571118
19. He, K., et al.: Measuring control plane latency in SDN-enabled switches. In: 1st ACM SIGCOMM Symposium on Software Defined Networking Research, Santa Clara, pp. 25:1–25:6. ACM Press (2015). https://doi.org/10.1145/2774993.2775069
20. Koumaras, H., et al.: 5GENESIS: the genesis of a flexible 5G facility. In: IEEE International Workshop on Computer-Aided Modeling Analysis and Design of Communication Links and Networks, Barcelona, p. 6. IEEE (2018). https://doi. org/10.1109/CAMAD.2018.8514956
21. Kreutz, D., Ramos, F.M.V., Esteves Verissimo, P., Esteve Rothenberg, C., Azodolmolky, S., Uhlig, S.: Software-defined networking: a comprehensive survey. Proc. IEEE **103**(1), 14–76 (2015). https://doi.org/10.1109/JPROC.2014.2371999. http://ieeexplore.ieee.org/document/6994333/
22. Mademann, F.: The 5G system architecture. J. ICT Stand. **6**(1), 77–86 (2018). https://doi.org/10.13052/jicts2245-800x.615
23. Mayer, G.: RESTful APIs for the 5G service based architecture. J. ICT Stand. **6**(1), 101–116 (2018). https://doi.org/10.13052/jicts2245-800x.617
24. Medhat, A.M., Taleb, T., Elmangoush, A., Carella, G.A., Covaci, S., Magedanz, T.: Service function chaining in next generation networks: state of the art and research challenges. IEEE Commun. Mag. **55**(2), 216–223 (2017). https://doi.org/ 10.1109/MCOM.2016.1600219RP
25. Merino, P., et al.: EuWireless: design of a pan-European mobile network operator for research. In: European Conference on Networks and Communications, EuCNC 2018, Ljubljana, p. 2. IEEE (2018)
26. Mueck, M.D., Srikanteswara, S., Badic, B.: Spectrum Sharing: Licensed Shared Access (LSA) and Spectrum Access System (SAS) (2015)
27. Next Generation Mobile Networks Alliance: 5G White Paper (2015)
28. Next Generation Mobile Networks Alliance: NGMN Overview on 5G RAN Functional Decomposition (2018)
29. O-RAN Alliance: O-RAN: Towards an Open and Smart RAN (2018)
30. Open Networking Foundation: Applying SDN Architecture to 5G Slicing (2016)
31. Ordonez-Lucena, J., Ameigeiras, P., Lopez, D., Ramos-Munoz, J.J., Lorca, J., Folgueira, J.: Network slicing for 5G with SDN/NFV: concepts, architectures, and challenges. IEEE Commun. Mag. **55**(5), 80–87 (2017). https://doi.org/10.1109/ MCOM.2017.1600935
32. Rios, Á., Valera-Muros, B., Merino-Gomez, P., Sobieski, J.: Expanding GÉANT testbeds service to support pan-European 5G network slices for research in the EuWireless project. Mob. Inf. Syst. **2019**, 1–13 (2019). https://doi.org/10.1155/ 2019/6249247
33. Robitza, W., et al.: Challenges of future multimedia QoE monitoring for internet service providers. Multimed. Tools Appl. **76**(21), 22243–22266 (2017). https://doi. org/10.1007/s11042-017-4870-z

34. Safianowska, M.B., et al.: Current experiences and lessons learned towards defining pan-European mobile network operator for research - based on EU project EuWireless. Przegląd Telekomun. I Wiadomości Telekomun. **2019**(6) (2019). https://doi. org/10.15199/59.2019.6.5

35. Sallent, O., Pérez-Romero, J., Ferrús, R., Agustí, R.: On radio access network slicing from a radio resource management perspective. IEEE Wirel. Commun. Netw. Conf. WCNC **24**(5), 166–174 (2017). https://doi.org/10.1109/MWC.2017. 1600220WC

36. Silva, A.P., et al.: 5GinFIRE: an end-to-end Open5G vertical network function ecosystem. Ad Hoc Netw. **93**, 101895 (2019). https://doi.org/10.1016/j.adhoc. 2019.101895. https://linkinghub.elsevier.com/retrieve/pii/S1570870518309387

37. Tehrani, R.H., Vahid, S., Triantafyllopoulou, D., Lee, H., Moessner, K.: Licensed spectrum sharing schemes for mobile operators: a survey and outlook. IEEE Commun. Surv. Tutor. **18**(4), 2591–2623 (2016). https://doi.org/10.1109/COMST. 2016.2583499

# Research Progress in the Processing
# of Crowdsourced Test Reports

Naiqi Wang[1,2], Lizhi Cai[1,2], Mingang Chen[2(✉)], and Chuwei Zhang[3]

[1] School of Information Science and Engineering,
East China University of Science and Technology, Shanghai, China
slytherinwnq@163.com
[2] Shanghai Key Laboratory of Computer Software Testing and Evaluating,
Shanghai Development Center of Computer Software Technology,
Shanghai, China
{clz, cmg}@ssc.stn.sh.cn
[3] Shanghai Foreign Affairs Service Center, Shanghai, China
zhangchuwei@sfasc.com.cn

**Abstract.** In recent years, crowdsourced testing, which uses collective intelligence to solve complex software testing tasks has gained widespread attention in academia and industry. However, due to a large number of workers participating in crowdsourced testing tasks, the submitted test reports set is too large, making it difficult for developers to review test reports. Therefore, how to effectively process and integrate crowdsourced test reports is always a significant challenge in the crowdsourced testing process. This paper deals with the crowdsourced test reports processing, sorts out some achievements in this field in recent years, and classifies, summarizes, and compares existing research results from four directions: duplicated reports detection, test reports aggregation and classification, priority ranking, and reports summarization. Finally explored the possible research directions, opportunities and challenges of the crowdsourced test reports.

**Keywords:** Software testing · Crowdsourced testing · Reports processing

## 1 Introduction

In 2006, Howe first proposed the concept of crowdsourcing, a distributed problem solving and production organization model in the Internet environment [1]. The company or organization outsources the tasks that were carried by the full-time staff to an unidentified, large-scale group to complete the task through an open Web platform.

Subsequently, in response to this definition, various circles have conducted a variety of researches on the working forms of crowdsourcing. The application of crowdsourcing to software testing has also become a new trend. A number of crowdsourced testing platforms have emerged on the Internet, such as Amazon Mechanical Turk, Baidu MTC, UTest, MoocTest and so on. Through these crowdsourced testing platforms, software testing can shorten the test cycle, increase the diversity of the test environment, and improve the quality of software products.

© ICST Institute for Computer Sciences, Social Informatics and Telecommunications Engineering 2020
Published by Springer Nature Switzerland AG 2020. All Rights Reserved
H. Gao et al. (Eds.): TridentCom 2019, LNICST 309, pp. 150–160, 2020.
https://doi.org/10.1007/978-3-030-43215-7_11

However, due to crowdsourced testing characteristics, crowdsourced testing still faces many challenges, such as the division of crowdsourced testing tasks, the incentives for crowdsourced workers, and crowdsourced test reports processing. Due to the large number of crowdsourced workers testing one software at the same time, and the uneven level of crowdsourced workers. The number of test reports received by developers is often large, the duplicate ratio is high, and the quality gap is large. This also makes it difficult for developers to quickly find effective information from these test reports and fix bugs based on these test reports.

Therefore, a lot of work is used to study crowdsourced test reports processing, such as test reports aggregation, classification, prioritization to select higher quality test reports, and multi-document reports summarization to enhance the efficiency of developer review reports. This paper retrieves the relevant papers of crowdsourced test reports processing from the three major databases: IEEE, ACM and SpringerLink, strives to carry out comprehensive summaries, and discusses the future work of crowdsourced test reports processing.

## 2  Background

### 2.1  Crowdsourced Software Testing

Mao et al. gave a complete interpretation of crowdsourcing work in the field of software engineering. They proposed that crowdsourcing software engineering is the behavior of external software engineering tasks in the form of public convening a large number of potential, undefined online workers [2].

In software testing, the developer as a task requester uploads the software to be tested and the test tasks list to the crowdsourced testing platform. After a large number of crowdsourced workers test it, the feedback is sent to the software developer. The procedure of crowdsourced software testing is shown in Fig. 1. A large number of online workers participate in the completion of test tasks, which can provide a good simulation of real application scenarios and real user performance, with short test cycles and relatively low costs [3]. These are some of the advantages of crowdsourced testing over traditional testing. However, due to the large number of crowdsourced workers required for the test project, the levels of crowdsourced workers involved in the test task are mixed, so the quality gap between the test reports submitted is also large. What's more, the measure of rewarding crowdsourced workers in most crowdsourcing platforms is the number of valid reports submitted by workers, which also leads to crowdsourced workers submitting as many reports as possible. All of the above reasons have led to the disadvantages of large gap in the quality of crowdsourced test reports, high duplicate ratio, and a low number of effective reports. Developers often need a lot of energy and time to review these crowdsourced test reports, and the efficiency of fixing bugs based on reports is very low.

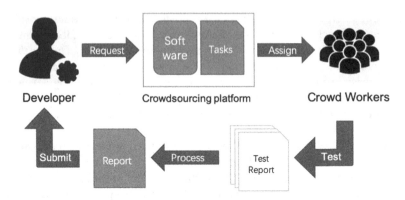

**Fig. 1.** The procedure of crowdsourced testing

### 2.2 Crowdsourced Test Reports

Unlike traditional test reports, Crowdsourced workers who receive test tasks in crowdsourced testing are often not professional software testers. Therefore, the length of the crowdsourced test reports is relatively short, including only the tester's test environment, input conditions, results, and whether or not the test passed.

In addition, as during the test, it is much more convenient to collect the results of the screenshot than to summarize the results into text, crowdsourced workers often use a large number of screenshots to help indicate the test results. Therefore, the crowdsourced test reports feature short text and rich screenshots [4, 5].

In the crowdsourced testing process, crowdsourced workers submit a large number of quality test reports, and crowdsourced testing platform auditors or task requesters will face difficulties in how to effectively integrate and process crowdsourced test reports [6]. Researchers have put a lot of effort in researching how to detect duplicate test reports and select higher-quality reports from the reports set.

## 3   Crowdsourced Test Reports Processing Research

This paper combines the research results of various scholars and summarizes the researches on crowdsourced test reports into four directions:

**Duplicate reports detection.** For a large number of test reports submitted by crowd- sourced workers, duplicate reports in the reports set are detected and further screened (See Sect. 3.1 for details).

**Clustering and classification of crowdsourced test reports.** Based on the duplicate reports detection of the test reports, similar test reports are clustered, or a classifier is constructed to classify the report (See Sect. 3.2 for details).

**Quality assessment and prioritization of crowdsourcing test reports.** Automate testing the content of a test report, conducting a quality assessment, and ranking all reports according to the quality of the reports within the report set (See Sect. 3.3 for details).

**Crowdsourced test reports summarization.** Multi-text summarization of crowd sourced test reports to simplify review of test reports (See Sect. 3.4 for details).

The crowdsourced testing reports processing flow is shown in Fig. 2.

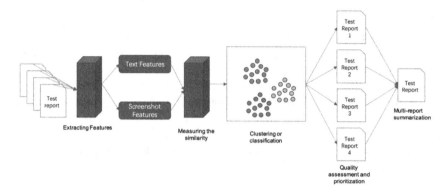

**Fig. 2.** The procedure of crowdsourced test reports processing

## 3.1   Duplicate Reports Detection

For the duplicate reports detection of test reports, researchers have proposed many methods to detect, such as using NLP [7–11], constructing discriminant [12], using information retrieval technology [13, 14] and using Machine learning techniques [12, 15–17].

**Using NLP.** In 2007, Runeson et al. first proposed the use of Natural Language Processing to achieve detection of similar defect reports [7]. They first segmented the reports text, removed all affixes and the stop words, replaced the synonyms. Each defect report is then characterized, converted into a bag-of-words and modeled as a feature vector, and each feature is a word of the report. The similarity between defect reports is calculated by the cosine distance between the feature vectors. Yang et al. used a combination of information retrieval and word embedding techniques to calculate the text similarity of the bug title and description part [8]; Rocha et al. used the bug attribute field calculation [9]; Hindle et al. used software quality context information, software structure items and system development to calculate the similarity between reports [10].

In addition to using the textual information of the test report itself, Wang et al. proposed the use of execution information to aid in the repeated detection of defect reports, Wang et al. set a similarity discrimination mechanism to determine the similarity between reports [11]. However, some studies have shown that only a small number of reports contain execution information, so relying on execution information to assist in detecting duplicate reports is not very effective.

**Using Information Retrieval.** Information Retrieval (IR) refers to the process and technology of obtaining information resources from the relevant information source set according to the needs of information users [13]. Sun et al. proposed a retrieval function (REP) to achieve detection of repeated defect reports. REP can not only use the summary of defect reports and textual similarity of description fields, but also use non-text fields for similarity analysis [14]; Nguyen et al. combines IR technology and topic models to achieve repeated reports detection [15]. They first used the BM25 algorithm to calculate the similarity between reports, and also used the topic model for calculations.

**Using Machine Learning.** The development of machine learning and artificial intelligence has brought about tremendous progress in the automatic classification of computers. Sun et al. constructed a discriminant and trained a discriminant model using a Support Vector Machine (SVM) to retrieve Top-K relevant similar reports from a set. Liu et al. used Learning to Rank (L2R) technique to build sorting models to achieve repetitive reports searches, while they also used knowledge in Wikipedia to discover semantic relationships between words and documents [16]. Banerjee et al. used multi-label classification to assign multiple duplicate predictions to each report and use fusion roles to combine the results [17].

### 3.2    Clustering and Classification of Crowdsourced Test Reports

Due to the working mode of crowdsourced testing, each test project will receive a large number of test reports. Therefore, how to effectively cluster and classify a large number of test reports is the focus of various scholars.

**Clustering of Crowdsourced Test Reports.** Clustering of crowdsourced test reports is the aggregation of similar reports into a cluster according to a similarity algorithm to condense a large number of scattered test reports into one cluster. Similar reports generally contain similar, identical bugs, so clustering similar reports can effectively classify test reports of the same type into the same reports cluster.

Wang et al. used a method of clustering and reclassification to process the crowdsourced test reports [18]. They first performed feature extraction on the test reports, including textual information, the sentiment orientation score of the reports and the experience of the crowdsourced workers as characteristics, and clustered using the K-means algorithm. Subsequently, the training data is constructed from the most similar clusters to construct the classifier, which can mitigate the impact of local bias on the classification effect.

The test reports submitted by the crowdsourced workers often have the following problems, the invalid problem, that is, the reports includes many non-error test reports and empty test reports that do not contain error information; the imbalance problem, that is, due to the difference between the worker levels, there is a big gap between language description and quality of the reports; multi-bug problem, that is, some workers submit reports containing multiple bugs, which need to be grouped into different clusters. In order to solve these problems, Jiang et al. proposed a new framework called the Test Report Fuzzy Clustering Framework (TERFUR) [19]. They first construct a filter to remove invalid reports, and then build a preprocessor to solve the test reports description too short. Finally, propose a two-stage merging algorithm to cluster redundant reports and multiple bug reports.

In response to the short text and rich screenshots of the crowdsourced test reports, Feng et al. divided reports into two parts, a text description part and a screenshot part [20]. The text description part is processed using NLP technology to obtain the distance vector between the text histogram and the text; the screenshot part distance is obtained by using the Spatial Pyramid Matching (SPM) [21] technique for the screenshot part. The two-part matrix is combined to obtain a mixed distance matrix. Hao et al. used this method to obtain the distance between test reports and cluster the reports using the Hierarchical Agglomerative Clustering (HAC) method [4]. Also, because in the case where such a cluster is not known in advance, the HAC can be adaptively clustered by setting a threshold value without first defining the number of clusters. The method proposed by Yang et al. is also using SPM to obtain the text and screenshot distance matrix, but in the clustering method selection, they chose a different way [22]. After obtaining the similarity value between all reports, they first choose two reports' similarity values. Then, they compare the first report in the remaining test reports with the existing two cluster representatives. This report is inserted if the similarity value is greater than or equal to the threshold they defined. In a cluster with a higher similarity value, if the similarity value is smaller than the threshold, a new cluster will be added. The next one is compared to similar values for the three existing clusters. In the comparison of similarity values and thresholds, if the similarity value is higher, it is added to the cluster of higher similarity values, otherwise, it is represented as a new cluster, so reciprocating until all the reports are traversed again.

In the selection of text clustering methods, Wang et al. used K-means clustering, but this method needs to pre-define the number of clusters that need to be clustered. Wang et al. use element silhouette to determine the number of clusters. The number of candidate K is set to 1–1000 to determine the best solution [18]. While Hao et al. used HAC to determine the number of clusters based directly on the threshold distance value, simplifies the process of clustering parameter setting [4]. However, in the method of image matching, the SPM method used in the papers above treats the features of different regions equally, and does not take into account the difference in the characteristics of different regions. What's more, this method does not fully play the role of the text information in the screenshot, and should be considered in future research.

**Classification of Crowdsourced Test Reports.** The classification of crowdsourced test reports is that the researchers extract features from the test reports set according to the features that need to be extracted, and construct a classifier from the extracted features. Reports repeatability testing, severity prediction, and bug triaging are available according to the capabilities of the classifier.

Wang et al. constructed a classifier for text features, sentiment features, and experience of workers in the results after clustering [18]. Later, they focused on the cross-domain issues faced by the crowdsourced test reports classifier [23]. Test reports in different fields often have their own special professional terms, and directly use different areas of test reports to build classifiers. These words will make the accuracy of the classifier reduced, so Wang et al. first trained a Stacked Denoising Autoencoders (SDA) model and generated advanced features of the reports based on the textual information of the reports, and finally trained the classifier on the advanced feature vector. In this way, the cross-domain problem in the crowdsourced test reports classifier training can be solved. They also proposed the Local Information Based Active Classification (LOAF) to classify true faults from crowdsourced test reports [24]. LOAF recommended a small number of instances that provide the most information in the local community, and continually asks users about their tags and then classifies them. LOAF utilizes an active learning approach that greatly reduces the amount of data that needs to be labeled and simplifies the annotation work required to build a classifier.

Wang et al. used text information and image information for classification too, but unlike [4, 22], they did not use SPM to calculate screenshot information. Instead, a SETU framework was proposed that combines information from screenshots and textual descriptions to detect duplicate population test reports. SETU extracts four types of features to characterize screenshots (image structure features and image color features) and text descriptions (TF-IDF features and word embedding features) and designs a hierarchical algorithm to detect four-based repeat similarities the scores come from four characteristics.

### 3.3   Quality Assessment and Prioritization of Crowdsourced Test Reports

In software engineering, it is very important to obtain software defect information from the defect reports for repair. The quality of the defect reports is also very important for the inspection reports [26, 27]. In the crowdsourced testing, although the crowdsourced test reports contain less information than traditional defect reports, due to its large number, how to conduct automated quality assessment of crowdsourced test reports to select higher quality reports and give priority to crowdsourced test reports is very important for the processing of the test reports.

**Quality Assessment for Crowdsourced Test Reports.** In the quality assessment for reports, some classification-based work has achieved the ability to classify reports according to reports quality. The classifier constructed by CURES [18], it's criteria for judging test reports are text features, emotional parameters, and worker experience. The text feature is the description of the bug by the crowdsourced workers. The sentiment parameter is a score of $-5$ to $5$, because studies have shown that the reported sentimental tendency may reflect the subjective feeling of the bug; the workers' experience is divided into the number of reports submitted, the number of true faults reported, and the proportion of true faults in the submitted reports. LOAF is the use of active learning methods to continuously learn the reports containing the true faults, so as to classify the reports [24].

Chen et al. proposed a framework for mobile applications called TERQAF [28]. They defined a series of indicators to measure the ideal properties of the test reports, and summarized the values of all the indicators to determine the test by using the step conversion function to judge the quality of the reports. To the best of the author's knowledge, this is also the first work to investigate the quality of test reports and to address the quality assessment of test reports.

**Prioritization of Crowdsourcing Test Reports.** For how to sort crowdsourced test reports, Feng et al. proposed a combination of risk strategy and diversity strategy considerations [29]. After modeling the test reports to vector, they first considered the risk strategy, that is, selecting the report with the highest risk value; Then considered the diversity strategy, that is, selecting the report with the largest distance from the selected report matrix in the candidate reports. Finally, they combined the two strategies and continually select reports to enter the reports set to complete the sorting task.

Feng et al. used text information and screenshot information, through the NLP and SPM to obtain the distance matrix [20]. They use a diversity strategy, when a developer reviews a report, the next one pushed is the one that is the most distant from the current review report. This strategy allows developers to find more errors in a short period of time.

For traditional test reports, Yu et al. trained neural network-based test reports priority prediction model [30], they added an additional layer in the neural network to learn the relationship between the severity and tester, used evolutionary learning to adapt to the addition of new features, and reused data between similar projects as an initial training set for new projects to speed up the training process.

## 3.4   Crowdsourced Test Reports Summarization

Text summarization has always been a hot issue in the field of NLP research. Text summarization is technically divided into extractive summarization and abstractive summarization, which is divided into single-document summarization and multi-document summarization from the abstracted document format. In the traditional test reports processing, because of its long text, it contains more information, single-document and multi-document summarization are both needed. However, the characteristics of the crowdsourced test reports are that the amount is large and the text is short. Therefore, the summarization work for the crowdsourced test reports is mainly a multi-document summarization.

In traditional test reports processing, Mani et al. applied four well-known unsupervised summarization algorithms for the error reports summarization in order to solve the problem that the supervised method requires manual annotated corpora and the generated digest may be biased toward training data [31]. To build a more efficient automatic summarizer to summarize bug reports, [32, 33] investigated whether the current conversation-based automatic summarizer is suitable for bug reports, and they found that the quality of the generated summary is similar to the summary generated by email or other conversations. They also trained an automatic summarizer for the bug reports, and achieved good results.

For the crowdsourced test reports summarization, Hao et al. clustered the reports firstly [4]. In each cluster, the PageRank algorithm is used to find a report with the largest amount of information as the main report, and the rest is used as the candidate reports. Separated the sentence with the screenshot in the candidate reports and cluster again. In each cluster, PageRank is used to sort the sentences and screenshots, and then the selected sentences are added to the master report to assist the review according to the set summary compression ratio. Jiang et al. first investigated the existing methods of attribute construction in Mining Software Repositories (MSR). Then, a new method called Crowd-Attribute is proposed to infer the valid attributes of the bug reports summary from the crowdsourced workers to generate reports data. Jiang et al. used Crowd-Attribute to construct 11 new attributes and proposed a new supervised algorithm, Logistic Regression with Crowdsourcing Attributes (LRCA) [34].

Currently, methods for crowdsourced test reports summarization are mostly extractive, multi-document summarization. Researchers use certain rules to extract the information they need from a large number of test reports and combine them into a single test report that helps developers to review submitted test reports more quickly.

# 4 Summary

This paper reviews the processing methods of crowdsourcing test reports in recent years. From the crowdsourcing test reports, duplicate reports detection, reports clustering and classification, report quality assessment and prioritization, and crowdsourced test reports summarization, we summarize the work in the four directions above. We can find that the quality of the report itself is uneven due to the large difference in the level of crowdsourced workers, which will affect the results of the crowdsourced test reports. And in the crowdsourced test reports processing, the methods currently used by researchers are more traditional, and the processing of text and screenshots is relatively simple. Therefore, future research on the processing of crowdsourced test reports can focus on the following points:

*(1) Using more advanced NLP models and image processing methods to process the reports:*

In recent years, NLP technology has developed rapidly. Based on the pre-trained model, BERT, XLNet have achieved excellent results in tasks such as text classification, reading comprehension, and short text matching, but the current text features extraction in crowdsourced test reports processing still uses a more traditional approach. Similarly, the current analysis of screenshots for crowdsourced test reports, the only documents available for review are the SPM method and the extraction of image structure and color. Therefore, how to use the more advanced NLP model and image processing method to process the crowdsourced test reports is the research directions that researchers can choose.

*(2) Constructing a recommendation system that combines the processed, classified test reports with the developer information. And assign bugs based on developer professionalism:*

Using clustering and classification methods can effectively bring together reports with similar characteristics, and similar reports often reveal the same bugs. In software engineering, different bugs are generally fixed by different developers. Therefore, pushing a test report that is highly relevant to a professional based on the developer's professional information can make it more efficient for developers to review the reports.

*(3) Generating test case based on the processed test reports:*

Mattia et al. proposed a method for automatically generating test cases based on bug reports of mobile applications. They used a combination of program analysis and natural language processing to generate executable test cases from bug reports, which can be correctly applied to most reports [35]. How to use the processed large-scale crowdsourced test reports to generate the corresponding test cases is also worth studying.

**Acknowledgment.** This work is funded by National Key R&D Program of China (No. 2018YFB 1403400).

# References

1. Howe, J.: The rise of crowdsourcing. Wired Mag. **14**(6), 1–4 (2016)
2. Mao, K., Capra, L., Harman, M., et al.: A survey of the use of crowdsourcing in software engineering. J. Syst. Softw. **126**, 57–84 (2017)
3. Latoza, T., Hoek, A.: Crowdsourcing in software engineering: models, motivations, and challenges. IEEE Softw. **33**(1), 74–80 (2016)
4. Hao, R., Feng, Y., Jones, J., Li, Y., Chen, Z.: CTRAS: crowdsourced test report aggregation and summarization. In: ICSE 2019 (2019)
5. Zhang, T., Chen, J., Luo, X., Li, T.: Bug reports for desktop software and mobile apps in GitHub: what is the difference? IEEE Softw. **36**, 63–71 (2017)
6. Zhang, X.F., Feng, Y., Liu, D., Chen, Z.Y., Xu, B.W.: Research progress of crowdsourced software testing. Ruan Jian Xue Bao/J. Softw. **29**(1), 69–88 (2018)
7. Runeson, P., Alexandersson, M., Nyholm, O.: Detection of duplicate defect reports using natural language processing. In: Proceedings of the 29th International Conference on Software Engineering, pp. 499–510. IEEE Computer Society (2007)
8. Yang, X., Lo, D., Xia, X., Bao, L., Sun, J.: Combining word embedding with information retrieval to recommend similar bug reports. In: ISSRE 2016, pp. 127–137 (2016)
9. Rocha, H., Valente, M.T., Marques-Neto, H., Murphy, G.C.: An empirical study on recommendations of similar bugs. In: SANER 2016, pp. 46–56 (2016)
10. Hindle, A., Alipour, A., Stroulia, E.: A contextual approach towards more accurate duplicate bug report detection and ranking. Empir. Softw. Eng. **21**, 368–410 (2016)
11. Wang, X., Zhang, L., Xie, T., et al.: An approach to detecting duplicate bug reports using natural language and execution information. In: ACM/IEEE 30th International Conference on Software Engineering, ICSE 2008, pp. 461–470. IEEE (2008)
12. Sun, C., Lo, D., Wang, X., Jiang, J., Khoo, S.-C.: A discriminative model approach for accurate duplicate bug report retrieval. In: Proceedings of the 32nd ACM/IEEE International Conference on Software Engineering, vol. 1. ACM (2010)
13. Information Retrieval. https://en.wikiipedia.org/wiki/information_retrieval. Accessed 10 Sept 2019
14. Sun, C., Lo, D., Khoo, S.C., et al.: Towards more accurate retrieval of duplicate bug reports. In: 26th IEEE/ACM International Conference on Automated Software Engineering, pp. 253–262. IEEE Computer Society (2011)
15. Nguyen, A.T., Nguyen, T.T., Nguyen, T.N., et al.: Duplicate bug report detection with a combination of information retrieval and topic modeling. In: 27th IEEE/ACM International Conference on Automated Software Engineering, pp. 70–79. ACM (2012)
16. Liu, K., Tan, H.B.K., Zhang, H.: Has this bug been reported? In: 20th Working Conference on Reverse Engineering (WCRE), pp. 82–91. IEEE (2013)

17. Banerjee, S., Syed, Z., Helmick, J., Cukic, B.: A fusion approach for classifying duplicate problem reports. In: ISSRE 2013, pp. 208–217 (2013)
18. Wang, J., Cui, Q., Wang, Q., et al.: Towards effectively test report classification to assist crowdsourced testing. In: ACM/IEEE International Symposium on Empirical Software Engineering and Measurement. ACM (2016)
19. Jiang, H., Chen, X., He, T., et al.: Fuzzy clustering of crowdsourced test reports for apps. ACM Trans. Internet Technol. **18**(2), 1–28 (2018)
20. Feng, Y., Jones, J.A., Chen, Z., et al.: Multi-objective test report prioritization using image understanding. In: 31st IEEE/ACM International Conference on Automated Software Engineering, pp. 202–213 (2016)
21. Lazebnik, S., Schmid, C., Ponce, J.: Beyond bags of features: spatial pyramid matching for recognizing natural scene categories. In: Computer Vision and Pattern Recognition, pp. 2169–2178. IEEE (2016)
22. Yang, Y., Yao, X., Gong, D.: Clustering study of crowdsourced test report with multi-source heterogeneous information. In: Tan, Y., Shi, Y. (eds.) DMBD 2019. CCIS, vol. 1071, pp. 135–145. Springer, Singapore (2019). https://doi.org/10.1007/978-981-32-9563-6_14
23. Wang, J., Cui, Q., Wang, S., et al.: Domain adaptation for test report classification in crowdsourced testing. In: International Conference on Software Engineering: Software Engineering in Practice Track. IEEE Press (2017)
24. Wang, J., Wang, S., Cui, Q., et al.: Local-based active classification of test report to assist crowdsourced testing. In: 31st IEEE/ACM International Conference. ACM (2016)
25. Wang, J., Li, M., Wang, S., Menzies, T., Wang, Q.: Images don't lie: duplicate crowdtesting reports detection with screenshot information. Inf. Softw. Technol. **110**, 139–155 (2019)
26. Nazar, N., Jiang, H., Gao, G., et al.: Source code fragment summarization with small scale crowdsourcing based features. Front. Comput. Sci. **10**(3), 504–517 (2016)
27. Jiang, H., Zhang, J., Ma, H., et al.: Mining authorship characteristics in bug repositories. Sci. China Inf. Sci. **60**(1), 012107 (2017)
28. Chen, X., Jiang, H., Li, X., et al.: Automated quality assessment for crowdsourced test reports of mobile applications. In: 25th International Conference on Software Analysis, Evolution and Reengineering (SANER). IEEE Computer Society (2018)
29. Feng, Y., Chen, Z., Jones, J.A., Fang, C., Xu, B.: Test report prioritization to assist crowdsourced testing. In: 10th ACM Joint Meeting on Foundations of Software Engineering, pp. 225–236 (2015)
30. Yu, L., Tsai, W.-T., Zhao, W., Wu, F.: Predicting defect priority based on neural networks. In: Cao, L., Zhong, J., Feng, Y. (eds.) ADMA 2010. LNCS (LNAI), vol. 6441, pp. 356–367. Springer, Heidelberg (2010). https://doi.org/10.1007/978-3-642-17313-4_35
31. Mani, S., Catherine, R., Sinha, V.S., Dubey, A.: AUSUM: approach for unsupervised bug report summarization. In: ACM SIGSOFT International Symposium on the Foundations of Software Engineering, pp. 1–11 (2012)
32. Rastkar, S., Murphy, G.C., Murray, G.: Automatic summarization of bug reports. IEEE Trans. Softw. Eng. **40**(4), 366–380 (2014)
33. Kokate, P., Wankhade, N.R.: Automatic summarization of bug reports and bug triage classification. Int. J. Sci. Technol. Manag. Res. **2**(6) (2017)
34. Jiang, H., Li, X., Ren, Z., et al.: Toward better summarizing bug reports with crowdsourcing elicited attributes. IEEE Trans. Reliab. **68**, 1–21 (2018)
35. Fazzini, M., Prammer, M., d'Amorim, M., Orso, A.: Automatically translating bug reports into test cases for mobile apps. In: 27th ACM SIGSOFT International Symposium on Software Testing and Analysis (ISSTA 2018), pp. 141–152. ACM (2018)

# Wireless, Networking and Multimedia Application

# Enabling Heterogeneous 5G Simulations with SDN Adapters

Thien Pham$^{(\boxtimes)}$, Jeremy McMahon, and Hung Nguyen

Teletraffic Research Centre, The University of Adelaide,
Adelaide, SA 5005, Australia
{thien.pham,jeremy.mcmahon,hung.nguyen}@adelaide.edu.au

**Abstract.** 5G networks are expected to consist of multiple radio access technologies with a Software-defined networking (SDN) core, and so simulating these networks will require connecting multiple subnetworks with different technologies. Despite the availability of simulators for various technologies, there is currently no tool that can simulate a complete heterogeneous 5G network. In this work, we develop a novel SDN adapter to enable seamless inter-working between different simulation/emulation tools, such as NS-3, Mininet-WiFi, Omnet++, and OpenAirInterface5G. Using the adapter, we have built a large scale 5G simulator with multiple networking technologies by connecting existing simulators. We show that our adapter solution is easy-to-use, scalable, and can be used to connect arbitrary simulation tools. Using our solution, we show that Mininet-WiFi exhibits unreliable behaviour when connected to other networks. We compare our solution against other alternatives and show that our solution is superior both in terms of performance and cost. Finally, and for the first time, we simulate a large heterogeneous 5G network with all of the latest technologies using only a standard commodity personal computer.

**Keywords:** Simulation · Cross domain · Interoperability · Network slicing · SDN · NFV · LTE · 5G NR

## 1  Introduction

5G networks will consist of multiple radio access technologies along with a Software Defined Networking (SDN) core to allow for a large number of end devices and flexible network deployment. A typical complete 5G is illustrated in Fig. 1 [4,5,24,25]. In this network, we have an SDN core where network function virtualization and network slicing are used to provide different services to different end users. Multiple access technologies such as WiFi-6, LTE, and 5G New Radio are being, and will be, used to connect end devices to the core.

Emulation software such as OpenAirInterface5G (OAI5G) [19] and srsLTE [14] have been used to evaluate the performance of 5G networks. They are, however, resource demanding and require actual RF transmission over the air

© ICST Institute for Computer Sciences, Social Informatics and Telecommunications Engineering 2020
Published by Springer Nature Switzerland AG 2020. All Rights Reserved
H. Gao et al. (Eds.): TridentCom 2019, LNICST 309, pp. 163–183, 2020.
https://doi.org/10.1007/978-3-030-43215-7_12

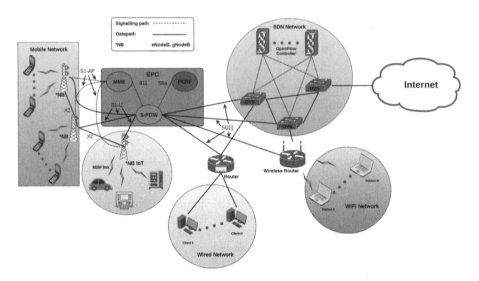

**Fig. 1.** The SDN-enabled 5G heterogeneous network

for real cellular connections. To run these emulations, end users must have a valid LTE spectrum license and furthermore, both tools support only up to 16 User Equipments (UEs).

Alternatively, network simulation tools provide a scalable and repeatable mechanism for researchers and engineers to test their ideas. Currently, there are no readily available simulation tools that can provide both heterogeneous access technologies and an SDN enabled core network. In the absence of a single tool fit for purpose, an alternative approach to simulate networks similar to those shown in Fig. 1 is to bridge multiple simulations together. As an example, we could bridge Mininet/Mininet-WiFi and Omnet++ so that we have the complementing access technologies of the separate tools together in a single network scenario. Nevertheless, bridging such tools is not necessarily simple. IP packets generated from one simulation often cannot cross to the other simulation over a simple interface for various reasons. Of the scenarios studied, these connectivity reasons include subnet differentiation, the lack of an address resolution mechanism (ARP), the network address translation process (NAT), and a missing external interface as the hook-in destination for simulator-side socket connections and the standard transport-level medium. To achieve this bridging, we investigate existing techniques but ultimately construct an SDN adapter for this bridging purpose. Our SDN adapter is versatile in both architecture and control logic, and is designed to address packet incompatibility issues at the transport level of the networks.

Our solution comes with a GUI to enable easy set up of the various simulation combinations. We show in this paper that the resulting 5G simulator with our SDN adapter is easy to use, scalable, and performs better than alternative solutions. Our 5G simulation solution, together with a number of examples where multiple simulations are combined together to produce a complete end-to-end 5G network are publicly available [26,27]. Our tool enables the end user to set up 5G networks simulations and performance validation with ease.

## 2    Background

There are more than 30 network simulation software packages available and each of these simulations is generally designed for a specific use case. For example, some simulators are developed for targeted networks, eg. WiFi networks. Furthermore, some simulators are resource demanding and are not suitable to simulate large scale networks with hundreds of nodes. Reviews and comparison studies of these tools can be found in [18,20,23]. Most importantly, there is no current tool that allows us to simulate large heterogeneous 5G networks.

### 2.1    Network Simulation Tools

We concentrate here on network simulation tools that have capabilities to simulate the latest 5G technologies, especially the ability to simulate heterogeneous networks such as those described in Fig. 1.

**NS3 - Network Simulator 3.** NS3 has been widely used by academia and industry [28] for building networks with different technologies such as WLAN, WiFi, LTE, 6LowPAN and physical layer properties including mobility and RF propagation. Recently, **OFSwitch13** was introduced into NS3 by Chaves et al. [9]. The NS3 **LENA** project [15,16] was designed to simulate 4G LTE and is not capable of modeling 5G New Radio. Although multiple technology stacks can coexist in the same network simulation source code (a C++ description of the simulation), some simulations require taking control of the global configuration states via **Config::SetDefault** and **GlobalValue::Bind** such as TCP SegmentSize, ChecksumEnabled, and ChannelType. Each simulation stack is designed and tested in very specific and narrow scenarios without interoperability consideration and intervention. For example, to simulate a heterogeneous network we would need to connect the simulated wired, WiFi and LTE networks to a common SDN-powered OFSwitch13 backhaul. We have found in our simulations that when enabling every configuration of the required networking stacks, the simulations terminated early due to incomplete configuration. If we turn off the configuration of either the LENA LTE or OFSwitch13 stack, the NS3 script is able to execute again. There is currently no published report of successful integration of LENA LTE with OFSwitch in NS3.

**Mininet-WiFi.** Mininet-WiFi is the most popular emulation tool for SDN-enabled WiFi networks [12,13]. Mininet-WiFi can emulate WLAN and WiFi networks but has no support for LTE and has an upper limit of 100 nodes supporting WiFi and 6LowPAN. As Mininet-WiFi itself does not provide LTE and other access technologies, to simulate a heterogeneous 5G network, we will need to connect Mininet-WiFi with other simulators. In this paper, we refer to Mininet-WiFi as Mininet.

**Omnet++.** Omnet++ with the INET plugin is the most versatile network simulation tool currently available to simulate modern network technologies [30,31]. To describe simulation scenarios, Omnet++ uses its own Domain Specific Language (DSL) called **Network Description** (NED). Plugins such as SimuLTE [32] are available for modelling LTE and LTE-Advanced networks. In terms of available SDN extensions, the OpenFlow 1.0 plugin was developed in [21] with performance analysis by Banjar et al. [8]. In 2015, the OpenFlow 1.3 update was introduced into Omnet++ [29] but no evaluation has been discussed for this update. Omnet++ lacks the richness of physical layer modelling provided by NS3 and furthermore, adding new models to Omnet++ is complex and time-consuming.

An overview of the aforementioned simulation tools' networking stacks are shown in Table 1.

**Table 1.** An overview of simulation tools' networking stacks

| Tool | Technology | | | | | |
|------|------|------|------|-------|-----|-------------------|
| | WAN | WiFi | LTE | 5G NR | SDN | External interface |
| NS3 | ✓ | ✓ | LENA✓ | ✗ | OFSwitch13 ✓ | TapDevice ✓ |
| Mininet | ✓ | ✓ | ✗ | ✗ | OpenvSwitch ✓ | (v)Ethernet ✓ |
| Omnet++ | ✓ | ✓ | SimuLTE ✓ | ✗ | OpenFlow 1.0 outdated ✗ | (v)Ethernet ✓ |
| OAI5G | ✗ | ✗ | ✓ | ✓ | ✗ | ✗ |

From Table 1, only NS3 is capable of simulating all required network technologies (except 5G NR), whereas Mininet cannot simulate LTE network technologies and Omnet++ does not support the de facto standard SDN protocol OpenFlow 1.3. As shown, there are no current tools that can simulate 5G heterogeneous networks with multiple access technologies and an SDN core. Our aim in this paper is to develop such a simulation tool.

## 2.2   Simulating Heterogeneous 5G Networks

There are two possible ways of building a heterogeneous 5G simulation tool. The first is extending one of the existing tools to incorporate the technologies that it lacks and the second is connecting multiple simulation tools with complementary technologies. The first option would be expensive with respect to both development time and maintenance time. For our proposed solution, we therefore choose the second option.

Connecting multiple simulated networks from different simulation packages, however, is not trivial. Despite numerous attempts, we did not succeed in producing a heterogeneous 5G simulations by simply linking NS3 with Omnet++ or Mininet-WiFi. We show in Fig. 2 the issues that were encountered when connecting networks from multiple tools. These include subnet differentiation, the lack of ARP proxy and responders, scalability and flexibility of the interplaying simulations. For example, if Simulator 1 has UEs connecting to Voice Server A which resides in a separate Omnet++ simulation, UEs cannot establish any connection to Server A as there are no ARP responders that help resolve Server A's MAC address. Similarly, if the Omnet++ simulation does not expose a common Ethernet interface sharing the same Ethernet data plane with Simulator 1, UEs from simulator 1 cannot reach Server A. Even if the two above mentioned problems are appropriately addressed, when Simulator 1 UEs trying to connect to NS3 Data Server B, due to different subnets in which Simulator 1's UEs and NS3 Data Server B belong to, they still cannot make connections without further network configuration changes.

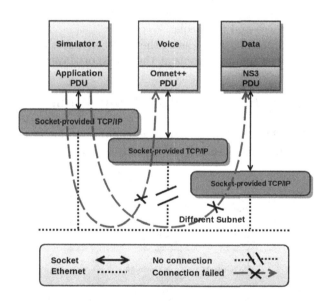

**Fig. 2.** Issues with connecting multiple simulated networks

## 2.3  Approaches to Connect Simulations and Networks

Network interoperability is a general issue that is not specific to simulation networks. To bridge multiple simulations in war games, the US Department of Defense (DoD) developed the **High Level Architecture** (HLA) and **Distributed Interactive Simulation** (DIS) framework [6]. In **DIS**, the application protocol is defined as binary formatted Protocol Data Units (PDUs) of state descriptions such as entity states, environmental processes, signal transmissions. The interconnected networks of simulations use traditional packet-based TCP/IP protocol stacks and only solve the interoperability at the application protocol level.

Several other approaches to inter-connect networks [7,22] use the RESTful API to express discrete and stateful communication between devices. They cannot be used to connect multiple simulations for 5G networks because simulations are connected at transport level whereas Restful APIs are at the session level.

The previously mentioned approaches solve interoperability issues at the application level and are not suitable for network simulations that work at the transport layer or below. Recently, Halba et al. [17] showed that one of the most efficient ways to connect incompatible networks is to use a transport level solution, exploiting the standard TCP/IP stack that is already implemented in most networks. They presented a solution for connecting multiple technologies in vehicle communications by converting CANbus payloads into IP-based packets before connecting to a SDN terminal for further transportation to the destination. By utilizing the SDN paradigm and packet-based conversion of legacy protocols, the automotive applications do not have to deal with tightly coupled vendor-specific interfaces and protocols.

We adopt the approach in [17] of using the latest advances in SDN to connect simulated networks from multiple tools at the transport layer.

## 3    SDN Adapter for Connecting Simulations

As explained in Sect. 2.2, using SDN to connect simulations at the transport layer is the most efficient method with respect to both time and cost. An overview of

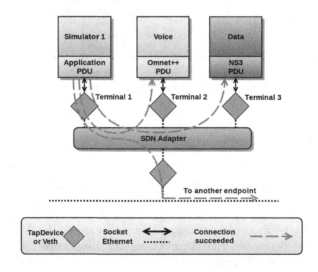

**Fig. 3.** SDN adapter integration

our SDN adapter solution is shown in Fig. 3. The issues identified in the previous section for connecting multiple simulation networks are resolved by using an SDN Adapter that intelligently forwards packets between simulated networks.

At the heart of our solution is a novel SDN adapter that acts as a bridge, allowing different simulation domains to communicate with each other.

### 3.1   Building Blocks

Our SDN adapter based solution consists of three key building blocks.

**The Wiring Block.** The various simulation modules bind to the interfaces at both ends of our SDN adapter to communicate with each other. The Open-Flow Controller will detect traffic and will perform appropriate stateful ARPs and SNAT/PNAT translation transparently and dynamically. For example, NS3 simulations for Wifi, SDN and LTE scenarios cannot be run as a single simulation, but can be separated into 3 isolated simulation processes and bridged together by our proposed SDN adapter. TapDevice works well with NS3 simulations but Mininet-WiFi and Omnet++ require *veth* devices for binding external interfaces as outlined in Fig. 4.

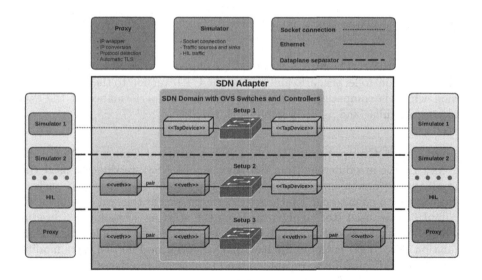

**Fig. 4.** Adapter architecture

**The Controlling Block.** OpenFlow controllers play a major role in interconnecting network domains. By providing ARP responders and NAT service, the controllers can actively manage the TCP/UDP states of ingress and egress traffic with OVS flows installation, provided all traffic is IP-based. Moreover, with the flexibility of SDN technology, the traffic can be easily routed and manipulated according to desired design specifications. The current implementation of OpenFlow controllers is in Ryu [3] with an ARP responder and a simple NAT application. A Ryu-version of the QoS controller mentioned in [9] is also implemented to support the performance evaluation with Mininet-WiFi.

**The Proxy Block.** SDN by nature is designed to work with IP-based traffic. Therefore, for legacy protocols or application protocols with flexible transport mechanism, an IP wrapper/conversion is needed to encapsulate the payload (e.g. PDUs) into TCP/UDP Ethernet frames before entering the SDN terminal [17]. The **Linkerd** project develops such a proxy for network statistics monitoring and reporting [2]. The proxy is also able to detect network protocol based on the payload header, as well as provide automatic TLS encryption between endpoints suitable for secure orchestration of large simulation scenarios across multiple subnets and public infrastructures. The incorporation of a proxy is however not required for the scenarios studied in this paper.

### 3.2   SDN Adapter for 5G Simulations

To simulate the desired scenario in Fig. 1, there are three essential components that must be built to support SDN, LTE/5G NR, and our SDN Adapter respectively, as demonstrated in Figs. 5 and 6.

**SDN Component.** The SDN component is inspired from [9] whereby we reused the NS3 QoS controller scenario and ported the C++ version to the Ryu Python version which is compatible with OpenvSwitch. The performance of the two versions are similar and agree in bandwidth results.

**Access Radio Component.** The LTE components of Omnet++/SimuLTE and NS3 LENA are different from one another. In NS3, we directly used the **lena-simple-epc.cc** example and modified the remote host in which packets are forwarded to an external TapDevice interface towards the real environment. In SimuLTE, we used **lteCoreExample** as the starting scenario then gradually added up to 8 eNodeBs, with 1 UE per eNodeB as the complete SimuLTE simulation. The router entity in the **lteCoreNetwork.ned** needed extra modification of the configuration to be able to bind to external interfaces, for example, the parameter *numExtInterfaces* must be set to 1. Additionally, a routing table must be changed to match the SDN Adapter veth IP/Subnet as the binding interface for the simulation.

**SDN Adapter Component.** We have three distinct setups for the SDN adapter with the main variation being its virtual peripheral type (Tap or Veth), and four different simulation combinations to reconstruct the scenario in Fig. 1.

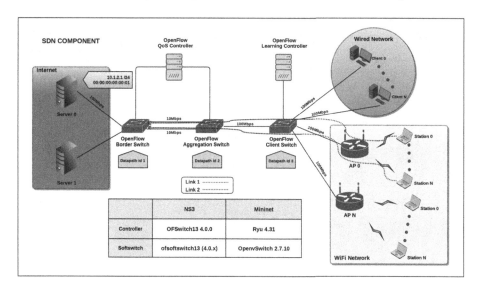

**Fig. 5.** SDN component

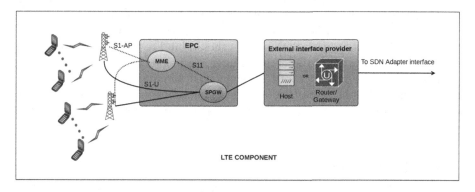

**Fig. 6.** LTE/5G NR component

## 3.3   Graphical User Interface for Setting up 5G Simulations

To facilitate easy set-up of 5G simulations with our SDN adapter, we have built a GUI that helps simplify the management of the simulation(s).

The SDN Adapter can be launched in most Linux distributions that support the creation of TUN/TAP devices, veth interfaces and the installation of OpenvSwitch. The process of creating the SDN Adapter is similar to Linux bridges. The SDN Adapter Designer GUI tool, shown in Fig. 7, allows end users to intuitively configure the adapter. This panel is used to design the layout and parameters for the SDN adapter such as IP and MAC addresses, interface type and name, and OpenvSwitch parameters. Once the design process is finished, the end user can start the creation process of the SDN adapter by running the

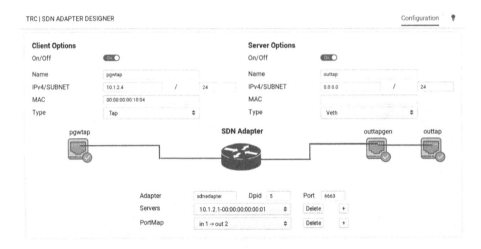

**Fig. 7.** SDN adapter designer configuration panel

auto-generated bash scripts displayed in the GUI as per Fig. 8. Then the user runs the Ryu controller with auto-generated code to control the SDN adapter.

At this stage, the user is able to start the simulations in arbitrary order. For example, the simulation with SDN servers should bind to the Server port of the SDN adapter by specifying the external interface name in the simulation code, then followed by the initiation of LTE simulation binding to the Client port of the SDN adapter in the same fashion. The whole process can be repeated if the user wants to add/remove ports to/from the SDN adapter for simulation binding modification.

## 4  Validation and Performance

We show in this section that our SDN adapter based solution can successfully connect multiple simulated networks to produce a 5G simulation with multiple network technologies. In order to simulate the scenario in Fig. 1, we can use the 4 combinations showed in Fig. 9 and those 4 scenarios are evaluated in this paper.

### 4.1  Measurement Settings

We replicate the methods used in [11] and treat the SDN adapter as a device-under-test (DUT) to measure the performance characteristics of the SDN adapter.

The VM is a VirtualBox image of Ubuntu 18.04.1 LTS with kernel 4.18.0-15-generic, 2 GiB of RAM and 1 CPU running at a constant rate of 3.5 GHz (Intel turbo boost disabled). The veths of the DUT are added into the VM as bridged adapters with driver **Paravirtualized Network** (virtio-net). The promiscuous

```
 0  #!/bin/bash
 1  # a tap device can be create by:
 2  sudo ip tuntap add name pgwtap mode tap
 3  # sudo ip tuntap add name outtap mode tap
 4  # ...
 5  # a veth pair can be create by:
 6  # sudo ip link add pgwtap type veth peer name pgwtapgen
 7  sudo ip link add outtap type veth peer name outtapgen
 8
 9  # OVS switch as SDN Adapter
10  sudo ovs-vsctl add-br sdnadapter
11  sudo ovs-vsctl set bridge sdnadapter protocols=OpenFlow13
12  sudo ovs-vsctl set bridge sdnadapter other-config:datapath-id=5
13  sudo ovs-vsctl set-controller sdnadapter "tcp:127.0.0.1:6663"
14  sudo ip link set sdnadapter promisc on
15  # Add port
16  sudo ovs-vsctl add-port sdnadapter pgwtap
17  # sudo ovs-vsctl add-port sdnadapter pgwtapgen
18  # sudo ovs-vsctl add-port sdnadapter outtap
19  sudo ovs-vsctl add-port sdnadapter outtapgen
20
21  # for example, if the we want the IP/HW MAC of pgwtap to be 10.1.2.4/24
22  # with mac address 00:00:00:00:10:04
23  sudo ip addr add 10.1.2.4/24 dev pgwtap
24  sudo ip link set pgwtap up address 00:00:00:00:10:04 promisc on
25  # sudo ip link set pgwtapgen up promisc on
26  # Similarly, for server port
27  sudo ip addr add 0.0.0.0/24 dev outtap
28  sudo ip link set outtap up promisc on
29  sudo ip link set outtapgen up promisc on
```

**Fig. 8.** Setup script autogen panel

mode must be turned on for both VM's vNIC and veth in order to pass packets freely between the two VMs.

Before the experiment, the Ryu controller needs to be configured with IP - MAC as:

- Client: **10.1.2.5/24 - 00:00:00:00:10:05**
- Server: **10.1.2.1/24 - 00:00:00:00:00:01**

Additionally, the Ethernet interfaces of the client VM and server VM must be configured with the same IP - MAC as shown above.

## 4.2   SDN Adapters Introduce Minimal Overheads

We show here that our SDN adapter provides an easy way to connect simulated networks without introducing overheads into the network. We cross compare our adapter based solution with a solution that uses a vanilla Linux bridge to connect trivial networks from multiple simulators. The setup is shown in Fig. 10a.

Ping is used to test latency as suggested by [10]. Using Iperf, we also measure the jitter performance (the difference in inter-arrival time of transmitting UDP packets).

The client successfully pings the server with performance shown in Fig. 10b. Using Iperf to measure the jitter level with a standard bandwidth of 10 Mbps and the results are shown in Fig. 10c.

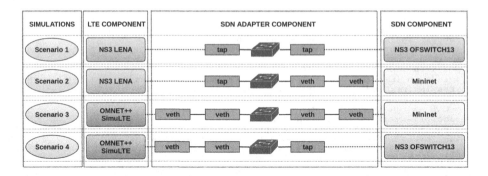

**Fig. 9.** Simulation combinations and their corresponding SDN adapter setups

The results show similar performance between our SDN adapter DUT and the vanilla Linux bridge DUT, indicating that our SDN adapters do not introduce any additional delay into the networks, which will in turn preserve simulation fidelity. Furthermore, our SDN adapter has a more stable ping RTT than the Linux bridge. On the other hand, the Linux bridge has less jitter than our SDN adapter by an approximate amount of $3\,\mu s$. This can be explained by the simplicity of the Linux bridge as the default data path behaviour is just forwarding from one port to the other.

Overall, the ping RTT and jitter overheads are limited to the micro-second scale which is very insignificant with respect to impacting simulation traffic.

### 4.3   SDN Adapter Integrated Scenarios and Evaluation

In this section, we show that the SDN Adapter can successfully interconnect different simulations with different technologies. To illustrate this capability, the scenarios will generally include an LTE component (8 & 100 UEs) and an SDN network core with two servers, 3 OVS switches and two OpenFlow Controllers as shown in Fig. 5. For SimuLTE, the LTE component will only incorporate 8 UEs and 8 eNodeBs. We will present a complete 5G network with 5G NR in a later section.

**NS3 Lena LTE and NS3 OFSwitch13.** Measurement results of the total throughput of both Server 1 and Server 2, with simulation time ranging from 1 to 100 s, are shown in Fig. 11a. The results illustrate that our SDN Adapter successfully enabled the two separate simulations to communicate.

The WAN clients are on the NS3 OFSwitch13 side which are responsible for keeping the simulation running, otherwise it will terminate prematurely due to empty event queues. In Fig. 11a, the value **ns3::LteEnbRrc::SrsPeriodicity** has been increased from the default value of 40 to 160 in order to support 100 connected UEs. The time scheduled for each UE has been reduced significantly due to the mismatch between simulation time and real clock time. This has caused the decline in LTE UDP throughput from 5 Mbps to 1 Mbps.

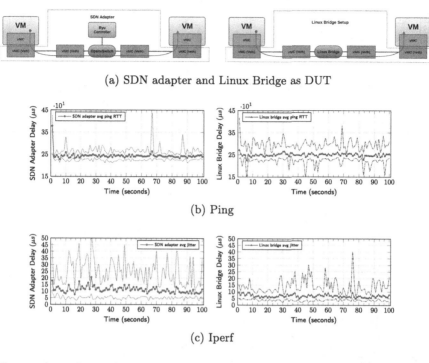

(a) SDN adapter and Linux Bridge as DUT

(b) Ping

(c) Iperf

**Fig. 10.** An end-to-end comparison of SDN adapter and Linux bridge performance

**NS3 Lena LTE and Mininet.** The performance results of this combination are shown in Fig. 11b. The results agree with those of Scenario 1 as the throughputs are very similar. Overall, the SDN Adapter has shown its ability to bridge NS3 LTE and Mininet SDN to form a complete SDN-enabled LTE network simulation. The simulation also highlights an issue with Mininet-WiFi that has not been reported before: for every 20 s, the measurement of the Mininet Iperf server throughput experiences unstable values. This issue appears more frequently with shorter report intervals, such as 1 s.

We perform further analyses of the Mininet-WiFi behaviors and summarize the findings below:

- The problem can be reproduced in up-to-date systems with several stable OpenvSwitch versions - we used OpenvSwitch 2.7 and 2.9 in Ubuntu 18.04.
- Network topologies are irrelevant to the cause of the problem as we have tested with different symmetric topologies ranging from 2 hosts - 1 switch, 4 hosts - 1 switch, and 4 hosts - 2 switches.
- OpenFlow Controllers have no contributing effects to this problem, as once the necessary flows get installed into the OpenvSwitch, it is not involved in packet processing logic.

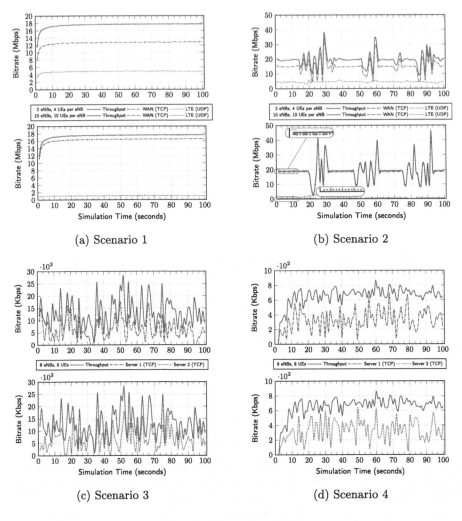

**Fig. 11.** Server bandwidth

- Increasing the connection bandwidth does reduce the variation e.g. 10 Mbps bandwidth will have larger bandwidth reading variations compared to 100 Mbps.

We believe this is a local issue of Mininet - a potential bug. From previous experiments, Mininet performance is on par or even better than NS3 OFSwitch13 with respect to some measures, but this measurement lag problem has introduced noise into our throughput results.

**Omnet++ SimuLTE and Mininet.** The performance results of this combination are shown in Fig. 11c. SimuLTE is inherently built on top of an INET extension of Omnet++ to provide LTE and LTE-Advance simulations. With the proven SDN stack in Mininet SDN, this scenario has the benefit of quickly introducing SDN into an Omnet++ simulation. The Omnet++ simulation needs to be run in **express mode**. Some other notable configurations are that the scheduler-class is real time (inet::cSocketRTSScheduler), the ppp queue frame capacity must be large enough (10000–100000 packets), and the external interface should be setup according to an **emulation** example.

**Omnet++ SimuLTE and NS3 OFSwitch13.** The results are shown in Fig. 11d. The two simulations can communicate with stable output results. Compared to Mininet SDN, however, the connection speed is slower and the throughput never increases more than 1 Mbps. Other measures such as packet drop and delay are insignificant as the reliable and bottleneck-free characteristics of the SDN adapter has been validated in Sect. 4.2.

### 4.4   Comparisons with Alternative Solutions

As there are no current solutions for connecting simulated networks, we are not so much comparing existing solutions but rather envisaging alternative approaches that could be taken by the end user. In particular we consider three alternative methods:

1. One or more routers (Cisco enterprises, small household routers)
2. Dedicated Linux hosts with manual configuration of local firewall (e.g. iptables)
3. Hand-crafted scripts/programs as middleware between simulators

As listed above, the physical routers provide NAT and ARP services for connecting simulators running on different hosts. Dedicated traditional computers with Linux installed can be used to replay routers' NAT and ARP services simply by using iptables with one NAT rule per subnet. Lastly, there is always a way for experienced users with highly-skilled computer literacy to manually create middleware-level software which replicates NAT and ARP services between simulators.

For comparison, our SDN Adapter can automatically resolve subnet incompatibility with only 2 flows per translation. With the embedded proactive ARP responders, it is able to activate "half connections" regardless of the starting order of simulations. A quick comparison can be also quantitatively estimated in Table 2. The $ sign is used to measure the scale of cost implementing the corresponding method.

In terms of cost, in both software and hardware required for connecting simulations, routers and dedicated Linux hosts are more expensive compared to hardware-less open source-based handcrafted scripts and our SDN adapter. Furthermore, enterprise-grade routers (such as Cisco) are more expensive than general computers running Linux. Most routers have embedded Web-based GUI to aid the setup and management which may result in shorter time cost. However,

**Table 2.** Comparison on alternative solutions to SDN Adapter

| Solution | Measure | | | | |
|---|---|---|---|---|---|
| | Cost | Time cost | Skill required | Scalability | Flexibility |
| Method #1 | $$$ | 1 h to days | Intermediate | Depends* | Low - Physical wiring |
| Method #2 | $$ | 1 h to weeks | Intermediate | Low | Low - Physical wiring |
| Method #3 | 0 | 1 week to months | Advanced | Depends* | High - Virtual wiring |
| SDN Adapter | 0 | Less than 1 h | Beginner | High | High - Virtual wiring |

*: Expensive and enterprise-grade routers have great scalability by design, while small household routers usually support less than 20 connected devices. Hand-crafted scripts may adjust to the level of scalability needed by the programmer, but usually have low scalability.

our SDN adapters also have an accompanying GUI called SDN Adapter Designer tool which significantly reduces the setup time to less than 1 h. To implement simulation connectivity using methods from 1 to 3, users need to have experience and at least an intermediate level of computer-based skills and literacy (programming, configuration, troubleshooting, etc). On the other hand, to use our SDN adapter, users are only required to have beginner skills in computer literacy with the ability to convert simulation specification into SDN adapter configuration and run the provided auto-generated codes. As already mentioned, for scalability and flexibility measures, users can freely spawn as many as SDN adapters they require, since our SDN adapter is hardware-independent and virtually controlled by software.

## 5    Complete 5G Simulations

We began our work with a requirement of simulating a heterogeneous 5G network. As the standalone 5G standard is not coming until mid 2020, we build our 5G network based on the non-standalone definition in [5] where 5G networks are comprised of multiple access technologies, 5G New Radio, LTE (e-gNodeB), virtualized and cloud-based solutions and a network slicing paradigm. Figure 12 shows the scenario of our complete 5G simulation implementation. In this figure, the simulated 5G network slice consists of sub-networks from different tools. OAI5G provides the flexible fronthaul, with simulated UEs (up to 256 UEs with expansion build) and one nFAPI gNodeB (Release 14–15). Note that OAI5G has recently integrated the open-nFAPI [1] introduced by Cisco and the specification can be found at the Small Cell Forum [4]. The NextEPC allows a fully featured EPC which is 100% virtualized. Moreover, the SDN adapter will bridge the NextEPC and Mininet-WiFi to incorporate an SDN backend into the slice. nFAPI enables Remote Radio Unit (e.g. a PNF entity) sharing between multiple vendors, allowing cost saving and increasing resource utilization.

## 5.1   Setting up the Simulations

**OpenAirInterface5G.** OAI5G is compiled to give **lte-softmodem.Rel14** and **lte-uesoftmodem.Rel14** which are the gNodeB and simulated UEs respectively. The standard configuration targeting nFAPI of the gNodeB and UEs has been listed below.

- Configuration: nFAPI-targeted configuration files
- Mobile Country Code - Mobile Network Code: 208 - 93 (Eurecom France)
- RF Band: 38
- MME address: s1utap's address or eth0 of the NextEPC VM
- UE profile: reused UE 0 (IMSI, SIM KEY, Operator Key)
- 5G NR link: through the oip[0-255] interfaces
- Note: **ue_ip.ko** kernel module must be loaded if NAS_UE_USE_TUN=0

The UE performance is tested using Iperf through the oip[n] interface (n = 0 to 255 in expansion mode, otherwise 0 to 15 in standard mode) exposing as the 5G NR link.

**NextEPC.** A VM running Ubuntu 18.04 is used to run NextEPC. The installation is through the Ubuntu package manager for NextEPC (HSS, SGW, PGW, MME, PCRF) and its Web GUI application which is used for adding new UE profile into the HSS's database. Following the Web UI and OAI5G UE configuration, we add the UE 0 profile into the HSS database. Without this step, the

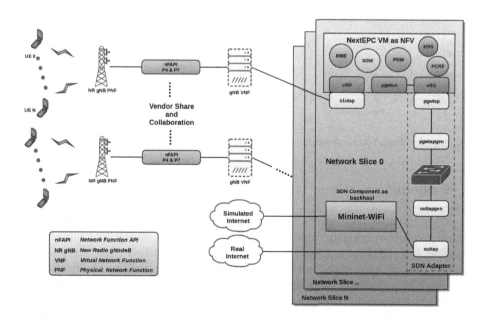

**Fig. 12.** A 5G network slice with OAI5G, NextEPC, SDN Adapter and Mininet-WiFi

simulated UE will be rejected during the attachment process. Lastly, the Nex-tEPC VM must be in forward mode (ip_forward is enabled). The NAT setup using iptables is not required since the SDN adapter already provides such functionality.

**Mininet-WiFi.** A Mininet-WiFi component is reused from the scenario shown in Fig. 5 as there is no additional modification required.

**SDN Adapter.** The SDN adapter setup is straightforward using our provided SDN Designer tool. The only additional step required is to switch the Client Port interface type to veth and then the end user can start running the bash scripts and the Ryu controller.

### 5.2 Performance

All of these components have been run on a commodity PC with 4 cores, 3.6 GHz CPU speed and 24 GB RAM. For this network, the UEs require 10.41 GB of RAM and the gNodeB requires 587.5MB. CPU loads are low, averaging 21% and 12.9% during Iperf and UDP tests respectively.

In Fig. 13 we present the throughput achieved by the UEs. As shown, most UEs have the stable throughput of 1 Mbps per UE in the simulation. For real UEs (e.g. mobile phones) with a software-defined radio-powered gNodeB, the throughput will be achieved with a higher rate than 1 Mbps.

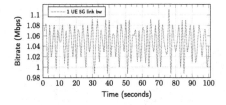 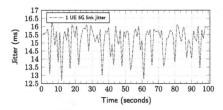

**Fig. 13.** Performance characteristics of a 5G network slice

## 6    Conclusion

5G non-standalone networks are currently being deployed worldwide, with standalone variants coming in 2020. Unfortunately, there is no current simulation tool that can simulate a complete 5G network with multiple radio access technologies and an SDN core. In this paper we have developed, for the first time, a 5G simulator that can be used to test all of these technologies simultaneously. Our solution connects multiple networks, provided by existing simulation tools, through a novel SDN adapter. We show that our adapter can connect different flavours of simulators and separate physical domains in a modern 5G network.

Our simulator can be run on commodity hardware and is easy to set up. We will make the simulator and all code used in this paper publicly available. Our SDN adapter also has potential beyond 5G simulations, for example, it can be used to connect Internet of Things (IoT) networks with different technologies. We intend to investigate these applications in future work.

# References

1. GitHub - cisco/open-nFAPI: An open source implementation of the Small Cell Forum's Network Functional API (nFAPI). https://github.com/cisco/open-nFAPI
2. Linkerd. https://linkerd.io
3. Ryu SDN Framework. https://osrg.github.io/ryu/
4. Small Cell Forum Releases. http://scf.io/en/documents/082_-_nFAPI_and_FAPI_specifications.php
5. What is 5G? https://www.cisco.com/c/en/us/solutions/what-is-5g.html
6. IEEE Standard for Distributed Interactive Simulation-Application Protocols. IEEE STD 1278.1-2012 (Revision of IEEE STD 1278.1-1995), pp. 1–747, December 2012. https://doi.org/10.1109/IEEESTD.2012.6387564
7. Alaya, M.B., Banouar, Y., Monteil, T., Chassot, C., Drira, K.: OM2M: extensible ETSI-compliant M2M service platform with self-configuration capability. Procedia Comput. Sci. **32**, 1079–1086 (2014). https://doi.org/10.1016/j.procs.2014.05.536. http://www.sciencedirect.com/science/article/pii/S1877050914007364
8. Banjar, A., Pupatwibul, P., Braun, R., Moulton, B.: Analysing the performance of the OpenFlow standard for software-defined networking using the OMNeT++; network simulator. In: 2014 Asia-Pacific Conference on Computer Aided System Engineering (APCASE), pp. 31–37, February 2014
9. Chaves, L.J., Garcia, I.C., Madeira, E.R.M.: OFSwitch13: enhancing Ns-3 with OpenFlow 1.3 support. In: Proceedings of the Workshop on Ns-3, WNS3 2016, pp. 33–40. ACM, New York (2016)
10. Emmerich, P., Gallenmüller, S., Raumer, D., Wohlfart, F., Carle, G.: MoonGen: a scriptable high-speed packet generator. In: Proceedings of the 2015 ACM Conference on Internet Measurement Conference - IMC 2015, pp. 275–287 (2015). https://doi.org/10.1145/2815675.2815692. arXiv:1410.3322
11. Emmerich, P., Raumer, D., Gallenmüller, S., Wohlfart, F., Carle, G.: Throughput and latency of virtual switching with open vSwitch: a quantitative analysis. J. Netw. Syst. Manag. **26**(2), 314–338 (2018). https://doi.org/10.1007/s10922-017-9417-0
12. Fontes, R.R., Afzal, S., Brito, S.H.B., Santos, M.A.S., Rothenberg, C.E.: Mininet-WiFi: emulating software-defined wireless networks. In: 2015 11th International Conference on Network and Service Management (CNSM), pp. 384–389, November 2015
13. Fontes, R.D.R., Rothenberg, C.E.: Mininet-WiFi: a platform for hybrid physical-virtual software-defined wireless networking research. In: Proceedings of the 2016 Conference on ACM SIGCOMM 2016 Conference, SIGCOMM 2016, pp. 607–608. ACM, New York (2016)
14. Gomez-Miguelez, I., Garcia-Saavedra, A., Sutton, P.D., Serrano, P., Cano, C., Leith, D.J.: srsLTE: an open-source platform for LTE evolution and experimentation. arXiv:1602.04629 [cs], February 2016

15. Gupta, R.: Real-Time LTE Testbed using ns-3 and LabVIEW for SDN in CROWD. Span (2015)
16. Gupta, R., et al.: LabVIEW based Platform for prototyping dense LTE Networks (2014)
17. Halba, K., Mahmoudi, C.: In-vehicle software defined networking: an enabler for data interoperability. In: Proceedings of the 2nd International Conference on Information System and Data Mining, Lakeland, FL, USA, ICISDM 2018, pp. 93–97. ACM, New York (2018). https://doi.org/10.1145/3206098.3206105
18. Imran, M., Said, A.M., Hasbullah, H.: A survey of simulators, emulators and testbeds for wireless sensor networks. In: 2010 International Symposium on Information Technology, vol. 2, pp. 897–902. IEEE, June 2010
19. Kaltenberger, F., Knopp, R., Nikaein, N., Nussbaum, D., Gauthier, L., Bonnet, C.: OpenAirInterface: open-source software radio solution for 5G. In: European Conference on Networks and Communications (EUCNC), Paris, France (2015)
20. Khana, A.U.R., Bilalb, S.M., Othmana, M.: A Performance Comparison of Network Simulators for Wireless Networks. arXiv:1307.4129 [cs], July 2013. arXiv:1307.4129
21. Klein, D., Jarschel, M.: An OpenFlow extension for the OMNeT++ INET framework. In: Proceedings of the 6th International ICST Conference on Simulation Tools and Techniques, SimuTools 2013, Cannes, France, pp. 322–329. ICST (Institute for Computer Sciences, Social-Informatics and Telecommunications Engineering), ICST, Brussels, Belgium (2013). http://dl.acm.org/citation.cfm?id=2512734.2512780
22. Kotstein, S., Decker, C.: Reinforcement learning for IoT interoperability. In: 2019 IEEE International Conference on Software Architecture Companion (ICSA-C), pp. 11–18, March 2019. https://doi.org/10.1109/ICSA-C.2019.00010
23. Kumar, A., Kaushik, S.K., Sharma, R., Raj, P.: Simulators for wireless networks: a comparative study. In: 2012 International Conference on Computing Sciences, pp. 338–342, September 2012
24. Lin, B.S.P., Lin, F.J., Tung, L.P.: The roles of 5G mobile broadband in the development of IoT, big data, cloud and SDN. Commun. Netw. **8**(1), 9–21 (2016). https://doi.org/10.4236/cn.2016.81002. http://www.scirp.org/Journal/Paperabs.aspx?paperid=63807
25. Maksymyuk, T., Dumych, S., Brych, M., Satria, D., Jo, M.: An IoT based monitoring framework for software defined 5G mobile networks. In: Proceedings of the 11th International Conference on Ubiquitous Information Management and Communication, IMCOM 2017, Beppu, Japan, pp. 105:1–105:4. ACM, New York (2017). https://doi.org/10.1145/3022227.3022331
26. Pham, T.: pthien92/sdn-adapter-designer-react-typescript, November 2019. https://github.com/pthien92/sdn-adapter-designer-react-typescript. Original-date: 2019-11-01T11:36:03Z
27. Pham, T.: pthien92/simulations-scripts, November 2019. https://github.com/pthien92/simulations-scripts. Original-date: 2019-11-01T12:15:51Z
28. Riley, G.F., Henderson, T.R.: The ns-3 network simulator. In: Wehrle, K., Güneş, M., Gross, J. (eds.) Modeling and Tools for Network Simulation, pp. 15–34. Springer, Heidelberg (2010). https://doi.org/10.1007/978-3-642-12331-3_2
29. Salih, M.A., Cosmas, J., Zhang, Y.: OpenFlow 1.3 extension for OMNeT++. In: 2015 IEEE International Conference on Computer and Information Technology; Ubiquitous Computing and Communications; Dependable, Autonomic and Secure Computing; Pervasive Intelligence and Computing, pp. 1632–1637, October 2015. https://doi.org/10.1109/CIT/IUCC/DASC/PICOM.2015.246

30. Varga, A.: INET Framework for the OMNeT++ Discrete Event Simulator (2012)
31. Varga, A., et al.: The OMNeT++ discrete event simulation system. In: Proceedings of the European Simulation Multiconference (ESM 2001), vol. 9, p. 65 (2001)
32. Virdis, A., Stea, G., Nardini, G.: Simulating LTE/LTE-advanced networks with SimuLTE. In: Obaidat, M.S., Ören, T., Kacprzyk, J., Filipe, J. (eds.) Simulation and Modeling Methodologies, Technologies and Applications. AISC, vol. 402, pp. 83–105. Springer, Cham (2015). https://doi.org/10.1007/978-3-319-26470-7_5

# Text Classification Based on Improved Information Gain Algorithm and Convolutional Neural Network

Mengjie Dong[✉], Huahu Xu, and Qingguo Xu

School of Computer Engineering and Science, Shanghai University,
Shanghai 200444, China
1151166299@qq.com, huahuxu@163.com, qgxu@t.shu.edu.cn

**Abstract.** Feature selection is an important step. It aims to filter some irrelevant features, improve the classifier speed and also reduce the interference during text classification process. Information gain (IG) feature selection algorithm is one of the most effective feature selection algorithms. But it is easy to filter out the characteristic words which have a low IG score but have a strong ability of text type identification. Because IG algorithm only considers the number of documents of feature items in each category. Aiming at this defect, we propose an improved information gain algorithm by introducing three parameters: intra-class word frequency, inter-class separation degree and intra-class dispersion degree. Then, the improved IG algorithm is used for feature selection, and important feature words with high IG value are selected according to the threshold value. Final, the important feature words in the text are expressed as two-dimensional word vectors and input into Convolutional Neural Network (CNN) to train and classify them. Therefore, a text classification model based on improved information gain and convolutional neural network is proposed and abbreviated as "I-CNN". Through experiments, we achieve good experimental results in THUCNews Chinese text classification corpus. Experimental results prove that the improved IG algorithm is better than the traditional feature selection algorithm.

**Keywords:** Text classification · Feature selection · Information gain · Convolutional Neural Network

## 1 Introduction

With the rapid development of Internet and cloud computing technology, the scale of data grows exponentially. There is a lot of important information hidden behind massive data. Facing the massive data, how to extract the key and effective information is the current research hotspot [1]. At present, most of the mainstream text representation is based on the VSM. But usually, the dimension of the vector space is very high, which can reach $10^5$ for Chinese corpus. And a text usually contains about $10^3$ words. It can be seen that the original vector space has the shortcomings of high dimensionality and sparseness, which will seriously affect the classification accuracy of common classifiers. Feature selection can solve the high dimensionality of text

© ICST Institute for Computer Sciences, Social Informatics and Telecommunications Engineering 2020
Published by Springer Nature Switzerland AG 2020. All Rights Reserved
H. Gao et al. (Eds.): TridentCom 2019, LNICST 309, pp. 184–198, 2020.
https://doi.org/10.1007/978-3-030-43215-7_13

representation and select a group of features from the feature set. Meanwhile, it can best express the meaning of the text without losing important information items.

Common feature selection algorithms include Document Frequency (DF), Information Gain (IG), Chi-square Test (CHI) and Mutual Information (MI). However, these algorithms perform in Chinese text not as well as in English text classification, because Chinese text has a higher feature space dimension and word correlation compared with English text. Research shows that theoretical information gain is the best feature selection method [2]. However, owing to the shortage of considering word frequency information of documents in class, the classification effect is not ideal. Literature [3] proposed that characteristics of different categories of data sets should be selected first. Then, different categories characteristics would be optimized and merged. Final, through the appearance of merged features, IG weights should be introduced. Literature [4] uses information entropy and information gain rate respectively as the heuristic information, and proposes an attribute reduction algorithm based on ACO. But it is easy for both to add redundant attributes to the reduced set as selected attributes. Ming [5] introduced the equalization ratio and intra-class word frequency position parameters. His algorithm solved the weakening classification and selection defect of local features problems caused by the traditional IG algorithm with ignoring word frequency distribution.

With the development of deep learning, Convolutional Neural Networks (CNN) have achieved great success in the field of image recognition. Kim [6] proposed that applying CNN to the field of text classification not only improves the classification efficiency but also makes the classification effect better than the traditional classification model. The greatest feature of CNN is that it can automatically extract features and share weights, while the traditional machine learning model with huge parameters needs to manually extract features. Using CNN as the classification model will greatly reduce the training time and improve the classification effect.

Based on the study of traditional IG algorithm and existing improved algorithm, a new improved IG algorithm is proposed in this paper. First, the improved IG algorithm should take into account the word frequency information to select words with high IG value and frequency. These words will be used as the important feature words in the classification. Second, representative feature words should be concentrated in a certain category. For example, "machine learning", "artificial intelligence" and other words that clearly represent IT texts should be concentrated in the IT category instead of sports, entertainment or other categories. This is called "inter-class separation degree". Furthermore, representative feature words such as "machine learning" should be evenly distributed in the IT class instead of only appearing in a few documents. This is called "intra-class dispersion degree". From here we see that, the representative feature words should have a larger degree of separation between classes and a smaller degree of dispersion within classes. Therefore, this paper introduces three parameters: word frequency information of feature items, inter-class separation degree and intra-class dispersion degree. After the feature extraction of the improved IG algorithm, the text is represented as a two-dimensional matrix which is similar to pictures and input into CNN for training. This model (I-CNN for short) can better extract important feature items and improve the classification effect.

The rest of this article is arranged as follows. In Sect. 2, we will describe the information gain algorithm and CNN classification model briefly. Section 3 proposes the improved information gain algorithm. Section 4 introduces the training steps of the proposed model. Section 5 is the experiment and result analysis. Final, there is a summary in Sect. 6.

## 2    Related Work

### 2.1    Information Gain Algorithm

Information gain [7] refers to the difference of information entropy, that is, the difference of information entropy whether each feature item appears in the text or not. The larger the information gain, the more important the feature item is in the text. IG algorithm is shown in formula (1):

$$
IG(t) = H(c) - H(c|t) = -\sum_{j=1}^{m} p(c_j) \times \log p(c_j) + p(t) \sum_{j=1}^{m} p(c_j|t) \log p(c_j|t)
$$
$$
+ p(\bar{t}) \sum_{j=1}^{m} p(c_j|\bar{t}) \log p(c_j|\bar{t})
$$

(1)

Where $c_j$ means the category attribute, $p(c_j)$ is the probability of the $i$th class value, $p(t)$ is the probability that feature $t$ occurs, and $p(\bar{t})$ is the probability that feature $t$ does not occur, $p(c_j|t)$ is the conditional probability that the class belongs to $c_j$ when the feature $t$ is included, while $p(c_j|\bar{t})$ is the conditional probability that the class belongs to $c_j$ when the feature $t$ is not included. $m$ represents the number of categories.

### 2.2    Convolutional Neural Network

Convolutional Neural Network (CNN) is a feedforward neural network composed of various combinations of convolutional layer, pooling layer (also known as the sub-sampling layer) and full connection layer. The spatial local correlation can be utilized by implementing a local connection mode between neurons in adjacent layers. At present, CNN has been widely used in image understanding, computer vision, language recognition, natural language processing and other fields [8]. Generally, CNN consists of one or more pairs of convolution layers and pooling layers and ends up with a completely connected neural network. The typical convolutional neural network structure [9] is shown in Fig. 1.

As we can see from Fig. 1, each neuron in the convolution layer is locally connected to the input layer. Convolution operation is the weighted sum of the convolution kernel parameters and the corresponding local input, then plus the offset value. The value will input to the activation function, and the output of the activation function is the value of the node in the next layer. This process is equivalent to the convolution process, hence the name of CNN [10]. The size and number of convolution kernels need to be customized. Each element on the convolution kernel is corresponded to a weight coefficient $w$ and a bias vector.

The pooling layer carries out a subsampling operation on the output feature graph of the convolution layer. It can compress the number of data and parameters, reduce overfitting and improve the fault tolerance and training speed of the model. Common pooling methods include Max Pooling and Average Pooling [11]. Max Pooling is taking the maximum value point in the local acceptance domain. Average Pooling is calculating the mean value of all values in the local acceptance field.

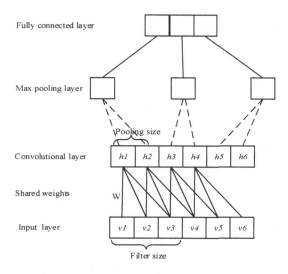

**Fig. 1.** Structure diagram of convolutional neural network.

The full connection layer can integrate the local information in the convolution layer or pooling layer. Then connecting all the local features and sending them to the classifier for classification [8].

CNN adopts local connection and weight sharing technology, which can not only extract feature information better, but also reduce network parameters and facilitate model training.

## 3 Improved Information Gain Algorithm

### 3.1 Disadvantage of IG

The IG value calculated by traditional algorithm only considers the document frequency of feature words and ignores the importance of word frequency information to classification. Therefore, it is easy to filter out the words with low IG value but high occurrence frequency and strong text recognition ability. To explain this, we assume that there are two feature words, $w_1$, $w_2$, and two document categories, $c_1$ and $c_2$. The document and frequency of feature words are shown in Table 1.

The feature words $w_1$ and $w_2$ in the table appear in the three documents $D_1$, $D_2$ and $D_5$. Calculated according to formula (1), $p(w_1) = p(w_2) = 3/8$, $p(\overline{w_1}) = p(\overline{w_2}) = 5/8$. The conditional entropy is $p(c_1|w_1) = p(c_1|w_2) = 2/3$, $p(c_1|\overline{w_1}) = p(c_1|\overline{w_2}) = 2/5$, $p(c_2|w_1) = p(c_2|w_2) = 1/3$, $p(c_2|\overline{w_1}) = p(c_2|\overline{w_2}) = 3/5$. The IG values calculated by formula (1) are the same, but the occurrence frequency of $w_1$ in the same document is significantly higher than that of $w_2$, which is more representative and IG values should be larger. The calculated results are inconsistent with logic. This may lead to the loss of important feature words in the text and the selection of words with lower frequency as feature words, resulting in worse classification effect.

**Table 1.** The distribution of feature words $w_1$ and $w_2$.

| Feature words | $c_1$ | | | | $c_2$ | | | |
|---|---|---|---|---|---|---|---|---|
| | $D_1$ | $D_2$ | $D_3$ | $D_4$ | $D_5$ | $D_6$ | $D_7$ | $D_8$ |
| $w_1$ | 12 | 10 | 0 | 0 | 5 | 0 | 0 | 0 |
| $w_2$ | 3 | 2 | 0 | 0 | 1 | 0 | 0 | 0 |

### 3.2  Improved IG by Three Parameters

**Intra-class Word Frequency.** The higher the occurrence frequency of feature items in a certain category y, the stronger the classification ability and the greater the weight should be. Set the feature set $F = \{w_1, w_2, w_3, ...., w_m\}$. There are $d_{ik}(1 \le k \le N_i)$ texts in class $c_i(1 \le i \le n)$ in the training set, $N_i$ is the total number of texts in class $c_i$, and the occurrence frequency of feature $w_j(1 \le j \le m)$ in text $d_{ik}$ in class $c_i$ is $tf_{ik}(w_j)$. Formula (2) uses data "min-max" standardization to linearly change the original data, so that the result value is mapped to between [0-1], and then there are weight parameters:

$$\alpha_{ij} = \sum_{i=1}^{N_i} \frac{tf_{ik}(w_j) - \min_{1 \le l \le m}(tf_{ik}(w_l))}{\max_{1 \le l \le m}(tf_{ik}(w_l)) - \min_{1 \le l \le m}(tf_{ik}(w_l))} \tag{2}$$

Considering the difference of the number of texts in different categories, formula (2) is normalized by "z-score" method.

$$\alpha = \frac{\alpha_{ij}}{\sqrt{\sum_{j=1}^{m} \alpha_{ij}^2}} \tag{3}$$

Formula (3) reflects that the larger the word frequency is within the category, the larger the weight a corresponding to the feature item is, the stronger the classification ability is.

**Inter-class Separation Degree and Intra-class Dispersion Degree.** If most of the feature words appear in a certain category and less in other categories, it means that the feature words can be well identified in this category. The separation degree of feature words is calculated as shown in formula (4):

$$CO(w) = \frac{\sqrt{\frac{1}{n}\sum_{i=1}^{n}(X_i(w) - \overline{X(w)})^2}}{\overline{X(w)}} \tag{4}$$

Where n represents the number of classes, $\overline{X_i(w)}$ represents the average number of features w appearing in all classes, and $X_i(w)$ represents the number of features w appearing in class $c_i$. From the above equation, it can be seen that the higher the value of the degree of separation between classes, the better the classification effect.

If a feature word appears in most articles of a certain category, it will be more representative of the class. The dispersion of characteristic words is calculated as shown in formula (5):

$$CI(w, c_i) = \frac{\sqrt{\frac{1}{m}\sum_{j=1}^{m}(X_{ij}(w) - \overline{X_i(w)})^2}}{\overline{X_i(w)}} \tag{5}$$

Where, m represents the number of documents in class $c_i$, $\overline{X_i(w)}$ represents the average of the occurrence of feature word w in each document in class $c_i$, and $X_{ij}(w)$ represents the occurrence of feature word w in the jth document in class $c_i$. As can be seen from the above equation, the smaller the value of dispersion within the class, the better the classification effect.

To sum up, it can be seen from the above two equations that the greater the degree of separation between classes and the smaller the degree of dispersion within classes, the better the classification effect is. Therefore, the degree of distinction of class $c_i$ by the feature word w can be defined as shown in formula (6):

$$\beta(w, c_i) = \frac{CO(w)}{CI(w, c_i)} \tag{6}$$

### 3.3 Improved IG Algorithm

Through the analysis of the first two sections, we introduce word frequency parameter $\alpha$ and distribution factor $\beta$. Not only the word frequency of feature words, but also the influence of feature word distribution on classification are considered. A new formula for calculating the information gain value is obtained, as shown in formula (7). The higher the word frequency, the higher $\alpha$. The larger the degree of separation between classes and the smaller the degree of dispersion within classes, the larger $\beta$ will be. For such words, the larger the IG value calculated by formula (7) is.

$$
\begin{aligned}
IG_{\text{new}}(t) = &- \sum_{j=1}^{m} p(c_j) \times \log p(c_j) + (p(t) \sum_{j=1}^{m} p(c_j|t) \log p(c_j|t) \\
&+ p(\bar{t}) \sum_{j=1}^{m} p(c_j|\bar{t}) \log p(c_j|\bar{t})) \times \alpha \times \beta
\end{aligned}
\tag{7}
$$

## 4  I-CNN Model Training

This section will explain the model training procedures proposed in this paper step by step. The text classification process is mainly divided into four steps: text preprocessing, feature extraction, text representation and classifier classification.

In the first step, "jieba" word segmentation tool is used in this experiment to segment the text. After word segmentation, use the stop word list to remove noise and filter out numbers, symbols, or other nonsense words from the text.

In the second step, feature extraction will use the improved IG algorithm proposed in this paper. It will set a threshold to remove the feature words with too high or too low information gain value.

The third step is that, after word segmentation and feature extraction, the text is a set of words or phrases. In order to represent the text and combine it into a two-dimensional matrix which is similar to image, word vectorization is required. "Word2vec" is an open source Google word vector generator. It maps words into low-dimensional spaces where semantically similar words are similar by modeling the context and semantic relations of words. Word2vec [12] has two models: CBOW and Skip-gram. In this paper, Skip-gram model is used to train word vectors, and the probability of context words is predicted by the central word. This model trains each word into a distributed word vector, such as: $[w_{i1}, w_{i2}, w_{i3}, \ldots, w_{ik}]$, $i$ represents the $i$th word in the text, and $k$ refers to the dimension of word vector. Thus, a text can be represented as a two-dimensional matrix $A_{lk}$, such as: $\begin{pmatrix} w_{11} & \cdots & w_{1k} \\ \vdots & \ddots & \vdots \\ w_{l1} & \cdots & w_{lk} \end{pmatrix}$. $l$ stands for $l$ words in a text. As shown in Fig. 2, assuming a short essay this after word segmentation and feature selection, extract the eight feature words {Sun, Yang, Asian, Games, winner, Chinese, gold, medal}. Each word will be trained as a 5 - dimensional word vector. The final text can be expressed as $8 \times 5$ two-dimensional matrix. After word vector processing, each short text can be expressed as a two-dimensional matrix similar to image, which can be used as the input layer of convolutional neural network.

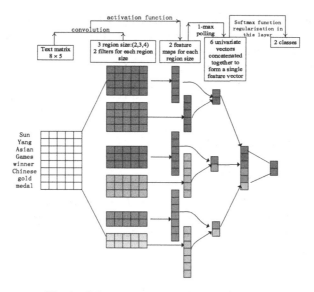

**Fig. 2.** Schematic diagram of model training.

The fourth step is to use convolutional neural network as classifier. The convolution kernel in the convolution layer will automatically extract more valuable features again. As shown in Fig. 2, convolution kernel with size (2, 3, 4) is set to convolve two-dimensional text matrix with two filters each. After convolution, 2 feature maps for each size. Among, ReLu [13] activation function is introduced for nonlinear processing to obtain convolution results, as shown in formula (8):

$$p = \text{Re}LU(A_{lk} \cdot w + b) \tag{8}$$

Where, $w$ is the parameter weight and $b$ is the bias. During the training, the values of $w$ and $b$ are constantly adjusted until the model converges. In the experiment, the feature graph after convolution is still very large and easy to over-fitting. Therefore, a pooling function needs to be introduced. In this experiment, the maximum pooling method is adopted to sample the Feature Map obtained by the convolution layer, as shown in formula (9):

$$p' = \max\{p\} \tag{9}$$

$p'$ is the Feature vector after pooling.

In Fig. 2, the pooled feature vectors need to enter the full connection layer to connect all the learned deep features. After several layers of full connection layers, the last layer is the softmax output layer, and you will get the probability that the text belongs to a class.

The above is the specific classification training steps in this paper. Feature selection method adopts the improved IG algorithm proposed in this paper to eliminate irrelevant and redundant features. So as to reduce the number of features and training or running time, then improve model accuracy. The classifier selects the CNN model. Since the convolution layer and input are locally connected and the weights are Shared [14], the number of parameters that CNN needs to learn is greatly reduced. Furthermore, the parameters are set manually and randomly. The CNN model can train the parameters by itself, which greatly improves the training speed. Therefore, the classification accuracy and training time of the I-CNN model are proposed in this paper.

## 5    Experiments and Results

### 5.1    Experiment Environment

In this experiment, a personal laptop is used to verify and test the I-CNN model, which combines the improved information gain feature selection algorithm and the text classification of convolutional neural network. Details of other experimental equipment are shown in Table 2:

**Table 2.** Details of experimental equipment

| | |
|---|---|
| The operating system | Windows 10 (64bit) |
| Central processing unit | Xeon E5-2620 v4 |
| Memory | 64G |
| The framework | TensorFlow |
| Integrated development environment | PyCharm |

### 5.2    Experiment Preparing and Parameter Settings

According to the procedure proposed in the previous Sect. 3, some super parameters should be set before the experiment. According to practical experience, the word vector dimension is set to 300. The number and size of convolution kernel, the number of convolution layer and pooling layer all affect the final classification results. Therefore, in this experiment, in order to obtain more local feature information of text through different convolution kernels, the hyperparameters were set as: 128 convolution kernels of 3, 4 and 5 respectively, and the learning rate of 0.01 [15]. The convolution layer and the pooling layer are placed alternately in two groups and classified through a layer of full connection layer.

The optimization objective of the experiment is to minimize the loss function. We will adopt the "cross entropy loss function" commonly used in the classification model of CNN. With the optimization target, it is necessary to update the weight parameters iteratively and train the accuracy of the model. Therefore, the optimization algorithm adopts the familiar "Stochastic Gradient Descent" (SGD) to conduct parameter training in the CNN classification process.

Meanwhile, in order to prevent over-fitting during training, the regularization method of "dropout" [16] was introduced into the full connection layer. The dropout's keep-prob ratio was set to 0.5.

This paper will make three experimental. In order to compare the effect of the improved IG algorithm on the selection of important feature items and the text classification effect of the I-CNN model. In experiment 1, SVM and KNN classical text classification model are used to verify the effects of different feature selection methods. In experiment 2, the traditional information gain algorithm is compared with the improved information gain algorithm, and CNN is used as the classification model for training. In experiment 3, the improved IG+SVM text classification model and classical CNN classification model are compared with the I-CNN model proposed in this paper.

### 5.3    Experiment and Result Analysis

The data set of this experiment adopts THUCNews Chinese short text data set provided by Tsinghua University. THUCNews is generated by filtering the historical data of Sina news RSS subscription channel from 2005 to 2011, including 740,000 news documents (2.19 GB), all of in utf-8 plain text format. This paper randomly selected five text categories: finance, education, current politics, entertainment and sports. 1000 documents for each category. The text set of each category is divided into training set, testing set and distributed randomly in the form of training set: test set rate equals 2:1. The training set is mainly used to train a classification model which need to be verified the performance by the test set.

The common evaluation indexes of text classification model performance include precision rate P, recall rate R and F1 value. P is the proportion of the number of documents properly classified to the test data set documents. R is the proportion of the number of documents properly classified to the actual number of properly classified documents. F1 value is the harmonic average of precision rate and recall rate. It can comprehensively evaluate the prediction accuracy and recall sample situation of the classification model on each type of text set. This paper will adopt these three indexes to evaluate the experimental results. The values of F1 are calculated as shown in formula (10):

$$F1 = \frac{2 \times P \times R}{P + R} \tag{10}$$

**Experiment 1.** Traditional feature selection methods such as IG, CHI and MI perform well in English text, but DF algorithm performs better in Chinese text. Therefore, Figs. 3 and 4 of this experiment respectively show the F1 mean curves of three feature selection methods on SVM and KNN classifier. The upper limit of feature number is set as 30000.

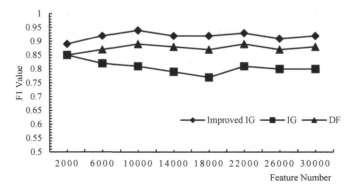

**Fig. 3.** Comparison of feature selection methods on SVM.

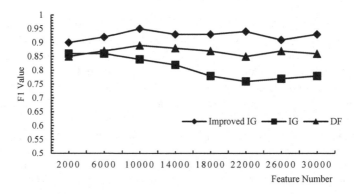

**Fig. 4.** Comparative performance of feature selection methods on KNN.

It can be seen from the figure that the improved IG algorithm not only performs better but also stably. F1 value in both classifiers is higher than other feature selection algorithms. However, the traditional IG algorithm is theoretically proved to be the best feature selection method, but its performance is the worst. The biggest reason is the neglect of word frequency information. Words that appear in many documents may not be representative words, but may be noise words.

Looking at the two figures, it can be found that the performance of the classifier reaches a maximum when the dimension of feature space is valued in the range of 5000 to 10000. It indicates that in the process of feature extraction, the dimension of feature space can be compressed to the original 10%–20%. And the remaining unnecessary words can be removed. This not only greatly reduces the dimension of feature space and memory occupation, but also improves the efficiency of classifier training without causing errors in classification results.

**Experiment 2.** In experiment 2, the traditional IG algorithm is compared with the improved IG algorithm. CNN is used as the classification model for training. It verifies whether the improved IG algorithm can effectively select representative words and improve the classification effect. The experimental test set selects 200 articles of finance, education, current politics, entertainment and sports respectively from the "THUC-News" data set. Use recall rate R and precision rate P as evaluation indexes. Correct classification number refers to the number of classified texts that really belong to this class. Actual classification number refers to the number of 1000 texts classified into this class after I-CNN model classification. According to the criteria of experiment 1, in the process of feature extraction, about 80–90% of unimportant feature words can be discarded. Some representative words are left as important features of the classification.

**Table 3.** Test results of traditional IG algorithms in test sets (unit: paper)

| Category | Test data set | Traditional IG algorithm | | | |
| --- | --- | --- | --- | --- | --- |
| | | Correct classification number | Actual classification number | P (%) | R (%) |
| Finance | 200 | 178 | 199 | 89.00 | 89.45 |
| Education | 200 | 164 | 181 | 82.00 | 90.61 |
| Current politics | 200 | 171 | 246 | 77.50 | 69.51 |
| Entertainment | 200 | 147 | 162 | 85.50 | 90.74 |
| Sports | 200 | 191 | 212 | 95.5 | 90.09 |
| Total | 1000 | 851 | 1000 | 85.9 | 86.08 |

**Table 4.** Test results of improved IG algorithms in test sets

| Category | Test data set | Improved IG algorithm | | | |
| --- | --- | --- | --- | --- | --- |
| | | Correct classification number | Actual classification number | P (%) | R (%) |
| Finance | 200 | 176 | 207 | 88.00 | 85.02 |
| Education | 200 | 187 | 211 | 93.50 | 88.63 |
| Current politics | 200 | 159 | 185 | 79.50 | 85.95 |
| Entertainment | 200 | 172 | 186 | 86.00 | 92.47 |
| Sports | 200 | 189 | 211 | 94.50 | 89.57 |
| Total | 1000 | 883 | 1000 | 88.30 | 88.33 |

As can be seen from Tables 3 and 4, in the current political data set, the actual classification number of the traditional IG algorithm is 246, while the correct classification number is only 171, resulting in the accuracy rate of only 77.5%. However, the actual and correct classification number of the improved IG algorithm are 159 and 185 respectively, and the accuracy rate is 79.5%. Also, the correct classification number, R and P of the improved IG algorithm in financial and sports categories have been decreased. But the average recall rate and average precision rate are higher than traditional algorithms. According to the calculation, the average recall rate of the improved IG algorithm increased by 2.25%. The average precision rate increased by

2.4%. The number of correctly classified samples increased by 32. Therefore, it can be seen that the improved IG algorithm has not only stable performance but also better feature selection effect.

**Experiment 3.** In experiment 3, an improved IG+SVM text classification model and a classic CNN classification model are compared with the I-CNN model. The F1 value of experimental results is shown in Fig. 5.

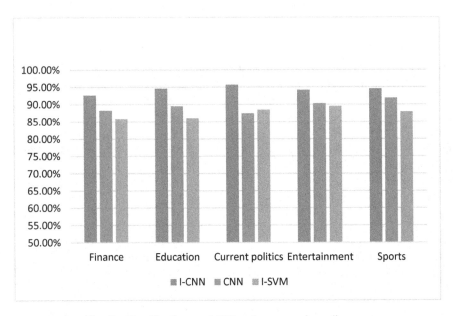

**Fig. 5.** Classification model F1 value comparison diagram.

It can be seen from the comparison experiment between CNN and I-CNN models, the CNN model lacks the feature extraction stage of improved IG algorithm. Although CNN can automatically extract features, the F1 value of CNN model is lower than that of I-CNN model. The F1 value of the I-CNN model in the current politics category reaches the highest value of 95.72%. While the CNN model in sports category only reaches 91.87%. And the classification effect is far less than that of the I-CNN model. Therefore, it can be seen that feature extraction is an indispensable part of the text classification process. Without feature extraction, there are a large number of noisy words and stop words in the text, which interfere with the training effect of the classifier.

According to the comparison experiment between I-CNN and I-SVM, when both have IG feature selection processing, the F1 value of CNN model is better than SVM model. The F1 value of the I-CNN model in the current politics category reaches the highest point of 95.72%. The F1 value of the I-SVM model in the entertainment category reaches only 89.52%. Moreover, the features of CNN local connection and weight sharing greatly reduce the number of parameters, make the model simpler and train faster. However, the traditional text classification model requires manual feature extraction. And weight is not shared, resulting in very large parameters. In contrast, the CNN model is fast in training. With the least parameters, the best classification effect can be trained, which is the reason why CNN is adopted as the classification model in this paper.

Therefore, this paper adopts CNN as classifier and combines it with the improved IG algorithm. According to the experimental results, the classification effect of the model is better than that of the traditional classification model.

## 6 Conclusion and Future Work

As a key technology of text classification, feature selection has a direct impact on the classification performance. In view of the shortcomings of traditional IG algorithm, this paper introduces the word frequency, inter-class separation degree and intra-class dispersion degree parameters. Then proposes a new improved IG algorithm. This algorithm solves the problem that the traditional IG algorithm neglects the word frequency distribution to weaken the classification. And added the parameter about the distribution of feature words. The classification accuracy has been improved. In this paper, we use CNN as the model. Because CNN can automatically identify local features, which makes up for IG algorithm's consideration of feature term relation. Combined with the features of weights sharing and local connection of convolutional neural network, the model training and classification are faster. The experimental results show that the I-CNN model is better to the traditional classification model.

Although the I-CNN model proposed in this paper has a better effect on text classification than the previous existing models, the classification effect is not accurate and fast enough. It is expected that the text classification model can well identify the categories of huge amount of text data on the network. And classify them accurately and quickly. So as to make the network information more organized and classified. Deep learning model is the general trend in the field of text classification. But the end-to-end thought of deep learning model makes the deeper things inside the model still need to be explored. Therefore, text classification is still a worthy research direction.

## References

1. Agnihotri, D., Verma, K., Tripathi, P.: Pattern and cluster mining on text data. In: 2014 Fourth International Conference on Communication Systems and Network Technologies, pp. 428–432. IEEE (2014)
2. Yang, Y., Pedersen, J.O.: A comparative study on feature selection in text categorization. In: ICML, vol. 97, pp. 35, 412–420 (1997)
3. Xu, J., Jiang, H.: An improved information gain feature selection algorithm for SVM text classifier. In: 2015 International Conference on Cyber-Enabled Distributed Computing and Knowledge Discovery, pp. 273–276. IEEE (2015)
4. Chen, Y., Chen, Y.: Attribute reduction algorithm based on information entropy and ant colony optimization. J. Chin. Comput. Syst. 36(3), 586–590 (2015)

5. Ming, H.: A text classification method based on maximum entropy model based on improved information gain feature selection. J. Southwest Normal Univ. (Nat. Sci. Ed.) **44**(03), 119–124 (2019)

6. Kim, Y.: Convolutional neural networks for sentence classification. arXiv preprint arXiv: 1408.5882 (2014)

7. Quinlan, J.R.: Induction of decision trees. Mach. Learn. **1**(1), 81–106 (1986)

8. Chang, L., Deng, X.M., Zhou, M.Q., et al.: Convolution neural network in image understanding. Acta Automatica Sinica **42**(9), 1300–1312 (2016)

9. Sainath, T.N., Mohamed, A., Kingsbury, B., et al.: Deep convolutional neural networks for LVCSR. In: 2013 IEEE International Conference on Acoustics, Speech and Signal Processing, pp. 8614–8618. IEEE (2013)

10. Lecun, Y., Bottou, L., Bengio, Y., et al.: Gradient-based learning applied to document recognition. Proc. IEEE **86**(11), 2278–2324 (1998)

11. Zeiler, M.D., Fergus, R.: Stochastic pooling for regularization of deep convolutional neural networks. arXiv preprint arXiv:1301.3557 (2013)

12. Mikolov, T., Sutskever, I., Chen, K., et al.: Distributed representations of words and phrases and their compositionality. In: Advances in Neural Information Processing Systems, pp. 3111–3119 (2013)

13. O'Shea, K., Nash, R.: An introduction to convolutional neural networks. arXiv preprint arXiv:1511.08458 (2015)

14. LeCun, Y., Bengio, Y., Hinton, G.: Deep learning. Nature **521**(7553), 436 (2015)

15. Kingma, D.P., Ba, J.: Adam: a method for stochastic optimization. arXiv preprint arXiv: 1412.6980 (2014)

16. Hinton, G.E., Srivastava, N., Krizhevsky, A., et al.: Improving neural networks by preventing co-adaptation of feature detectors. arXiv preprint arXiv:1207.0580 (2012)

# Correlation Study of Emotional Brain Areas Induced by Video

Huiping Jiang$^{(\boxtimes)}$ ⓘ, Zequn Wang ⓘ, XinKai Gui ⓘ,
and GuoSheng Yang ⓘ

Brain Cognitive Computing Lab, School of Information Engineering,
Minzu University of China, Beijing 100081, China
{jianghp,Yangguosheng}@muc.edu.cn

**Abstract.** Emotions are physiological phenomena caused by complex cognitive activities. With the in-depth study of artificial intelligence and brain mechanism of emotion, affective computing has become a hot topic in computer science. In this paper, we used the existed emotional classification model based on electroencephalograph (EEG) to calculate the accuracy of emotion classification in 4 brain areas roughly sorted into frontal, parietal, occipital, and temporal lobes in terms of brain functional division, to infer the correlation between the emotion and 4 brain areas based on the accuracy rate of the emotion recognition. The result shows that the brain areas most related to emotions are located in the frontal and temporal lobes, which is consistent with the brain mechanism of emotional processing. This research work will provide a good guideline for selecting the most relevant electrodes with emotions to enhance the accuracy of emotion recognition based on EEG.

**Keywords:** Brain areas · EEG · Correlation · Emotion

## 1 Introduction

Emotional state affects human cognition and behaviour to a great extent. In the past few decades, most of the relative research works existed in the fields of psychology and cognitive science. With the development of information technology and artificial intelligence, emotional computing has been proposed by Professor Picard [1], who defined it as "the calculation of factors related to emotion, triggered by emotion or able to affect emotion." Emotion recognition using computer technology is the crucial factor to realize advanced human-computer interaction, which will be of considerable significance to the study of Brain-like Intelligence.

Facial expressions, phonetic intonation, body posture, and physiological signals are commonly used in affective computing. Electroencephalograph (EEG), one of the physiological signals, are extensively studied in the research field of affective computing because of its distinguished characteristics of non-expensive, time resolution,

H. Gao et al. (Eds.): TridentCom 2019, LNICST 309, pp. 199–212, 2020.
https://doi.org/10.1007/978-3-030-43215-7_14

bearable space resolution, and higher recognition rate than other physiological signals [2], and many research methods based on the EEG, such as stimulus selection, categories of induced emotions, acquisition equipment, feature extraction methods, different dimensionality reduction, classification algorithms, and so on, has been proposed, along with a mass of achievements of significant research results.

Although a mass of significant research results based on the EEG has been achieved, brain research is still in the exploratory stage, the mechanism by which emotions are generated is somewhat unclear. All of these have become the bottleneck in selecting most relevant electrodes with emotions to enhance the accuracy of emotion recognition based on EEG.

Therefore, first of all, this paper will explore the recognition accuracy of the universal emotional recognition system based on EEG, and then seek the correlation between emotions and brain areas with the higher accuracy of emotion recognition based on EEG, to provide the guideline for selecting most relevant electrodes with emotions to enhance the accuracy of emotion recognition based on EEG.

## 2 Related Works

### 2.1 Research on Affective Computing

EEG signals contain sufficient emotional information and can directly reflect the electrical activity of the brain. There are many methods to extract EEG features, such as time-frequency distribution, fast Fourier transform, eigenvector method, wavelet transform, and autoregressive method, and so on [3, 4]. Feature extraction means minimizing the most critical loss in the original signal, so the feature extraction method should minimize the complexity of application to reduce the consumption of information processing.

Duan et al. [5] performed a short-time Fourier transform on the EEG signals to obtain the Fourier transform coefficients for each electrode in each frequency band, and then train and classify them with support vector machine. The average accuracy of emotional classification using differential entropy as an emotional feature is 84.22%. Nie et al. [6] decomposed the original EEG signal into five bands: delta, theta, alpha, beta, and gamma. The five groups of the original EEG signal were transformed by Short-time Fourier Transform (STFT) with a one-second open window. The power spectrum of each electrode in five frequency bands was obtained, which will be trained and classified using SVM, and the average accuracy of the five groups is 87.53%. Murugappan et al. [7] carried out a 5-layer discrete wavelet transform on the original EEG signal, calculated the energy of each frequency band through the wavelet coefficients of each frequency band, and then selected three modified emotional characteristics, which are the ratio of power to total energy in each frequency band, logarithm of energy ratio and the absolute value of logarithm of energy ratio, and then KNN and linear discriminant analysis are used to classify the above three emotional features. The results show that the KNN classification method with the absolute value of the logarithm of energy ratio is the highest accuracy.

Zheng et al. [8] performed short-time Fourier transform (STFT) on the original EEG signal using 1 s uncovered Hamming window, and took the differential entropy of each electrode at five frequency bands as EEG characteristics, that were classified by a classifier combined with depth trusted network and hidden Markov model. The average accuracy was 87.62%.

The classification of EEG emotion is essentially a pattern recognition problem. At present, the commonly used classification methods are linear discriminant analysis (LDA), support vector machine (SVM), BP neural network and deep learning model [8, 9]. The concept of deep learning originates from an artificial neural network, which is a general term for such learning algorithms as a deep neural network and is a research hotspot in the field of machine learning. At present, the commonly used deep learning models include deep belief network (DBN), self-coding model (AE), convolutional neural network (CNN) and recurrent neural network (RNN) [10–12]. Deep belief network is a multi-layer neural network model formed by stacking multiple restricted Boltzmann machines (RBM), which effectively overcomes the problem of inadequate training effect of the multi-layer neural network. Still, it has not been widely used in EEG. Zheng Weilong et al. used the DBN model to classify positive and negative emotions in EEG signals, and the average classification accuracy is 87.62% [13]. Because EEG signals are composed of multi-channel signals and contain a large amount of time-frequency information, if deep learning can make full use of this feature, it may achieve better results.

## 2.2   Study on Emotional Brain Areas

As early as the 18th century, scientists in the field of psychology and physiology proposed many emotional theories to explain how emotion originated and produced, such as Darwin's Three Principles Theory of 1872 [14] and James-Lange theory of 1884 [15]. Izard [16] proposes that emotions are caused by neural circuits, reflective systems, and cognitive behaviours through the investigation of existing literature.

Current brain nerve research suggests that the process of emotion is mainly related to the amygdala. The amygdala is divided into deep cortical pathways for deep processing and subcortical pathways for shallow processing [17]. When studying the mechanism of emotional development in patients with cognitive impairment, it was found that temporal lobe plays a vital role in effective signal detection and depression [18]. Also, it was found that there exists a strong correlation between forehead and emotion. The left prefrontal lobe produces intense EEG activity for positive music, and the right prefrontal lobe produces intense EEG activity for negative music [19].

Studies on the mechanism of emotional production in the brain are mainly focused on the functions of brain areas based on the functional division of the brain. But the research on the external physiological signals corresponding to the particular brain area is not much.

Researchers on emotion recognition based on EEG are interested in extracting features from the external physiological signals corresponding to the particular brain area, and feature classification, but pay little attention to the mechanism of emotional production in the brain. Because we are still not fully aware of the mechanism of the emotional output in the brain and the degree of association between different brain areas, we naturally think that it is necessary to use all electrodes (64 leads/128 leads, etc.) to obtain more emotional information to improve the recognition rate of emotions, besides studying new recognition algorithms. This may not be true. When all electrodes are used, it is possible that some redundant (or even useless) information will be mixed with the useful information, which will increase the complexity of the algorithm and occupy more computational resources and time.

Therefore, making use of what we have done previously [20, 21], this paper explores the correlation between emotional information and different brain areas based on the existing rough functional division of brain areas and the results of emotional recognition with high accuracy and obtains the optimized location of electrodes corresponding to a certain emotion, which provides credible, stable and streamlined information data for emotional recognition based on EEG source.

# 3  Research Methodology on Correlation Between Emotions and Brain Areas

## 3.1  Brain Areas

As usual, the brain can be divided into four areas: the frontal lobe, the parietal lobe, the occipital lobe, and the temporal lobe. But there is no strict division among the four brain areas. The electrode name on the 64-channel electrode cap is composed of letters plus numbers. The endless amount of notes is 1 to 2, which represents the coronal line of the skull, that is, the initials of the English word in the brain areas to which the electrode belongs. The numbers represent the sagittal lines, and the electrodes containing the same number represent the electrodes in the same sagittal line. The electrodes included in the four brain areas selected in this experiment are shown in Fig. 1-a, -b, -c, and -d.

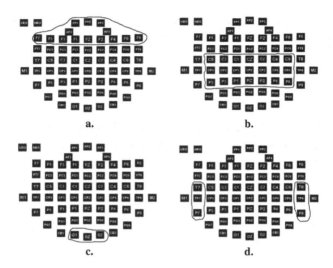

**Fig. 1** a. Frontal electrodes, b. Parietal electrodes, c. Occipital electrodes, d. Temporal electrodes

The partition electrodes of the four brain areas were utilized to obtain the emotion information data on which feature extraction and classification are performed to get emotion recognition result.

## 3.2    Feature Extraction

To get a reasonable emotion recognition rate, it is very crucial to extract emotional EEG features. As usual, EEG features can be time-domain features, frequency domain features, and time-frequency features. Because of the most significant correlation between frequency domain features and emotion, the EEG features selected in this paper are frequency domain features. The frequency-domain signals of EEG transformed from time-domain signals are classified into ones with 5 bands, named as $\delta$, $\theta$, $\alpha$, $\beta$, and $\gamma$. Therefore, the EEG features selected in this paper include frequency band energy, frequency band energy ratio, frequency band energy ratio logarithmic and differential entropy.

A 5-layer wavelet transforms with the selected wavelet basis is performed on the EEG signals in each brain area. The approximate coefficient (AC) and the detail coefficient (DC) of each frequency band are obtained, shown in Table 1.

**Table 1.** Wavelet decomposition result

| Wavelet coefficient | Five bands + Noise | Frequency range (Hz) |
|---|---|---|
| CD1 | Noise | 64–125 |
| CD2 | Gamma | 32–64 |
| CD3 | Beta | 16–32 |
| CD4 | Alpha | 8–16 |
| CD5 | Theta | 4–8 |
| CA5 | Delta | 0–4 |

Frequency band energy feature: the frequency band energy $cE_{ik}$ is the sum of the squares of the wavelet coefficients of *the* $i$-th band in the $k$-th brain area, expressed as Eq. (1):

$$E_{ik} = \sum_{j=1}^{n_i} \left( d_{ij}^k \right)^2 \tag{1}$$

Where $d_{ij}^k$ is the j-th wavelet coefficient of the i-th frequency band in k-th brain area, $i = 1, 2, 3, 4,$ *or* $5$, $n_i$ is the number of wavelet coefficients of the i-th frequency band, and $k = 1, 2, 3,$ *or* $4$.

a. Frequency band energy ratio feature: the frequency band energy ratio $REE_{ik}$ is the ratio of $E_{ik}$ to the total energy of 5 bands in the k-th brain area, expressed as Eq. (2):

$$REE_{ik} = \frac{E_{ik}}{\sum_{j=1}^{5} E_{ik}} \tag{2}$$

b. Frequency band energy ratio logarithmic feature: the frequency band energy ratio logarithmic $LREE_{ik}$ is the logarithm of the $REE_{ik}$ expressed as Eq. (3):

$$LREE_{ik} = log_{10}^{REE_{ik}} \tag{3}$$

c. Differential entropy feature: the differential entropy $DE_{ik}$ is the logarithm of the $LREE_{ik}$, expressed as Eq. (4):

$$DE_{ik} = log_{10}^{E_{ik}} \tag{4}$$

### 3.3    Emotional Classification

Currently, there are many classifiers in the field of machine learning, and each classifier has a suitable application field. Support vector machine (SVM) performs better performance when dealing with a small sample and high-dimensional classification problems. Therefore, this study will use SVM as emotional classifier because of the small sample size of the EEG signal and the high dimension of the signal feature.

Selecting kernel functions is the key to successful use of SVM. Standard kernel functions include polynomial kernel functions, linear kernel functions, Gaussian radial basis kernel functions, and sigmoid kernel functions. Compared with polynomial kernel function, Gaussian radial basis kernel function has fewer parameters (only two parameters: penalty factor, gamma function parameters) and can perform the same as linear kernel functions with one parameter (penalty parameter). The parameter selection of the sigmoid kernel function is too complicated. Thus the kernel function selected in this experiment is a Gaussian radial basis kernel function. And the trained SVM was used to analyze the training set, and to predict the sample type of the test set: shown as Eq. (5).

$$f\left(X^T\right) = \sum\nolimits_{i=1}^{l} y_i a_i x_i X^T + b_0 \tag{5}$$

Where $y_i$ is the class label of the support vector $x_i$, $X^T$ is the test sample, $l$ is the number of support vectors, and $a_i b_0$ are parameters.

### 3.4    Correlation Between Emotion and Brain Areas

**Accuracy Rate.** In this paper, the accuracy rate $R_a$ is defined as the ratio of the number of correct emotion classification $N_c$ to the total number of the test samples $N_{ts}$, expressed as Eq. (6):

$$R_a = \frac{N_c}{N_{ts}} \tag{6}$$

**Correlation Method.** In this pape. The correlation method is divided into several steps, explained as follows:

Step1: Pick up EEG features from each brain area to construct a vector $V_i(i = 1, 2, 3, 4)$ respectively;

Step 2: Cascade two vectors from selected two brain areas with higher $R_a$ in the four brain areas to build a vector $V_{22}$;

Step 3: Cascade three vectors from selected three brain areas with more senior $R_a$ in the four brain areas to construct a vector $V_{33}$;

Step 4: Cascade 4 vectors from the four brain areas to build a vector $V_{44}$;

Step 5: Perform the emotion recognition on $V_i$, $V_{22}$, $V_{33}$, and $V_{44}$, respectively, and calculate the maximum of recognition rate, which corresponds to the most relevant correlation between emotion and brain areas.

All of this processing is shown in Fig. 2.

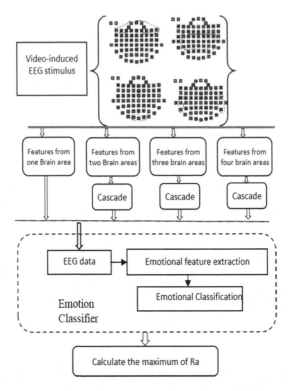

**Fig. 2** Schematic diagram of the correlation method

## 4 Experiments and Discuss

### 4.1 Stimuli Materials

Emotional induction is a vital issue in affective computing, and the choice of emotional stimuli affects the effectiveness of emotions evoked. In the existing research, the relevant stimulus materials commonly used include visual, auditory, and olfactory stimuli. Because the video stimuli material combines the characteristics of vision and hearing, it can better induce the emotions of the subjects. Therefore, this paper plans to use video clips to influence emotions to ensure the effectiveness of emotion-induced.

As stimuli, we selected a total of 30 video clips to induce the emotions of the subjects, including joy, sadness, and neutral video material. The length of each video clip is 1 min.

Fifty-three undergraduates were selected to watch 30 target videos in the emotional database, and a questionnaire survey was conducted on the pleasure, arousal, and dominance of each video using the 9-point scale to complete the quantitative evaluation [24].

Six clips were selected as positive emotion video from high to low, six clips were selected as negative emotion video from low to high, and the average arousal degree of the 12 clips was about 8, indicating that the 12 clips can effectively evoke the emotions of the subjects. The 12 movie clips selected were shown in Tables 2 and 3.

**Table 2.** Video stimulating material 1

| Movie clips | Name | Start and end time |
|---|---|---|
| | Lost on Journey | 0:44:07–0:45:07 |
| | Shaolin Soccer | 0:22:56–0:23:56 |
| | Flirting Scholar | 0:31:13–0:32:13 |
| | Dad's lies | 0:00:10–0:01:10 |
| | Packing articles of "Going Home" | 0:00:16–0:01:16 |
| | A Dog's Tale | 1:22:05–1:23:05 |

**Table 3.** Video stimulating material 2

| Movie clips | Name | Start and end time |
|---|---|---|
| | A Chinese Odyssey | 0:41:33–0:42:33 |
| | Crazy Stone | 0:46:56–0:47:56 |
| | Shaolin Soccer clip 2 | 0:31:13–0:32:13 |
| | Beijing Love Story Movie | 0:44:43–0:45:43 |
| | Dearest | 0:17:29–0:18:29 |
| | Titanic | 2:47:44–2:48:44 |

## 4.2   Subjects

EEG data in this study were recorded from three women and three men aged around 22. They are physically and mentally healthy, right-handed, and clearly understood the experimental content. All of the subjects were undergraduate students from the Minzu University of China and were informed about the purpose of this experiment. Ample sleep and mental concentration were ensured before the trial. And this study protocol was approved by the institutional review boards (ECMUC2019008CO) at Minzu University of China. All participants provided IRB-approved written informed consent after they were explained the experimental procedure.

## 4.3   Data Collection

Let a subject view a piece of movie clip lasting no more than 1 min, and collect the EEG signals by SynAmps2 and Scan4.5 developed by Neuroscan company. The sampling rates are $f = 500\,\text{Hz}$ for EEG. The experimental procedure includes a training phase and a formal testing phase. The recorded EEG data is divided into training data group and testing data group in term of the ratio of 4:1.

## 4.4   Feature Extraction

A 5-layer wavelet transforms with the selected wavelet basis is performed on the EEG signals in each brain area. The selection of wavelet basis in the wavelet transform is a crucial issue, and each wavelet base has its characteristics. In this experiment, four standard wavelet basis of db4, db8, sym8, and coif5 are selected to calculate EEG features with the Eqs. (1)–(4). The emotional classification results (subject cyf) are shown in Table 4.

**Table 4.** CYF's emotional classification accuracy

| Subject | Feature | Wavelet | Accuracy |
|---------|---------|---------|----------|
| cyf | Energy | db4 | 76.39% |
| | | db8 | 80.56% |
| | | sym8 | 73.61% |
| | | coif5 | 75% |
| | REE | db4 | 75% |
| | | db8 | 77.78% |
| | | sym8 | 75% |
| | | coif5 | 65.28% |
| | LREE | db4 | 79.17% |
| | | db8 | 77.78% |
| | | sym8 | 73.61% |
| | | coif5 | 69.44% |
| | DE | db4 | 83.33% |
| | | db8 | 79.17% |
| | | sym8 | 84.72% |
| | | coif5 | 80.56% |

The results show that the differential entropy feature, along with the wavelet function sym8 has the highest emotion recognition rate. Thus the differential entropy feature along with the wavelet function sym8 is selected to perform the emotional recognition in this paper.

### 4.5 Brain Areas and EEG Correlation

In this experiment, the differential entropy is taken as the EEG feature, and sym8 is selected as the wavelet function. According to the method presented in Sect. 3, correlations between brain areas and emotions are performed on EEG feature vectors of $V_i(i = 1, 2, 3, 4)$ and calculate recognition rate $R_a$ respectively. The classification results are shown in Fig. 3-(a, b, c, d, e, f).

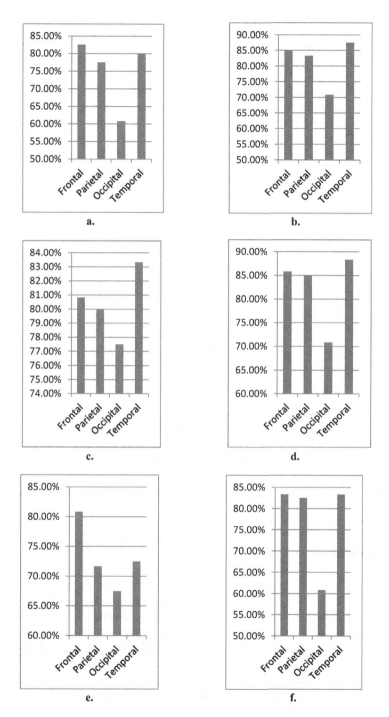

**Fig. 3** a. Accuracy of four brain areas of cyf, b. Accuracy of four brain areas of fxs, c. Accuracy of four brain areas of fyh, d. Accuracy of four brain areas of lzs, e. Accuracy of four brain areas of sxl, f. Accuracy of four brain areas of zq

The above results indicate that the accuracy of emotional classification of the six subjects in the four brain areas is different. However, it can be seen that the emotion classification on the frontal and temporal lobes is the highest, followed by the parietal lobe, and the occipital lobe is the lowest.

To find the brain areas most associated with emotion. The emotion classification accuracy was calculated by stacking brain areas in the order of high to low precision. That is to calculate the emotional classification accuracy of the three groups of brain areas: frontal and temporal lobes; frontal, temporal and parietal lobes; frontal, temporal, parietal, and occipital lobes. The experimental results of the six subjects are shown in Fig. 4.

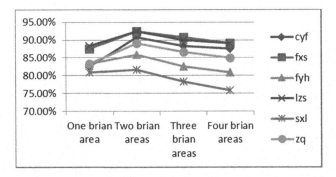

**Fig. 4**  Accuracy of the four brain areas of the six subjects

Figure 4 shows that the accuracy of emotional classification when joining data from frontal and temporal lobes is the highest; the accuracy of emotional classification when joining data from frontal, temporal and parietal lobes is higher; the accuracy of emotional classification when joining data from frontal, temporal, parietal, and occipital lobes is lower; the accuracy of emotional classification with only one brain area is the most economical.

## 5  Conclusion

In this work, we have explored the recognition accuracy of the standard emotional recognition method based on EEG, and then sought the correlation between emotions and brain areas with the higher accuracy of emotion recognition based on EEG, to provide the guideline for selecting most relevant electrodes with emotions to enhance the accuracy of emotion recognition based on EEG. Both the theoretical analysis and experiment have demonstrated that the brain areas most related to emotions are located in the frontal and temporal lobes. This conclusion can be further developed by correlating emotions with electrodes in the most relevant brain area.

**Acknowledgement.** Huiping Jiang has been supported by the National Nature Science Foundation of China (NO. 61503423). And this work has been supported in part by the Leading Talent Program of State Ethnic Affairs Commission, and Double First-class Special Funding of MUC.

# References

1. Picard, R.W.: Affective Computing. MIT Press, London (1997)
2. Nie, D., Wang, X.W., Duan, R.N., Lu, B.L.: A survey on EEG based emotion recognition. Chin. J. Biomed. Eng. **31**(4), 595–606 (2012)
3. Upadhyay, D.: Classification of EEG signals under different mental tasks using wavelet transform and neural network with one step secant algorithm. Int. J. Sci. Eng. Technol. **2**(4), 256–259 (2013)
4. Kim, B.K., Lee, E.C., Suhng, B.M.: Feature extraction using FFT for banknotes recognition in a variety of lighting conditions. In: International Conference on Control, pp. 698–700 (2014)
5. Duan, R.N., Zhu, J.Y., Lu, B.L.: Differential entropy feature for EEG-based emotion classification. In: 2013 6th International IEEE/EMBS Conference on Neural Engineering (NER), pp. 81–84. IEEE (2013)
6. Nie, D., Wang, X.W., Shi, L.C., Lu, B.L.: EEG-based emotion recognition during watching movies. In: Proceeding of the 5th International IEEE EMBS Conference on Neural Engineering, pp. 667–670 (2011)
7. Murugappan, M., Ramachandran, N., Sazali, Y.: Classification of human emotion from EEG using discrete wavelet transform. J. Biomed. Sci. Eng. **2**(4), 390–396 (2010)
8. Gupta, A., Agrawal, R.K., Kaur, B.: Performance enhancement of mental task classification using EEG signal: a study of multivariate feature selection methods. Soft. Comput. **19**(10), 2799–2812 (2015)
9. Subasi, A., Gursoy, M.I.: Comparison of PCA, ICA and LDA in EEG signal classification using DWT and SVM. Exp. Syst. Appl. **37**(37), 8659–8666 (2010)
10. Yanagimoto, M., Sugimoto, C.: Recognition of persisting emotional valence from EEG using convolutional neural networks. In: IEEE International Workshop on Computational Intelligence & Applications, pp. 27–32 (2017)
11. Baghaee, S., Onak, O.N., Ulusoy, I.: Inferring brain effective connectivity via DBN and EEG time series data. In: International Scientific Conference of Iranian Academics in Turkey (2014)
12. Seijdel, N., Ramakrishnan, K., Losch, M.: Overlap in performance of CNN's, human behavior and EEG classification. J. Vis. **16**(12), 501 (2016)
13. Zheng, W.L., Zhu, J.Y., Peng, Y., et al.: EEG-based emotion classification using deep belief networks. In: IEEE International Conference on Multimedia and Expo, pp. 1–6. IEEE (2014)
14. Darwin, C., Ekman, P.: The Expression of the Emotions in Man and Animals. Oxford University Press, New York (1872/1998)
15. James, W.: What is an emotion? Mind **9**(34), 188–205 (1884)
16. Izard, C.E.: The many meanings/aspects of emotion: definitions, functions, activation, and regulation. Emot. Rev. **2**(4), 363–370 (2010)
17. LeDoux, J.: Emotional networks and motor control: a fearful view. Prog. Brain Res. **107**, 437–446 (1996)

18. Sturm, V.E., Yokoyama, J.S., Seeley, W.W., et al.: Heightened emotional contagion in mild cognitive impairment and Alzheimer's disease is associated with temporal lobe degeneration. Proc. Natl. Acad. Sci. **110**(24), 9944–9949 (2013)
19. Schmidt, L.A., Trainor, L.J.: Frontal brain electrical activity (EEG) distinguishes valence and intensity of musical emotions. Cogn. Emot. **15**(4), 487–500 (2001)
20. Lu, Y., Jiang, H., Liu, W.: Classification of EEG Signal by STFT-CNN Framework: identification of right-/left-hand Motor Imagination in BCI Systems. In: 7th International Conference on Computer Engineering and Networks, Shanghai, China, 22–23 July 2017 (2017)
21. Zhou, Z.: Research on EEG signal characteristic representation in emotion recognition. Master Thesis, Minzu University of China (2015)

# Activity Recognition and Classification via Deep Neural Networks

Zhi Wang[1], Liangliang Lin[2,3], Ruimeng Wang[4], Boyang Wei[5],
Yueshen Xu[6], Zhiping Jiang[6], and Rui Li[6(✉)]

[1] School of Software Engineering, Xi'an Jiaotong University,
Xi'an 710049, China
zhiwang@xjtu.edu.cn
[2] School of Computer Science and Technology, Xi'an Jiaotong University,
Xi'an 710049, China
lin_ll@126.com
[3] Informatization Office, Xi'an Conservatory of Music, Xi'an 710061, China
[4] School of Photovoltaic and Renewable Energy Engineering,
The University of New South Wales, Sydney, NSW 2052, Australia
brianrwangmsecs@gmail.com
[5] Geogetown University, Washington DC 20007, USA
bw558@georgetown.edu
[6] School of Computer Science and Technology, Xidian University, Xi'an, China
rli@xidian.edu.cn

**Abstract.** Based on the Wi-Fi widely separated in the world, Wi-Fi-based wireless activity recognition has attracted more and more research efforts. Now, device-based activity awareness is being used for commercial purpose as the most important solution. Such devices based on various acceleration sensors and direction sensor are very mature at present. With more and more profound understanding of wireless signals, commercial wireless routers are used to obtain signal information of the physical layer: channel state information (CSI) more granular than the RSSI signal information provides a theoretical basis for wireless signal perception. Through research on activity recognition techniques based on CSI of wireless signal and deep learning, the authors proposed a system for learning classification using deep learning, mainly including a data preprocessing stage, an activity detection stage, a learning stage and a classification stage. During the activity detection model stage, a correlation-based model was used to detect the time of the activity occurrence and the activity time interval, thus solving the problem that the waveform changes due to variable environment at stable time. During the activity recognition stage, the network was studied by innovative deep learning to conduct training for activity learning. By replacing the fingerprint way, which is used broadly today, with learning the CSI signal information of activities, we classified the activities through trained network.

**Keywords:** Channel state information · Pearson correlation coefficient · Deep convolutional neural networks · AlexNet network

© ICST Institute for Computer Sciences, Social Informatics and Telecommunications Engineering 2020
Published by Springer Nature Switzerland AG 2020. All Rights Reserved
H. Gao et al. (Eds.): TridentCom 2019, LNICST 309, pp. 213–228, 2020.
https://doi.org/10.1007/978-3-030-43215-7_15

# 1    Introduction

The rapid development and wide application of the Internet of Things (IoT) around the world stimulate the study on wireless activity awareness. At present, the two main study directions in the field of wireless activity awareness are device-based activity awareness systems and device-free activity awareness systems. The device-based activity awareness systems collect data mainly through built-in sensors of mobile phones, smart bracelets, smart watches or other sensing devices to obtain the activity status of people or other targets. And the device-free activity awareness systems obtain people's activity status mainly through the impact of people's activities on wireless networks. However, the device-based systems are limited by many conditions, for example, the senior and the infant are typically loath to carry a device, and those devices are not suitable for bringing into private occasions. Therefore, the device-free wireless-based activity awareness systems are needed in more and more scenarios and have ever-increasing research value. At the same time, recognizing activities with wireless networks also faces a lot of challenges.

As the number of mobile smart device increases rapidly around the globe, and the wireless network devices are popularized and widely used in people's life, the methods for activity awareness are diversified (including RFID [9], Wi-Fi [1] and radar), and the characteristic that the wireless signal can spread over the space without any impact on persons lays a solid foundation for the device-free activity awareness system.

At present, many institutions and companies at home and abroad have conducted researches in the field of activity awareness and achieved diversified solutions. The WiTrack [8] system, published by the Massachusetts Institute of Technology at the NSDI International Conference in 2014, performs activity awareness for targets by applying wireless technologies of frequency modulated continuous wave and radar reflection in the Wi-Fi field. The WiTrack 2.0 [15] system, presented at the NSDI International Conference in 2015, allows more than one person to present in the scenario to conduct location awareness. Similarly, WiSee [2] system and WiHear [14] use wireless technologies to perform activity awareness on human body in whole or in part. Currently, in the field of activity awareness, limited by technologies and scenarios, most of the device-free activity awareness systems are still being developed, with strong demands in commercial application.

Despite relatively sluggish progress on commercial application development, the activity awareness system has broad prospect and will become a huge innovative point in commercial application. The wireless activity awareness system can be widely applied in many scenarios, such as a nursing home, where the senior can be protected from dangers by activity monitoring, and safety precaution can be made when the senior suffer from sudden illness. In the private spaces such as washroom and bedroom, the wireless-based activity awareness system can not only monitor the target activity in real time, but also detect and alarm abnormities. From this, as an emerging product, the wireless activity awareness system has a promising commercial prospect thanks to its low hardware cost, high accuracy, convenient installation and other advantages.

The research in this paper contributes to the following aspects: (1) using extensive commercial routers to differentiate more detailed activities; and (2) using deep learning methods to perform activity awareness and recognition with good fault tolerance and stability. Meanwhile, many challenges still remain in the research. The work direction will be: (1) supervised learning, as the people's activities need to be learned thoroughly; and (2) the system is unable to recognize and distinguish activities of several persons at once.

## 2  Related Work

There are many researches in the field of activity awareness [1–10]. Related researches mainly include video-based, mobile device-based, radar-based and wireless fingerprint-based activity awareness systems.

The products of video-based activity awareness system are relatively mature. Key of this system lies in using video images to recognize and identify the target [11–13]. The user's behaviors are obtained by analyzing activities of human bodies. Among these systems, Kinect [4] and Leap Motion [5] are widely used in commercial application. Kinect collects human images mainly through video and infrared, and it simulates people's activities by constructing collected images into a 32-node model. The moving activities in the depth direction can not be detected by plane images. The video-based activity recognition uses a depth camera to detect the activities in the depth direction other than the plane motion. To recognize the detailed local motion, a camera and a depth camera are used to detect the edge of human body and construct a denser dot matrix into a network model to obtain the local motion activity. Leap Motion uses facial activity recognition based on binocular vision. It simulates binocular vision effects via dual cameras to capture two pictures simultaneously to realize 3D modeling and sense the 3D activities out of 2D planes. Applying different technologies, the above two widely-used commercial products ultimately aim at recognizing activities via video. More importantly, they overcome the key problems in detection of 3D activities through image recognition under the relatively mature conditions. Application of these two products, however, is constrained by strict environmental requirements, such as sufficient light and no obstruction.

The mobile device-based activity awareness system mainly relies on the sensor module built into the mobile device [16–25]. Especially during the current period when the mobile phone is commonly used, this system typically detects the people's activities by the compass, gyroscope, the acceleration sensor and the sensors in the telephone which cooperate with each other. With the direction indicated by the compass, the device status in 3D space indicated by the gyroscope, the velocity indicated by the acceleration sensor, and detailed displacement distance calculated by time, this system can obtain the user's specific motions, but the activity details cannot be detected. This is the most widely-used method at this stage, with inability to directly detect fine activities as its chief drawback. Individual's ongoing activities can only be inferred by these built-in sensors of the mobile phones. For example, the system can detect that a person is exercising, climbing the stairs or sleeping, but it is unable to sense the specific activities such as standing up, sitting down or raising hands. In addition to mobile phones, today's most popular activity awareness devices are smart bracelets which are designed for monitoring. The bracelets are equipped with various sensors, such as the heartbeat sensor to detect the heart rate and the temperature sensor to detect the body temperature. Representative products include Apple Watch, Huawei Sports Watch and Xiaomi Sports Bracelet. These wearable devices are sufficient as a simple activity awareness device, but they are unacceptable as a part that must be carried by human body, especially for children, the new born and the senior, because it is undesirable for theses persons, both physically and mentally, to wear such a special device.

The radar-based activity awareness system senses the surrounding environment through high-frequency radar signals. When the target is active in the area, it causes reflection of radar signals. Through the collection of high-frequency signal, people's motion at every moment can be obtained. By combining these motions together, a continuous activity is formed and thus the activity of the target is obtained. As a sophisticated technical means, radar is highly sensitive to people's activities. But it is very expensive with strict application requirements. What's more, the high-precision radar system is gigantic and difficult to deploy, restricting its application only to the military field. Despite its high precision, its huge size and high cost make this system not suitable for the current commercial environment.

The technical solution we studied is mainly based on 2.4 GHz wireless RF signals, similar to detecting target activity with RF fingerprints. Earlier, researches of wireless-based activity awareness were mainly through wireless RSSI information. For example, the SigComm conference published an article about using RSSI to detect people's heartbeat [9] in 2011, but the RSSI had rigorous requirements on environment and the content of information was insufficient, so it was difficult to get more valuable information from it. There are many methods for activity recognition, such as application of sensor-based activity recognition systems [1, 2], but the sensors either require to be carried by the target, or deployed around the activity area of the target. The systems applying acceleration sensors to detect the motion speed of human body are easily disturbed, for example, the GrandCare will be disturbed by the motion of doors. There are other wearable device systems that use BodyScop as a sound sensor to classify people's activities to identify eating, coughing and other people's activities.

# 3  Wireless Activity Recognition System

To design a relatively universal system and enable the system to recognize the activities of the target in a low-power Wi-Fi environment, we proposed a better method to record changes of Wi-Fi signals. Besides, we carried out training based on collection of a large amount of data for the purpose of being suitable for more extensive scenarios.

## 3.1  Architectural Design of Wireless Activity Recognition System

This system uses wireless signals to recognize the people's activities. Based on existing wireless router and CSI signal monitoring means, there are many insuperable difficulties for the system to rely only on the channel of the Wi-Fi signal to monitor the people's activities. First of all, when recognizing people's activities, data needs to be learned, thus requiring a large amount of stable data. When collecting data, factors including environment and equipment must be changed singly, so that we can determine that the signal is affected by people's activities rather than change of environment. In addition, the stability of the data must be ensured during data filtering. Second, it is critical to determine when the motion changes. After receiving the data of the target motion, it is necessary to recognize the time at which the motion occurs and the time at which the motion ends. For example, within a video surveillance area, when a quiescent person suddenly stands up from different positions at different speeds, the start and end time of the motion and the type of motion are required to be accurately recognized by the algorithm. The environment has changed due to people's motion, regardless of whether they become quiescent again (Fig. 1).

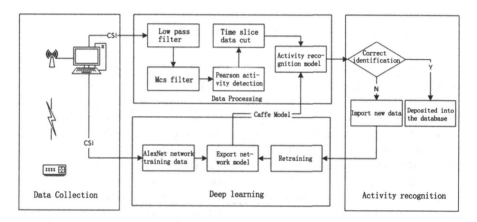

**Fig. 1.** System architecture diagram

We mainly studied two aspects of the wireless activity recognition system. On the one hand, as home wireless routers become more and more popular, watching TV, playing computer games, surfing the internet and other daily applications can be supported by the Wi-Fi signals provided by devices. With more stable Wi-Fi signal and enhanced network bandwidth, finer granularity of data can be achieved through a better way under 802.11n MIMO system. With the standard 20 MHz signal and 40 MHz signal, the 802.11 system provides 52 and 128 OFDM subcarriers respectively. In this system, we are able to collect 30 subcarriers, and the CSI impact on people's activities is shown in Fig. 2. On the other hand, the far-reaching application of the system is to recognize and differentiate target groups through activity recognition, that is, distinguishing targets through recognition of target activities, a series of meaningful activities and statistics. By tracking one's activities, a time series-based portrait of the target person is created, through which the characteristics of the target groups in the current scenario are identified.

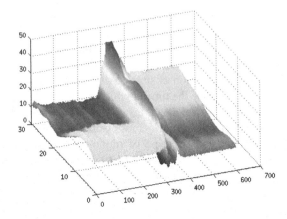

**Fig. 2.** Chart of CSI fluctuation caused by people's activities

We collected data by using a commercial wireless router based on the 802.11n MIMO system at a frequency of 2.3 GHz to 2.4 GHz. At this frequency, although it was not easy to obtain subtle motions, the impact of major motion of human body on wireless signals was very obvious. Besides, the difficulty in feature extraction was reduced through deep learning, thus compensating the poor recognition accuracy. The basic conception of the system is to recognize the human body motion based on signal characteristics and sequences by deeply learning the characteristics of the CSI link signal. We collected data of 30 channels through the network card, and after data preprocessing, we deeply learned the convolutional network. By modifying the parameters, the data was trained for several times to obtain an activity recognition model, through which the activity can be accurately recognized.

In the actual operation of the system, the following problems need to be solved. First one is data collection. Because the wireless signals, which can be received, are invisible, and can only be described by human imagination. In scientific research, the most common method for data collection is control variable method, by which other factors are controlled as much as possible during data collection to make the wireless signal fluctuate only by people's activities. To this end, we strictly controlled the environmental change during data collection. At the same time, the sampling rate is also essential for data collection. The sampling rate concerns the accuracy of the system's recognition of people's activity. Of course, the higher sampling rate causes a more complicated calculation, so the sampling rate shall be determined in line with the time required by the motion. Therefore, we determined a proper sampling rate by investigating the time of each motion made by target groups. The core of the system lies in learning the CSI through deep learning method, which has more advantages for target recognition, including the capability to judge a more detailed behaviors of the users and distinguish different target users. The core part of the system is activity recognition, which includes the learning and recognition of the activity. Activity recognition is divided into two parts: one is the recognition of the activity start & end time of the system to distinguish two different motions. Generally speaking, when the activity occurs, the CSI link will change drastically. And the end time of the activity is usually not easy to determine.

## 3.2   Design of Deep Learning Network Model

The model for activity recognition in the system performs image learning recognition by converting data into grayscale images. Therefore, the network model AlexNet is a more advantageous network structure model, which is the classic model of CNN in image classification.

The network model is shown in Fig. 3. You can see that this network structure uses two GPU servers (of course one GPU is also acceptable), so there are two processes. From the perspective of network structure, the entire AlexNet network model has a total of 8 layers, of which 5 layers are located in the convolutional layer, and the remaining 3 layers are fully connected layers. Each convolutional layer includes the excitation function and normalized function as partial response, and then pooling processing is conducted to simplify the calculation.

The input images are 224 × 224 × 3 pixel pictures, and change to 227 pixels after preprocessing to facilitate the convolution kernel selection and calculation of the network, and then the pooling layer is used to simplify the calculation. The network uses a 5 × 5 convolution kernel for feature extraction. The 48 in the figure means that each GPU uses 48 convolution kernels because two GPU are used for processing. In addition, although the size of the convolution kernel is 5 × 5, since the general training image uses an RGB three-channel image, the corresponding convolution kernel also has three layers in the third dimension.

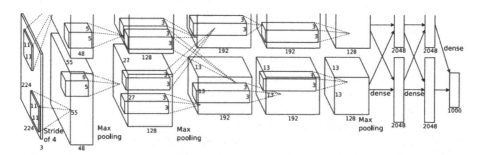

**Fig. 3.** AlexNet network structure

## 3.3   Design of Activity Recognition Scheme

In CSI, the number of subcarriers available in the system was 30, so the data used was a matrix of n × 30. The feature for activity recognition was 30 subcarriers.

$$h = s_0 + s_1 \times x_1 + s_2 \times x_2 \cdots + s_{30} \times x_{30}$$

where $x_i$ is a vector representing the ith data. Appropriate parameters can be obtained by the gradient descent method.

Within the context of CSI, the impact of motions performed by targets within the region on CSI is a relatively stable distribution of CSI, and the impact can represent the activity and the activity time of this target. At the same location, CSI waveform distributions caused by different activities vary. CSI waveforms caused by the repetitive motion of the target and the different postures of the user are also different. First, the CSI waveforms of the same motion are compared to see if the CSI fluctuations caused by the same motion are related or similar. Then the CSI fluctuations caused by different motions are compared to observe whether it is possible to distinguish the two motions. Through real experimental comparison, it can be observed that the waveform similarity between the same motions is much higher than that between different motions, so it is theoretically possible to complete activity recognition by wireless means.

For known activities, only the known raw data are needed during data collection. After filtering and noise reduction, the occurrence time of the activity is obtained through an activity detection model, and then the current target activity is obtained through two schemes, one of which only compares the CSI fingerprint information from fingerprint database by a proper algorithm, and obtains the target motion from the nearest CSI waveform distribution. Comparing the waveform distribution or the ratio of wave peaks to waveforms are favorable fingerprint match algorithms. The second is to conduct supervised learning in advance by learning algorithm. When training known activity data by learning algorithms, namely, using data as training samples, the samples of the activities themselves are very similar during training and learning. The valid recognition can even be realized after data conversion by the traditional comparison method using fingerprint matching, so it can be very easy to recognize the known activities after using the CNN. During the learning of the model, complete matching will not be conducted to avoid overfitting, which is problematic for a highly accurate recognition with tiny error. However, it is very suitable here, because the impacts of the same activity on CSI are different, including the error of the hardware and effect of noise in the scenario. What more, when different persons do the same motion, the local details of their bodies vary obviously. This is conducive to the recognition accuracy of the learning algorithm, which can further recognize the very detailed local features to obtain the target within the current region.

The recognition of unknown target activities is the research priority of this system. For the fingerprint matching system, the fingerprint database stores all the active fingerprints. Although there are many targets and different active fingerprints, it is impossible to include fingerprints of all persons. In this case, the signal fingerprints formed by the same activity of different targets established by the fingerprint matching system are eventually similar despite distinction. A problem raises therefore. Although the fingerprints on images of different targets may be similar, errors are still remaining. Through comparison of fingerprint database, the risk of error will be relatively high. Such risks may reduce as the fingerprint library increases, but as the types of activity increase, similar activities have increasingly higher requirements for fingerprint match algorithm. The approach of deep learning that we proposed also focuses on this point. Deep convolutional neural networks can extract local features well by convolution operations of convolution kernels.

# 4 Implementation of Wireless Activity Recognition System

The wireless activity recognition system first collects data, then preprocesses the original data collected to obtain smoother data before learning the activity data of targets, including the same activity of different targets and different activities of the same target, and finally improves the accuracy of the system with higher frequency.

## 4.1 Data Collection

The initially received CSI data are $30 \times N \times M$ and each data is plural, N is the number of antennae and M is the number of data packets received. The scenario for data collection represents an important factor, and the representations of CSI signals are different in different scenarios. To recognize activities of targets in different scenarios, a large amount of data need to be collected in these scenarios to ensure the learning model used can better improve its accuracy. When collecting data, stable scenario shall be ensured, and data of different persons in the same scenario and data of the same person in different scenarios shall be collected to ensure the comparability of the data.

## 4.2 Data Preprocessing

Given the instability of hardware itself and the impact of ambient noise contained in the original CSI data collected, the original CSI data need to be preprocessed. Observation shows that wireless signal is vulnerable to the environment, for example, changes in location of items in the environment and sway of clothes and other items affected by wind will cause a great deal of noise to the original CSI data, resulting in the inability to obtain more effective information. For data training, dimension conversion of data is the main task. After receiving the original CSI data, the wireless signal data are converted and the signal information of 30 subcarriers is extracted. For a sequence, the whole data are the data set of 2D data $30 \times n$, and when training data, the data set needs to be converted into a data set of 3D data to facilitate the data training. The training sample and Label file are input to perform training. Data preprocessing is designed to improve the reliability of CSI data, and the data representing noise in the original CSI data are removed to allow CSI data to better reflect the activity of the target. The noise mostly comes from the Wi-Fi device transmitting in the indoor environment.

(1) Low-pass filtering

Low-pass filtering is a method to filter data, and its principle features that low frequency signals are allowed to pass while high frequency signals reaching the threshold will be blocked or weakened, and the amplitudes of blocking and weakening varies according to frequency and filtering process. High-pass filtering is a filter relative to low-pass filtering. The calculation formula of its critical frequency is as follows.

$$f_c = \frac{1}{2 R_2 C}$$

The low-pass filtering is used to remove the high frequency noise not caused by people's activities. Relatively, people's activities generally affect low frequency, so high frequency ambient noise needs to be removed. We used an exponential smoothing filter (DESF) which can smooth data changes of samples by exponential smoothing based on changes in original samples, and can remove high frequency noise and protect CSI data changes caused by people's activities from being removed.

(2) Filtering of modulation and coding index

CSI data are not only influenced by people's activities and ambient noise, but also modulation and coding index. We found in our experiment that modulation and coding index may also cause fluctuation of CSI signal and change fluctuation of CSI data due to signal fluctuation resulting from inherent unstable wireless signals, so CSI needs to be filtered when minimum impact was imposed on CSI by people's activities. When this part of impact not caused by human factors is removed, more accurate data will be obtained. The activity behavior data are only caused by people's activities, so it is impossible to remove all noise, but greatest efforts can be made to highlight the CSI signal data affected by people's activities.

(3) Trigger of detection activities

In this system, activities occur and stop randomly, so it is an ongoing monitoring process. It keeps collecting data during operation and people's activity itself is a random event, so the time when the activity is going to happen or stop and when the next activity is to happen shall be monitored in order to recognize people's activities via wireless signals. By observing the fluctuation of CSI signals, we can see that every time one activity happens, the wireless signal produces a violent fluctuation, so we can know the start and end time of people's activities by only detecting the time when the wireless signal begins to fluctuate and when the fluctuation turns to be relatively quiet (not totally still). There are two ways for detecting fluctuation, and one is threshold method. This method is very simple: an initial threshold is set and during receiving CSI signals, activities are considered to happen when one or more signals exceeding the threshold are detected, while activities are considered to have stopped when stable one or more signals below the threshold are detected.

The Pearson product-moment correlation coefficient is mainly used to measure the correlation between two variables, and the correlation coefficient between two variables is defined as the quotient of covariance and standard deviation between two variables. The calculation formula is as follows.

$$\rho_{X,Y} = \frac{\text{cov}(X, Y)}{\sigma_X \sigma_Y} = \frac{E[(X - \mu_X)(Y - \mu_Y)]}{\sigma_X \sigma_Y}$$

The formula above defines the overall correlation of X and Y, and covariance and standard deviation of the samples is represented by r, and the calculation formula is as follows.

$$r = \frac{\sum\limits_{i=1}^{n} (X_i - \bar{X})(Y_i - \bar{Y})}{\sqrt{\sum\limits_{i=1}^{n} (X_i - \bar{X})^2} \sqrt{\sum\limits_{i=1}^{n} (Y_i - \bar{Y})^2}}$$

The Pearson correlation coefficient does very well at the beginning. After data preprocessing, we got the image shown in Fig. 4 by detection of Pearson correlation coefficient, and we can see from the image that Pearson correlation coefficient does a very good job in detecting the time when the fluctuation starts and ends. However, things are not always the same. Pearson correlation coefficient is outstanding when sound data are available and the time when the activity happens and stops can be easily judged. However, data are not always that sound, and environmental changes and fluctuation of hardware itself or minor irregular movement caused by wind blowing curtains and other items can also cause undesired data. As shown in Fig. 5, the judgment of the time when the activity starts and ends is very important for activity recognition, and when such case of Fig. 5 happens, it is difficult to know the occurrence time of the data. Although Pearson correlation coefficient serves well in judging the occurrence of activities when sound data are available, some errors may happen due to the instability of the signal itself and presence of noise. To reduce such misjudgment caused by the instability of the signal itself, we modified the data content of the algorithm, namely the sum of three data packets were used to judge the fluctuation, as shown in Fig. 6.

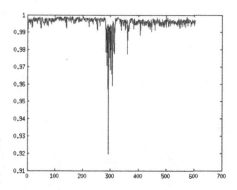

**Fig. 4.** Pearson correlation coefficient

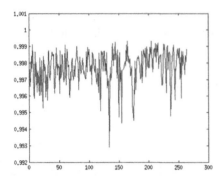 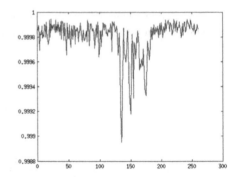

**Fig. 5.** CSI under Pearson correlation coefficient    **Fig. 6.** Performance of Pearson coefficient

## 5 Performance Evaluation

Since we used a deep learning-based convolutional neural network to recognize activities and the accuracy of the time when activities happen is the key indicator of the whole system, it is necessary to evaluate the performance of activity detection of the system.

(1) Performance of Pearson correlation coefficient model
   As the time in the activity detection model was obtained by comparing the lowest coefficient points within the most recent time window, the model had nothing to do with the environment, and the overall waveform of CSI would not be impacted by environmental changes, To get more detailed performance evaluation, we chose two test sites to conduct the test and obtained the performance evaluation analysis of the activity detection model. We carried out two groups of experiments in each of the two sites, and collected adequate data and established an activity detection model for each group of experiments. The true activities and the time when the activities happened were compared to obtain the accuracy rate of the activity detection models and the time error of detection activities. For detection activity trigger, accuracy rate of 95% was acceptable, and the time error of its activity detection was about 0.1 s, as shown in Fig. 7.

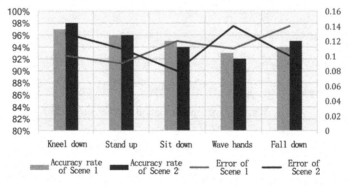

**Fig. 7.** Accuracy rate and time error of different activity detections

During the model detection, the system was randomly tested when the test target squatted down, stood up, sat down and waved hands, and the time when activities happened was detected by testing the models. After filtering the data collected, the detection model calculated the time error of activity occurrence, which was compared with the actual time when environmental activities happened. Each activity was sampled for 200 times with 1000 experiments conducted in total. It can be seen that the fluctuation time point was detected in a relatively accurate way. The figure above shows that the average error of this detection model is about 0.1 s.

(2) Performance of activity recognition model

We analyzed five deep learning network models including AlexNet and VGG, and conducted a multi-dimensional and detailed comparison on their similarities and their own advantages and disadvantages. Figure 8 shows the training comparison between the two deep convolutional network models namely AlexNet and VGG. We found through comparison that under the same data situation, AlexNet can achieve relatively high accuracy when much less learning data were needed in the network learning while VGG network showed high depth, so when less single data are available, it is very like to cause overfitting. That is to say, it works very well when learning, but when it comes to actual classification, the accuracy rate may fall.

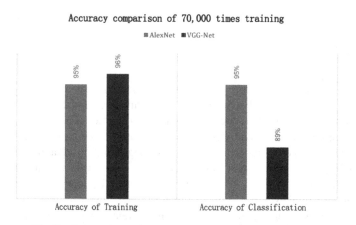

**Fig. 8.** Comparison of accuracy between AlexNet and VGG

After the system was deployed in Scenario 1, we respectively sampled data samples with 50 actions as a group by systematic data collection and training, and each sampling lasted 10 s and data transmission rate was 50 kpt/s. If the classification was right, the results were considered to be right, otherwise the results were considered to be wrong regardless of any other classification. Experiments showed that among the total 250 matching calculations, the accuracy rate was

98%, which mainly resulted from unstable hardware. Expensive device failed to conform to the design purpose of the experimental system, and the inexpensive commercial routers with an accuracy rate of 92% was acceptable. In Scenario 2, we conducted the same experiment with a consequent accuracy rate of 95% and a false positive rate of 3%, which were mainly due to the unstable fluctuation of the hardware itself. Compared to other systems like WiSee [1], an accuracy of 94% was obtained by very expensive device (USRP) (Fig. 9).

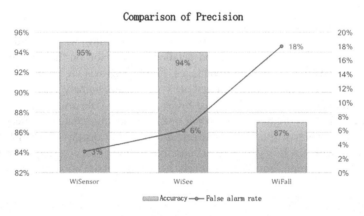

**Fig. 9.** Comparison of accuracy among WiSensor, WiSee and WiFall

## 6 Conclusion

By comparing and analyzing the existing activity recognition technologies, we summarized and analyzed the advantages and disadvantages of the current scheme and proposed to carry out activity recognition by training wireless CSI signals by means of the deep learning methods, and designed an activity recognition system. The comparison of various schemes in terms of their advantages and disadvantages showed that wireless activity recognition had better suitability and stability. And we chosen a network model most suitable for the current system by comparing various deep learning network models.

The authors used the means of converting wireless signals into pictures in an innovative manner. The activity detection model was used to obtain the time slice of activity occurrence which was clipped before being converting into pictures, and then the pictures were classified by means of the deep learning methods, thus the results and the classification of activities were obtained simultaneously. This means compensated for the inconsistency of waveforms of wireless signals at different time points. All waveforms, high or low, can be removed during training as backgrounds of pictures. Such scheme largely resolves the inconsistency of waveforms when signals are stable.

# References

1. Wang, Y., Liu, J., Chen, Y., et al.: E-eyes: device-free location-oriented activity recognition using fine-grained WiFi signatures. In: Proceedings of the 20th Annual International Conference on Mobile Computing and Networking, pp. 617–628. ACM (2014)
2. Pu, Q., Gupta, S., Gollakota, S., et al.: Whole-home gesture recognition using wireless signals. In: Proceedings of the 19th Annual International Conference on Mobile Computing & Networking, pp. 27–38. ACM (2013)
3. Zheng, X., Wang, J., Shangguan, L., et al.: Smokey: ubiquitous smoking detection with commercial WiFi infrastructures. In: IEEE INFOCOM 2016-The 35th Annual IEEE International Conference on Computer Communications, pp. 1–9. IEEE (2016)
4. Ren, Z., Meng, J., Yuan, J., et al.: Robust hand gesture recognition with kinect sensor. In: Proceedings of the 19th ACM International Conference on Multimedia, pp. 759–760. ACM (2011)
5. Weichert, F., Bachmann, D., Rudak, B., et al.: Analysis of the accuracy and robustness of the leap motion controller. Sensors 13(5), 6380–6393 (2013)
6. IEEE Std. 802.11n-2009: Enhancements for higher throughput (2009). http://www.ieee802.org
7. Silver, D., Veness, J.: Monte-Carlo planning in large POMDPs. In: Advances in Neural Information Processing Systems, pp. 2164–2172 (2010)
8. Adib, F., Kabelac, Z., Katabi, D., et al.: 3D tracking via body radio reflections. In: NSDI, vol. 14, pp. 317–329 (2014)
9. Gollakota, S., Hassanieh, H., Ransford, B., et al.: They can hear your heartbeats: noninvasive security for implantable medical devices. ACM SIGCOMM Comput. Commun. Rev. 41(4), 2–13 (2011)
10. Asadzadeh, P., Kulik, L., Tanin, E.: Gesture recognition using RFID technology. Pers. Ubiquit. Comput. 16(3), 225–234 (2012)
11. Tongrod, N., Lokavee, S., Kerdcharoen, T., et al.: Gestural system based on multifunctional sensors and ZigBee networks for squad communication. In: 2011 Defense Science Research Conference and Expo (DSR), pp. 1–4. IEEE, 2011
12. Wang, Y., Wu, K., Ni, L.M.: Wifall: device-free fall detection by wireless networks. IEEE Trans. Mob. Comput. 16, 581–594 (2016)
13. Molchanov, P., Gupta, S., Kim, K., et al.: Short-range FMCW monopulse radar for hand-gesture sensing. In: 2015 IEEE Radar Conference (RadarCon), pp. 1491–1496. IEEE (2015)
14. Wang, G., Zou, Y., Zhou, Z., et al.: We can hear you with Wi-Fi! IEEE Trans. Mob. Comput. 15(11), 2907–2920 (2016)
15. Adib, F., Kabelac, Z., Katabi, D.: Multi-person localization via RF body reflections. In: NSDI, pp. 279–292 (2015)
16. Xie, Y., Li, Z., Li, M.: Precise power delay profiling with commodity Wi-Fi. In: Proceedings of the 21st Annual International Conference on Mobile Computing and Networking, pp. 53–64. ACM (2015)
17. Krizhevsky, A., Sutskever, I., Hinton, G.E.: ImageNet classification with deep convolutional neural networks. In: Advances in Neural Information Processing Systems, pp. 1097–1105 (2012)
18. Kleisouris, K., Firner, B., Howard, R., Zhang, Y., Martin, R.P.: Detecting intra-room mobility with signal strength descriptors. In: ACM MobiHoc (2010)
19. Lei, J., Ren, X., Fox, D.: Fine-grained kitchen activity recognition using RGB-D. In: ACM UbiComp (2012)

20. Keally, M., et al.: PBN: towards practical activity recognition using smartphone based body sensor networks. In: ACM SenSys (2011)
21. Adib, F., Katabi, D.: See through walls with WiFi! In: ACM SIGCOMM (2013)
22. Yatani, K., Truong, K.N.: BodyScope: a wearable acoustic sensor for activity recognition. In: Proceedings of the ACM UbiComp (2012)
23. Halperin, D., et al.: Tool release: gathering 802.11n traces with channel state information. ACM SIGCOMM CCR **41**(1), 1 (2011)
24. Xia, P., Zhou, S., Giannakis, G.B.: Adaptive MIMO-OFDM based on partial channel state information. IEEE Trans. Signal Process. **52**(1), 202–213 (2004)
25. Hong, J., Ohtsuki, T.: Ambient intelligence sensing using array sensor: device-free radio based approach. In: CoSDEO Workshop (2013)

# A Link Analysis Based Approach to Predict Character Death in Game of Thrones

Swati Agarwal[1]([✉])[ID], Rahul Thakur[2], and Sudeepta Mishra[3]

[1] BITS Pilani, Goa Campus, Goa, India
agrswati@ieee.org
[2] IIT Roorkee, Roorkee, India
rahul@ieee.org
[3] BITS Pilani, Hyderabad Campus, Hyderabad, India
sudeepta@hyderabad.bits-pilani.ac.in

**Abstract.** Mysterious and uncertain deaths in the "Game of Thrones" novel-series have been stupefying to the vast pool of readers and hence interested researchers to come up with various models to predict the deaths. In this paper, we propose a Death-Prone Score model to predict if the candidate character is going to die or stay alive in the upcoming book in the series. We address the challenge of high-dimensional data and train our model on the most significant attributes by computing feature importance in the vector space. Further, we address the challenge of multiple interactions between characters and create a social network representing the weighted similarity between each character pair in the book. The proposed model takes similarity and proximity in a social network into account and generates a death-prone score for each character. To evaluate our model, we divide the characters data into training (characters died before year 300) and testing (characters died in the year 300 and characters alive till year 300). Our results show that the proposed Death-Prone Score model achieves an f-score of 86.2%.

**Keywords:** Character similarity · Death prediction · Feature importance · Game of Thrones · Social network analysis · Weighted vector space model

## 1 Introduction

'A Game of Thrones' is a novel series were written by renowned American novelist George R. R. Martin[1] can be regarded as the most popular book series of the contemporary generation if not of all time. The novel deals with various royal families, diplomats, and bureaucrats with a blending of numerous major

---

[1] http://www.georgerrmartin.com/grrm_book/a-game-of-thrones-a-song-of-ice-and-fire-book-one/.

© ICST Institute for Computer Sciences, Social Informatics and Telecommunications Engineering 2020
Published by Springer Nature Switzerland AG 2020. All Rights Reserved
H. Gao et al. (Eds.): TridentCom 2019, LNICST 309, pp. 229–244, 2020.
https://doi.org/10.1007/978-3-030-43215-7_16

and minor characters instead of a handful of characters which adds to its dimensions [11]. Among various occurrence trends in the series, sudden, abrupt, and mind-boggling deaths have been fascinating events for the readers. For instance, in the first book of the series, *Ned Stark* appeared to be the main protagonist of the series. However early, in the beginning, he is beheaded by a boy *King Joffrey* signalling that anyone can die in the series at any time. Such sudden deaths led to great impacts in the series as well as among the audiences [18]. In this particular case, the beheading of *Ned Stark* led to the origin of *The War of Five Kings*[2] while there was a buzz on social media as well as on the relevant blogs and forums[3]. Following the sequence of many such sudden incidents (death of *Khal Drogo, King Joffrey,* and *King Robb Stark*), audiences started guessing and gauging the upcoming deaths, trying to understand author's writing patterns, character psychology, and interrelations. The immense popularity of the series and many such unexpected events stirred researchers and analysts to analyze this interesting series.

**Background and Motivation:** We conduct a literature survey in three lines of research: (1) studies conducted on Game of Thrones (GoT) books or tv series, (2) predicting characters' death for GoT as well as other similar series, and (3) character analysis conducted on other movies, tv-series, and books. Beveridge et al. [2] performs a context-based analysis on the books and create a social network of all characters and their houses. They use social network measures and compare their results against the importance of each character in the respective book. Inspired by the above article, Bonato et al. [4] performed a social network analysis on four different books; Twilight by S. Meye, S. King's The Stand, and J.K. Rowling's Harry Potter and the Goblet of Fire. They used social network measures and supervised learning-based models to investigate character modelling in these books and identify the most influential characters. Over the last two years, many researchers conducted experiments on the dataset of GoT series and published their results on blogs. Janosov [10] created a social network (approximately 400 nodes and more than 3000 edges) of all the characters pairs based on their interaction (appearing together in a scene). He used various network measures (PageRank, degree, weighted degree, clustering, betweenness, closeness, and eigen centralities) as features and applied SVM algorithm for predicting the next character to be dead in the series. Similarly, Phillip Tracy used the application of modularity and clustering network measures to predict the death risk of a character before an event happened [20]. In [19], Joel Shurkin surveys various social network analysis based approaches proposed for 18th century English novels and concludes that the degree distribution of a character in the network follows the Power Law [9]. Unlike other book series such as *Lord of the Rings, Twilight,* or *Harry Potter,* predicting characters' death in *Game of Thrones* is a technically challenging due to the following three major reasons: (1) the vast domain of characters, complex relation, and ratio of their importance with their interactions, (2) automating the interpretation of the interactions of

---

[2] https://awoiaf.westeros.org/index.php/War_of_the_Five_Kings.

[3] https://www.vox.com/2016/6/1/11669730/tv-deaths-character-best.

characters (based on their appearance in a scene, similar houses, etc.), and (3) the absence of ground truth for upcoming portions of the series. Furthermore, the existing studies ignore the fact of the relative importance of different types of interactions between characters. For example, the importance of belonging to the same "house" over fighting as an opponent in the same "battle". Inspired by the existing literature, we formulate the problem of character death prediction as network analysis and classification problem. Social Network Analysis on the network of characters of Game of Thrones depicts different natural and behavioural aspects of the actors, thus providing a logical base of analysis. Understanding the relationship and network bindings between the dead characters and the remaining ones provide us with a likelihood of an existing actor's death. The Algorithmic approach lays a mathematical foundation of depicting proneness of a character's death in the upcoming series.

## 2    Novel Research Contributions

In contrast to the existing work, the work presented in this paper makes the following novel contributions:

1. *A utility matrix-based model for generating a character profile:* While existing studies use one relation as a notion of similarity between characters, we propose to create a character profile from all attributes present in the character-attribute utility matrix. We further assign the weights to each attribute based on their importance in predicting the death of a character in the upcoming novel.
2. *A link analysis-based model for computing the similarity between character profiles:* We create a social network of all the characters and propose a Death-Prone Score (DPS) model that assigns a score to each node (or character) in the network. The proposed model is a function of proximity (distance in the graph) and similarity (character profile) with connecting dead nodes for predicting the death of the candidate character.
3. *A probabilistic model to compute DPS for disconnected profiles:* We design a joint probability and damping factor based DPS model to address the challenge of no direct edge between a dead and alive character pair. Such model removes the biases in the prediction that only the nodes within proximity to the dead node are highly likely to die next unlike the existing studies where centrality is the primary measure used for the prediction.

Computing DPS is not limited to the predicting the death of a character in a novel or television series, but it has its applications in many domains [15]. Therefore we expect our results to be useful for the communities that analyze the impact of one event on another linked in a network (similar to knock-on effect in percolation theory) [14,17]. For example, we expect our model to be useful for cellular network users or operators to predict the failure of a device based on the failure of some existing devices in the network. The proneness of failure can be predicted by computing the weighted similarity between the failed and active devices [22]. Similarly, in case of a malicious attack happened in a network, the proposed approach can be used to detect the devices to be attacked next. Also, based on the similarity between user profiles hacked on a social network, the model will be able to capture the next accounts to be hacked. Similarly, based on the information about some channels posting fake news on social media and their links with other channels can be exploited to determine the diffusion of fake news and the identification of potential channels uploading fake news [21].

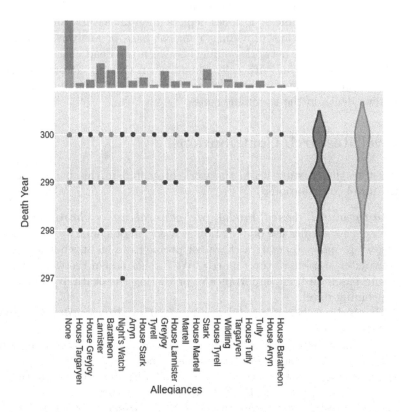

**Fig. 1.** Illustrating the statistics of the dataset in character-deaths.csv file. X-axis represents the various allegiances in the book and their death year is represented on Y-axis. The Violin plot on the right side and the histogram plot on the top represent the individual statistics of death year and allegiances respectively.

## 3    Experimental Setup

We conduct our experiments on an open source data downloaded from Kaggle[4]. The available dataset is created by combining multiple datasets initially collected by different groups and teams and published online for public use. The dataset on Kaggle consists of three CSV files (battles.csv, character-deaths.csv, and character-predictions.csv) collectively created for first four books

---

[4] https://www.kaggle.com/mylesoneill/game-of-thrones.

from the series (A Game of Thrones, A Clash of Kings, A Storm of Swords, and A Feast for Crows).

- **battles.csv:** This file is a comprehensive collection of all the battles fought in the series in four books. The dataset is created from the *"The War of the Five Kings"* dataset[5] collected initially by Chris Albon. The dataset contains details about 38 battles fought in three years in 10 different regions. The dataset includes a total of 25 attributes including battle name, attacker king, defender king, region, location, and year of the battle, number of major deaths, the outcome of the battle, etc. The dataset reveals that there are four different types of battles while the number of participants information is available only for three types of battles. Similarly, for some of the battles no information is available on the attacker or defender kings causing missing values in our dataset. Since the dataset is generated from the original book scripts, the missing values cannot be filled using pre-processing or statistical measures.

- **character-deaths.csv:** This file contains the exhaustive list of the characters and when they died. The file was created by Erin Pierce and Ben Kahle as a part of their Bayesian Survival Analysis [16]. The file contains a total of 917 characters featured using 13 attributes such as year of death, book and chapter number, appearances in different books in the series, etc. We conduct an exploratory data analysis to identify some features that are useful for the prediction model. Figure 1 shows the basic statistics of the exploratory data analysis. The scatter plot in the Figure shows characters died in Year 297–300 from various house groups (None represents the unknown house information). The Violin graph on the Y-margin represents the number of characters died in each year filtered based on the gender of the characters. The violin graph reveals that maximum number of male characters died in year 299. While, the maximum number of female characters died in year 300 while in 297 year, no female characters had died. We combine this meta information with the histogram plotted in X-margin. The overall graph reveals that the majority of the characters who died in first three books do not have their house (Allegiances) information available in the dataset irrespective of their gender. The graph also reveals that maximum number of male characters who died in year 297–300 are from Night's Watch house followed by Lannister and Baratheon groups with relatively higher ratio of female characters. The variation in number of characters died from a house and the ratio of female and males indicates that allegiances and the gender are the two strong indicators for predicting the next characters to die in the series.

- **character-predictions.csv:** This file contains the comprehensive list of all 1946 characters and their metadata. For example, *name, house, culture, title, family relations* (parents, siblings, spouse), *dead* or *alive, title, gender*, date of birth, etc. This dataset was created by the team '*A Song of Ice and Data*' and later made available for research community on Kaggle[6].

---

[5] https://github.com/chrisalbon/war_of_the_five_kings_dataset.
[6] http://awoiaf.westeros.org/index.php/Main_Page.

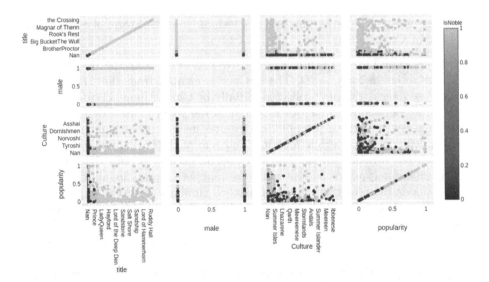

**Fig. 2.** A matrix based graph amongst various features from the dataset. The relation between attributes is exploited to determine the weight and priority of each feature for the prediction mode. The color parameter in the graphs shows the binary score of attribute IsNoble representing whether the character who died with different characteristics (popularity, culture, title, and gender) belong to noble class or not. (Color figure online)

We merge all the files to create our experimental dataset. The dataset consists of 53 attributes including four categorical and 49 numeric attributes. We convert each categorical attribute into a numeric format. Since *name* is a nominal categorical attribute, we assign a unique ID to each name. For *title*, *house*, and *culture* attributes, we convert them to an ordinal attribute and assign a priority to each field based on their frequency within the attribute. If a field (title type, house type, or culture type) is more frequent in the dataset (across all characters), we decrease its priority over the fields occurring less frequently. Figure 2 shows the graph of relation between various characteristics from utility matrix. The graphs are further labeled based on the status of the characters (isNoble = 0 or 1). The sub-graph [3, 1] demonstrates the relationship between various titles and cultures. The colors in the sub-graph [3, 1] reveals that any dead character that has a title or a culture is possibly a noble as well. Whereas, all the characters with unknown title or unknown culture are highly likely to be a no-noble person. The sub-graphs [4, 3] and [3, 4] reveals that many characters who have an unknown culture are still popular in the book while majority of them are male characters. Whereas, there are many female characters who belong to a culture and have high popularity as well. The sub-graph [3, 4] reveals that there are many no-noble characters who are more popular in the series in comparison to the characters who belong to a particular culture. The sub-plot [2, 3] shows that across all the cultures, majority of the dead female characters are not from noble house. Similarly, sub-plot [2, 4] reveals that most popular characters

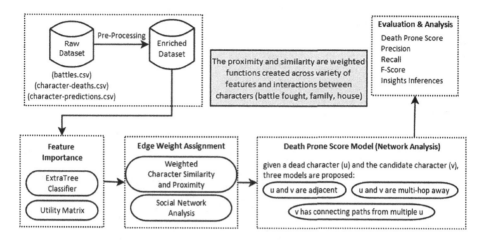

**Fig. 3.** A general high-level framework proposed for the prediction of dead and alive characters in the dataset.

who belonged to noble family are male while only a very few female characters are from noble family and popular as well. Otherwise, majority of the female characters who died are neither popular nor belong to the noble family.

We further normalize all priority scores to avoid the dominance in high-value attributes. We use the following function to compute the priority of each attribute value within an attribute: $Priority_x = f(x) = \frac{1}{TF_x} \times k$, where $TF_x$ represents the column-wise frequency of $x$ attribute value, and $k$ represents the normalizing constant. The final dataset after merging consists of 1947 characters. To conduct our experiments, we divide our dataset into training and testing data. Since the year 300 is the most recent year in the downloaded dataset we use the characters present in the year 300 as our testing dataset and the remaining characters from previous years are used for training the model. Thus our dataset contains a total of 83 and 1864 characters in testing and training data, respectively. We formulate the problem of character death prediction as a social network analysis and classification problem [6,8]. Figure 3 illustrates the high-level architecture of the proposed research framework. The proposed architecture is a multi-step process consisting of four major phases: feature importance, edge weight assignment in the social network of characters, death-prone score model, and prediction and evaluation. We discuss each of these phases in the following subsections:

## 3.1 Feature Importance

As discussed in Sect. 3, each character in the series has a variety of features describing the profile of each character. For example, house, culture, battle fought as an attacker or a defender, siblings, appearance in the book and many more. The same set of features defines the notion of similarity between two characters in the series. The existing studies assign equal weight to each attribute for computing the interactions between characters and ignore the fact of the relative

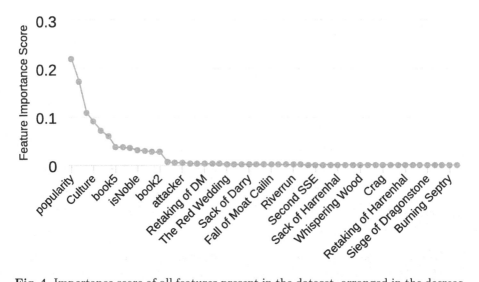

**Fig. 4.** Importance score of all features present in the dataset, arranged in the decreasing order of the score.

importance of different types of interactions. For example, the importance of belonging to the same *house* over fighting as opponents in the same *battle* or the *spouse* relation over belonging to different house or culture. In this paper, we propose to use the relative importance of each attribute and assign them weights to compute the similarity between the two characters. Each character in the dataset is represented as a vector in a $k$-dimensional space where $k$ represents the number of attributes. The similar vector can be visualized as a Utility matrix where column represents the $k$ attributes and rows represent the characters. The similarity computation is technically challenging due to a sparse utility matrix.

We compute the importance of each feature and assign a normalized weight to them. The tree-based classification, correlation, and leave-p-out methods are some of the most standard algorithms used for determining the importance of the features. We use ExtraTree Classifier- a tree-based ensemble method to compute the weight of each feature [7]. ExtraTree Classifier [1] focuses on randomizing both the attribute and split point for the tree node. We use ExtraTree Classifier as it outperforms Random Forest and Decision Tree-based methods by reducing computational complexity linked to the determination of optimal cut-points (tree pruning). Unlike bagging approach in the random forest algorithm, it finds the best fit among various random splits for the random set of attributes. The more randomness of the algorithm addresses the challenge of bias and minimizes the errors (less correlated) made by baseline models. Based on the feature importance calculated in our dataset (refer to Fig. 4) we find that *popularity, culture, house, isnoble*, role of an *attacker* in the battle, and appearance in *books number* 2 and 5 are some of the most significant attributes in the dataset.

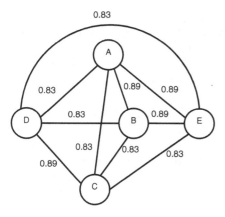

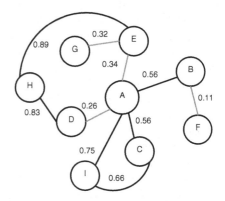

**Fig. 5.** A snapshot of top 10 weighted edges between 5 different characters in the social graph

**Fig. 6.** A Snapshot of the discarded edges due to the relatively low similarity between characters

## 3.2 Edge Weight Assignment in the Social Network

The existing studies create a social network for different relations between characters to predict their death. However, for individual feature or relation, the predictions are made differently for the same character [2]. Further using one attribute for a network generates a combination of directed and undirected graphs for different relations. For example, for *house* or *culture* attributes, the graph has undirected edges with weakly connected components. While for *battle fought* as a relation, the graph has directed edges with many isolated nodes since not all characters participated in the battles. We extend the idea of creating a social network for one feature and instead represent the relation between two nodes as one single edge that depicts the similarity between two characters. In prior literature, all edges have an equal cost of 1. We, however, propose to assign different weights to each edge equal to the similarity between two nodes in the network. We create a character profile from the utility matrix [12] of all the features and their associated importance in the dataset. Thus each character is represented as a vector $u = [\alpha_1 A_1, \alpha_2 A_2, ...., \alpha_n A_n]$ where $\alpha_i$ represents the importance of attribute $A_i$. We take each character profile from the character-attribute utility matrix and use centered cosine similarity to compute the similarity every character pair. The centered cosine similarity addresses the challenge of zero-valued vectors (features of a character) and computes the similarity normalized across all attributes, thus keeping a check on the dominance of high magnitude- attributes over other attributes.

Figure 5 shows a concrete example of the edge weight computes between character pairs. Figure 5 illustrates that reciprocal links between only four characters ranked the highest in weights. We conduct a manual inspection on the dataset and observe the patterns in these characters (A: Stafford Lannister, B: Tybolt

Lannister, C: Damon Lannister (lord), D: Gerold Lannister, E: Daven Lannister). The pattern reveals that these characters belong to the same family, hold the similar titles and the popularity. Further, they have same gender, present in the first four books, and have participated in the battles together. Such a degree of similarities justifies the weights the edges between them hold. We further discard the links that have negligible similarity between two characters. The similarity computation is a function of type of interaction and the frequency of interaction in the book series. For example, two characters who fought multiple battles together. The higher the frequency of interaction increases the score of the edge weight. However, the edge weight further depends on the importance of the interaction. For example, two character having same gender is less important than the two different gender characters belonging to the same house. Thus, we expand the idea of weighted TF-IDF and exploit the application of ExtraTree Classifier and User Profile Utility Matrix to compute the edge weight. Some character pairs who have higher frequency but do not have high rated interactions are linked via less weight edges. To improve the performance of out model and avoid overfitting in prediction, we discard edges from the network consisting of negligible weights. To compute the threshold for removing edges, we compute the mean of all edge weights. Figure 6 shows the concrete examples of characters with very low similarity and hence not having a direct connecting edge in the network. For all the characters, we had approximately 1.8 million character pairs. We take only top 6000 similarity scores and plot their social network.

Figure 7 shows a snapshot (sample) of the character pairs present in our dataset. Figure 7 reveals that despite having a different culture, book or battle attributes, many characters end-up connected in the network due to the weighted feature importance and character similarity model. Since house and culture are two of the most significant attributes in the dataset, the majority of the characters in the sample network belong to the same house (Stark family). The width of the edge in the network represents the similarity score between two characters based on a variety of parameters such as house, battle, culture, and many more. Colour represents the clusters of characters having similar behaviour within parameters. The size of a node represents the number of interactions in series (degree of a node in the network).

### 3.3   The Proposed DPS Model

As discussed in Sect. 3, we divide our experimental dataset into two parts: all the characters died before year 300 are used as training nodes while other characters (died in the year 300 or still alive) are used as the testing nodes. To predict the death of characters present in the testing dataset, we propose to compute the death-prone score of each character and determine how likely a character is going to die next. We extend the idea of PageRank [5, 13] and damping factor [3] to compute the Death-Prone Score (DPS) of each character. We propose to quantify the proneness of death by integrating the idea of PageRank with the proximity between dead and unknown/candidate characters in the social

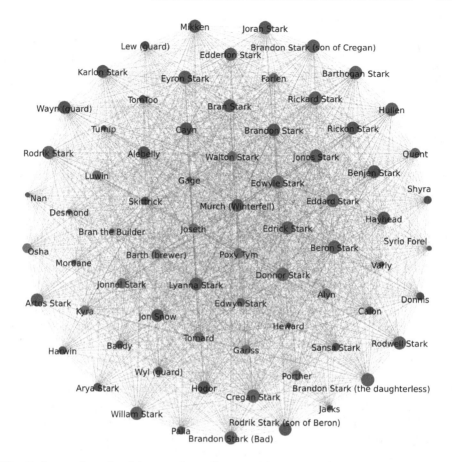

**Fig. 7.** A snapshot of social network graph created for various characters in the dataset. The width of the edge represents the weight of the overall interaction based on the priority of various interactions. (Color figure online)

network. We take each dead node $(u)$ in the network present in the training dataset, and it's neighbouring candidate characters $(v)$ are assigned a DPS of

$$DPS(v) = \frac{\alpha \times \sum_{i=0}^{N} \prod_{j=0}^{k-1} \frac{w(u_j, u_{j+1})}{2^j \times deg(u_{j+1})}}{N} \qquad (1)$$

where $PR(u) = \sum_{x \in X} \frac{PR(x)}{deg(x)}$ denotes the PageRank of a node $u$. The PageRank value for a node $u$ is dependent on the PageRank values for each node $x$ contained in the set $X$ (the set containing all nodes linking to node $u$), divided by the number $deg(x)$ of links from node $x$. In Eq. 1, $k$ is the number of hops between the dead node $\{u\}$ and the candidate node $\{v\}$, the value of $j$ represents the intermediate nodes, $i$ represents the number of dead nodes (N) connected to $v$, and $\alpha$ represents the damping factor set to the standard value as 0.5. We divide

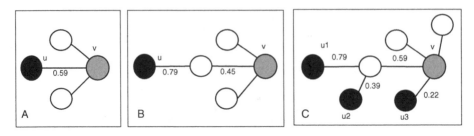

**Fig. 8.** Shows different scenarios of candidate characters (red node) to be connected with dead character (black node) for computing the death prone score in the social network (Color figure online)

the weighted score by $deg(v)$ and $N$ to normalize the effect of many counts of neighbors of $v$.

Based on the closeness of a dead character ($u$) to the candidate character ($v$) in the network, we evaluate our model for the following possible scenarios:

1. **u and v are the adjacent nodes:** Figure 8 shows a snapshot of the network in which a dead node $u$ (represented as black node) and testing character $v$ (represented as red node) are one hop away from each other. In such a network, $v$ might be connected to other nodes (represented as white nodes) as well. As shown in Fig. 8, the DPS of $v$ strictly depends on the proximity and similarity to $u$. For the given similarity score in Fig. 8, we compute the DPS of $v$ to proofread our proposed formula of DPS score. Since $v$ is connected to only one dead node, the value of $N$ is equal to 1. Further, the nodes are adjacent to each other hence, the value of $k$ is 1. For such nodes, we compute the death-prone score of alive character as

$$DPS(v) = \alpha \times \frac{w(u,v)}{deg(v)} \qquad (2)$$

   Given the 59% similarity between nodes $u$ and $v$, the death-prone score of $v$ is $0.5 \times 0.59/3 = 0.098 = 9.8\%$.
2. **u and v are multi-hop away:** Given a network where the dead node and the candidate node characters are two or multiple hops away (have one or multiple intermediate nodes in between), the $DPS(v)$ does not only depends on the similarity from the $u$ but also depends on the proximity of intermediate nodes from $u$. Therefore, we use the joint probability measures and compute the $DPS(v)$ as a product of $DPS(u,x)$ and $DPS(x,v)$ where $x$ represents the intermediate node. The product of DPS with the intermediate score signifies that as the closeness between a dead node and candidate node decreases the contribution of the trail of weights should also be decreasing as the number of intermediate nodes increase. For the given similarity scores in Fig. 8B, we compute the $DPS(v)$. For such a network, we simplify the formula as

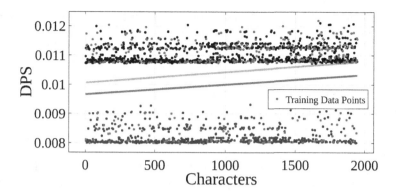

**Fig. 9.** Death Prone Score of each character in the dataset. Demonstrates the linearly separated characters based on their DPS value.

$$DPS(v) = \alpha \times \prod_{j=0}^{k-1} \frac{w(u_j, u_{j+1})}{2^j \times deg(u_{j+1})} \tag{3}$$

Given the similarity score of $u$ and $v$ with intermediate nodes (79% and 45%, respectively), the death prone score of $v$ is 1.48% (($0.79/2$) × ($0.45/2 \times 3$) × $0.5 = 0.0148$) which is relatively lower than the DPS of intermediate node which turns out to be 19.8%.

3. **$v$ has a connecting path from multiple dead nodes:** Considering a real-world scenario, we analyze the possibility of the network where a character can have connecting edges from multiple dead nodes and can also have intermediate nodes in between the dead node and itself. Figure 8$C$ shows an example of such network. Similar to above points, in such case, the death prone score of candidate node is affected by the proximity of each connecting dead node and the intermediate node. For the intermediate nodes, we use the above formula, while for multiple connecting dead nodes, we use the weighted average of $DPS(v)$ computed explicitly w.r.t. each dead node computed using Eq. 3. Therefore, for such cases, we use our generalized formula proposed in Eq. 1. Given the similarity scores of $v$ and intermediate node with various dead node characters, the death prone score of $v$ is (($0.395 \times 0.073$) + ($0.195 \times 0.073$) + ($0.55 \times 0.5$))$/3 = 0.296/3 = 0.098 = 9.8\%$. While considering the intermediate node as our candidate node, the DPS turns out to be 32% which makes sense since the node is adjacent to more dead nodes ($u_1$ and $u_2$) than $v$ and has higher character similarity.

### 3.4   Classification and Results

Figure 9 shows the death-prone score of all the characters present in our dataset and reveals that there is a fair discriminatory line separating the characters with low DPS from the characters with high DPS value. Since the data points are

**Table 1.** Confusion Matrix and prediction results for alive and dead characters present in the testing dataset

| | | Predicted | | | Metrics | Accuracy |
|---|---|---|---|---|---|---|
| | | Alive | Dead | | Precision | 95.6% |
| Actual | Alive | TP = 1138 | FN = 313 | | Recall | 78.4% |
| | Dead | FP = 52 | TN = 85 | | F-score | 86.21% |

linearly separable, we find the least square fit in the dataset (optimal linear parameters) and draw the line separating data points. We apply the simple rule-based classifier to label each character. All the characters below margin are predicted alive while the characters with a DPS appearing above margin line are labeled dead in the year 300. We check the performance of our proposed methodology and DPS model against the ground truth available for year 300 data. We use the standard measures in information retrieval and report the accuracy in the form of precision and recall. Table 1 shows the confusion matrix for the classification and prediction results. Table 1 reveals that among 1588 characters present in our testing dataset, 85 are correctly identified as dead while 1138 are correctly predicted as to be alive in the upcoming year or book. The model, however, reports a misclassification of 37% and 21% in predicting dead and alive characters, respectively. The proposed model achieves a precision of 95.6 and a recall of 78.4%. We further compute the f-score of our model and achieves an accuracy of 86.21%.

## 4    Conclusions and Future Work

In this paper, we exploit the application of social network analysis for the prediction of dead and alive characters in the novel book series named "A game of thrones". We address the challenge of the vast domain of features and sparsity in the dataset by assigning a weighted score to each feature referred to as feature importance. We automate the interpretation of the relationship between characters by computing the weighted similarity between every character pair in character-features utility matrix. We create a social network of all characters present in our dataset and propose a network measure based model to predict the characters that are highly likely to die or stay alive in upcoming chapters or novel in the series. We propose a Death-Prone Score model that takes proximity and similarity between characters as inputs and generate a score. We further use this score to predict the death of a character. We also test our model for various situations of a candidate character in the network such as direct proximity with a dead node (character), two or multi-hop away from a dead node, and connected with multiple dead nodes. The idea is to improve the performance of our prediction model by giving more weightage to the characters having multiple links with a dead node. Our results show that computing feature importance normalizes the factor of biases towards character profile and house, are the most discriminatory and significant attributes in the dataset to find the character similarity in GoT book series. Further, unlike the different proximity score for each relation, an aggregated weight can be assigned to each node pair in the network that is an efficient approach to find similar characters in the series despite the lesser number of interactions and direct similarity. Our results reveal that the proposed DPS model achieved an accuracy of 86.21% while reporting precision and recall of 95.6% and 78.4%, respectively.

Future work includes performing an event-based analysis for the prediction of the character's death. The work presented in this paper predicts the death of a character based on the static analysis of year 300. We plan to extend the analysis and forecast the death of character B in the testing dataset when character A has died from the same year and thus capture the dynamic changes in the network. Our future work also includes training a supervised classifier model to automatically predict the characters' death based on their metadata and death prone score model. Computing death-prone score is not limited to predicting the death of characters but has its application in a variety of domains. The future work includes testing the model for cellular and femtocell network architecture. The aim is to capture the devices with similar configuration and predict the next devices to be attacked in case of an earlier malicious attack happened on one or more devices.

# References

1. Athey, S., Tibshirani, J., Wager, S., et al.: Generalized random forests. Ann. Stat. **47**(2), 1148–1178 (2019)
2. Beveridge, A., Shan, J.: Network of thrones. Math Horiz. **23**(4), 18–22 (2016)
3. Boldi, P., Santini, M., Vigna, S.: PageRank as a function of the damping factor. In: Proceedings of the 14th International Conference on World Wide Web, pp. 557–566. ACM, New York (2005)
4. Bonato, A., D'Angelo, D.R., Elenberg, E.R., Gleich, D.F., Hou, Y.: Mining and modeling character networks. In: Bonato, A., Graham, F.C., Prałat, P. (eds.) WAW 2016. LNCS, vol. 10088, pp. 100–114. Springer, Cham (2016). https://doi.org/10.1007/978-3-319-49787-7_9
5. Chakrabarti, S.: Dynamic personalized pagerank in entity-relation graphs. In: Proceedings of the 16th International Conference on WWW, pp. 571–580 (2007)
6. Farine, D.R.: When to choose dynamic vs. static social network analysis. J. Anim. Ecol. **87**(1), 128–138 (2018)
7. Geurts, P., Ernst, D., Wehenkel, L.: Extremely randomized trees. Mach. Learn. **63**(1), 3–42 (2006)
8. Haghani, S., Keyvanpour, M.R.: A systemic analysis of link prediction in social network. Artif. Intell. Rev. **52**(3), 1961–1995 (2019)
9. Ibnoulouafi, A., Haziti, M.E., Cherifi, H.: M-centrality: identifying key nodes based on global position and local degree variation. J. Stat. Mech.: Theory Exp. **2018**(7), 073407 (2018). http://stacks.iop.org/1742-5468/2018/i=7/a=073407
10. Janosov, M.: Network science predicts who dies next in game of thrones. Department of Network and Data Science Group at Central European University (2017). https://networkdatascience.ceu.edu/article/2017-07-08/network-science-predicts-who-dies-next-game-thrones

11. Jia, R., Liang, P.: A game of thrones: power structure and the stability of regimes. In: Wärneryd, K. (ed.) The Economics of Conflict: Theory and Empirical Evidence. CESifo Seminar Series, pp. 79–104. MIT Press, Cambridge (2014)
12. Lakiotaki, K., Delias, P., Sakkalis, V., Matsatsinis, N.F.: User profiling based on multi-criteria analysis: the role of utility functions. Oper. Res. Int. J. 9(1), 3–16 (2009)
13. Liben-Nowell, D., Kleinberg, J.: The link-prediction problem for social networks. J. Am. Soc. Inf. Sci. Technol. 58(7), 1019–1031 (2007)
14. Maurella, C., et al.: Social network analysis and risk assessment: an example of introducing an exotic animal disease in Italy. Microb. Risk Anal. 13 (2019). https://doi.org/10.1016/j.mran.2019.04.001. ISSN: 2352-3522
15. Moradabadi, B., Meybodi, M.R.: Link prediction in weighted social networks using learning automata. Eng. Appl. Artif. Intell. 70, 16–24 (2018)
16. Pierce, E., Kahle, B., Downey, A.: Bayesian survival analysis for "game of thrones". A blog by Allen Downey (2015). http://allendowney.blogspot.com/2015/03/bayesian-survival-analysis-for-game-of.html
17. Sah, P., Mann, J., Bansal, S.: Disease implications of animal social network structure: a synthesis across social systems. J. Anim. Ecol. 87(3), 546–558 (2018)
18. Schubart, R., Gjelsvik, A.: Women of Ice and Fire: Gender, Game of Thrones and Multiple Media Engagements. Bloomsbury, New York (2016)
19. Shurkin, J.: Using social networks to analyze the classics. Inside Science (2012). https://www.insidescience.org/news/using-social-networks-analyze-classics
20. Tracy, P.: Using big data to accurately predict death in the 'game of thrones' series. Intelligence on all things wireless, RCR Wireless News (2016). https://www.rcrwireless.com/20160915/big-data-analytics/game-of-thrones-tag31-tag99
21. Tschiatschek, S., Singla, A., Gomez Rodriguez, M., Merchant, A., Krause, A.: Fake news detection in social networks via crowd signals. In: Companion Proceedings of the The Web Conference 2018, pp. 517–524. International World Wide Web Conferences Steering Committee (2018)
22. Zhang, Y., Mu, L., Shen, G., Yu, Y., Han, C.: Fault diagnosis strategy of CNC machine tools based on cascading failure. J. Intell. Manuf. 30(5), 2193–2202 (2019)

# Author Index

Printed in the United States
By Bookmasters